NATIONWIDE APPLAUSE FOR YOUR FILM ACTING CAREER

"The next time anyone asks me how to break into the business, I am just going to recommend that they buy *Your Film Acting Career*."

—*THE CELEBRITY BULLETIN*

"Incredibly informative and marvelously witty—a rare combination."

—*LAWRENCE B. MARCUS, SCREENWRITER*
(THE STUNTMAN, PETULIA, ETC.)

"Full of solid advice for folks who are bull-headed or confident enough to tackle Hollywood."

—*CATHERINE RAMBEAU, DETROIT FREE PRESS*

"A nuts-and-bolts handbook (that) takes a very pragmatic look at breaking into the business. M.K. and Rosemary Lewis bring their years of experience to bear on the subject, anticipating most every difficulty the novice will encounter ... A thorough overview of the business side of acting."

—*MARK LOCHER, SAG NEWSLETTER*

"If only M.K. Lewis' marvelously informative handbook had been around a few years ago when I first came to Hollywood from San Diego, maybe it wouldn't have taken me 20 years to hit my stride!"

—*MARION ROSS, HAPPY DAYS*

"*Your Film Acting Career* is brutally honest and necessary advice that no novice can afford to miss. This is mandatory reading for any actor who is even considering taking a crack at Hollywood."

—*TONY SHEPHERD, DIRECTOR OF TALENT AND CASTING,*
AARON SPELLING PRODUCTIONS, INC.

"An excellent book. I suspect that it will end up being a [standard] textbook."

—*HAROLD GREENE, KABC-TV, AM LOS ANGELES*

"This is a splendid book—bright and breezy with just enough factual detail—a great gift for a star-struck teenager or a regular viewer of TV and movies and a must for the rookie trying to get through his first jobs. It's a lively textbook from a couple who graduated from the school of hard knocks."

—*CHRISTINA VELLA, TEMPO*

"This is a great book. Just chock full of information."

—*LORI LERNER, KRTH L.A.*

"Even successful actors and actresses should read this enlightening book!"

—*JUNE ALLYSON*

YOUR FILM ACTING CAREER

YOUR FILM ACTING CAREER

M.K. Lewis
& Rosemary R. Lewis

HOW TO BREAK INTO THE MOVIES & TV & SURVIVE IN HOLLYWOOD

 GORHAM HOUSE PUBLISHING
Santa Monica, California

SAMUEL FRENCH TRADE, Distributors
Hollywood, California

Published by Gorham House Publishing,
2210 Wilshire Blvd., Suite 777, Santa Monica, California 90403 U.S.A.

Distributed by Samuel French Trade,
7623 Sunset Blvd., Hollywood, California 90046 U.S.A.

Illustrated by Rosemary R. Lewis
Typesetting by DynaType
Printed in the United States of America

Library of Congress Cataloging in Publication Data

Lewis, M.K.
Your Film Acting Career.
Includes index.
1. Moving-picture acting—Vocational guidance.
2. Acting for television—Vocational guidance.
I. Lewis, Rosemary R. II. Title.

Library of Congress Catalog Card Number: 88-81684
ISBN 0-929149-00-9

(Previously published by Crown Publishers, Inc.,
ISBN 0-517-549115 [cloth], ISBN 0-517-549123 [paper])

10 9 8 7 6 5 4 3

First Revised Edition

To Marguerite and Jozef
for the talent and background,
and
To Mama Ru and Papa Ru
for their loving support.

CONTENTS

FOREWORD

For me, the choice to become an actress was clear almost at birth. I never longed to be a doctor, firefighter, scientist or politician. I like being an actress. Acting is a joyous adventure.

Over the years I have eagerly read or reviewed countless books on the technique of acting, most being exclusively geared to the stage actor. Some of them have been excellent, for example, Uta Hagen's *Respect for Acting*, Stanislavski's *An Actor Prepares*, etc. Sanford Meisner, to me without question the master teacher, has a book ready for publication this year. [The Meisner book, *Sanford Meisner on Acting*, is now available.]

Any serious actor should have more than a passing knowledge of the technique and craft expressed by these formidable artists/teachers. In my opinion, one should also possess a sound background in theatre and film history from the earliest times to the present. The Greek theatre, German playwrights, Scandinavian filmmakers should be studied, and certainly much emphasis should be placed on our cousins in the English-speaking world. However, an actor's research should not ignore American theatre, film and television. We tend to belittle our own cultural contributions, when, in fact, they have been enormous—in all fields.

It is most useful to be familiar with the approach other actors take to their work. The recently published *Actors On Acting* is excellent.

We have also experienced a proliferation of "star turn" books in recent years, written with or without the actor's permission. If one cares to wade through the sex lives, illnesses, traumas, and disappointments over which these actors have triumphed, one might receive some small measure of information about how it all came together for them—but I seriously doubt it. *Being a voyeur does not prepare one for a career.*

I have had the privilege of addressing university students in recent years and have been astonished by their lack of information about the artists' role in the United States—no practical application to add to Strindberg and Brecht. The mere mention of unions, agents, or how to survive outside the ivory towers seems to be considered pedestrian and out of place. In most universities, the film department is separated from the theatre department. Television, cable and satellite television are only touched upon in the communications departments. A curious exercise in "territorial rights" seems to block the student from the interchange which is essential for making decisions that affect life choices in the arts.

We come to New York or Hollywood ill-prepared to survive the shock of the commercial world.

M.K. and Rosemary Lewis' book deals exclusively with the film capital— Hollywood. It was not written by renowned stars or academicians. It was written by two people who have worked the system and, in an intelligent and entertaining fashion, have chronicled that experience. As a professional actress and longtime advocate of the actor's role in American society, I welcome their contribution.

Wherever and however our creative lives begin, we must have a foundation of preparation—total preparation. To "wing it" is more an expression of how we got by than how we prevailed.

Is the "joyous adventure" for you? The chapters that follow are a map with clues. Only you have the answers within you.

If you decide the answer is yes ... relish the journey.

Welcome!

KATHLEEN NOLAN

KATHLEEN NOLAN has appeared in every form of entertainment—showboats, tent shows, repertory companies, Broadway, film, and television. She came to national prominence as Kate on the long-running TV series *The Real McCoys*. After 16 years' service on the board of directors of the Screen Actors Guild, she was elected president of SAG in 1975 and served two terms—the first woman president in its [then] 50-year history. She has been a presidential appointee to the Corporation for Public Broadcasting and a panelist for the National Endowment for the Arts.

PREFACE

It's enough to make you stand in the middle of the patio of Mann's Chinese Theatre, shouting . . .

"How do you crack this town?!?"

Each year, hundreds of actors point themselves in the general direction of Hollywood and Vine. Thousands more all over the country are thinking about it. Their shapes, sizes, talents, educations, and egos are as varied as their chances, but almost all have one thing in common: no idea how to start (or establish) a career.

Maybe you're among them.

Even if you've been to college, you're probably as lost as the 16-year-old starlet with stars in her eyes. You can graduate with a Ph.D in Drama (having written a dissertation on the costumes Minnie Maddern Fiske wore in *Our American Cousin*) and still not know what a *Daily Variety* looks like or be able to recognize an agent if he fell on you.

"The universities are pumping out well-trained repertory theatre actors that the world never needed in the first place," says drama critic John C. Mahoney.

This lack of knowledge often leads to paying phony "agents" to take you on; using photos that belong in a high school yearbook; attending so-called "acting classes" that do you no good and sometimes great psychological harm. And on and on.

Ultimately, your pocket—not to mention your mind—gets picked so much that you either jump on a bus or off a building, shouting all the way down . . .

"How do you crack this town?!?"

Even "old pros," newly migrated to L.A., can get totally frustrated. Suddenly what you did for years not only doesn't work any more, it works against you; sometimes it hurts you. And as you walk away from that stern-faced guard at the Burbank Studios, that *creep* who wouldn't let you onto the lot to drop off a picture, for crying out loud, you might just be tempted to cry out loud . . .

"How do you crack this town?!?"

In an effort to help, in 1976 we began to teach a course called "The Hollywood Actor's Survival Seminar." Over those years, besides drawing on our own experiences, we've engaged in hundreds of hours of interviews with producers, directors, agents, casting directors, personal managers, publicists, and the like—even a cinematographer or two—so our students would hear the opinions of the most important people of all—those who do the hiring. And some student would inevitably say, "You know, you ought to write a book."

Well, here it is. We can't promise it'll make you "crack this town"— but it might help to bend it a little.

M.K. LEWIS has been teaching over 20 years at his own studio and also has taught at the California Institute of the Arts, Sherwood Oaks Experimental College, and both theatres which he founded. Now devoting himself to writing and teaching, he has appeared in, directed or written hundreds of theatrical productions (including *The Hero*, which he wrote and directed, at the Walnut Street Theatre in Philadelphia).

His film and TV credits include *Hard Times, Death Hunt, Raise The Titanic*, episodes of *Policewoman, Baretta, Delvecchio, The Blue Knight*, etc. He was placed into contention for an Emmy nomination in 1980.

A former member of the SAG Conservatory Committee and a frequent guest speaker at SAG Seminars, he has been interviewed by over 40 radio and TV stations nationwide (*The CBS Morning News, AM Los Angeles, The Michael Jackson Show*, as well as *People* magazine, *The Los Angeles Times*, etc.).

ROSEMARY R. LEWIS is a writer-cartoonist who has worked in public relations, TV (WDSU-TV News) and newspapers (as action line columnist and feature writer for the daily *New Orleans States-Item*).

Currently a free-lance writer and illustrator, she illustrates Liz Scott's award-winning humor column "Modine Gunch" for *New Orleans Magazine*, continuing a long-distance partnership that began with the cookbook *Getting Into New Orleans' Seafood*.

With acting credits of her own (*The Blue Knight, General Hospital*, etc.), in 1976 she and M.K. Lewis founded the ongoing Hollywood Actors Survival Seminar, upon which their book is based.

ACKNOWLEDGEMENTS

Hollywood is a selfish city?

This book, both the original and revised editions, could not have been written without the generosity of hundreds of members of the Hollywood community. Many graciously took the time to speak at one of our seminars (a few more than once); to grant us interviews at their offices or over the phone; to appear as guest speakers at other seminars or classes we attended. And they all had one thing in common . . .

. . . They all donated their time.

Grateful thanks to: Ellie Abrahamson, Laurel Adams, Donna Allen, Eddie Applegate, Maxine Arnold, Simon Ayer, Kevin Baar, Sean Bainbridge, Vikki Bandlow, Arthur Bartow, Deborah Barylski, Fran Bascom, Angela Bath, Miriam Baum, Mel Becker, Paul Bengston, Jim Bennett, Barbara Best, Noel Black, Merritt Blake, Mel Blank, Susan Bragg, Buddy Bregman, Kevin Michael Brown, Michael Campus, Pamela Campus, Reuben Cannon, Diana Carpenter, Bonnie Carstensen, Louise Chamis, Warren Christensen, Don Ciminelli, Jerry Cohn, Susan Conners, Patrice Cormier, Cynthia Ann Crawford, Diana Daves, Becki Davis, Sally Dennison, Debbie Devine, Karen DiCenzo, Angie Dickinson, Bernie Distler, Michael Dixon, Pat Doty, Georg Duuglas, Sylvie Drake, Bill Eaton, Bill Edwards, John Edwards, Van Epperson, Pamm Fair, Jane Feinberg, Kim Fellner, Mike Fenton, Margaret Ferier, John Fisher, Roxanne Fitzgerald, Larry Fonseca, Jerry Franks, Bud Friedman, Tracy Fuller, Joseph Garber, Melinda Gartzman, J. Carter Gibson, Edmund Gilbert, Susan Glicksman, Susan Goldstein, Lora Granett, Jim Green, Bob Harbin, Marci Helzig, Nancy Hereford, Norman Herrman, Bob Hester, Sharon Himes, Bobby Hoffman, Beth Holmes, Judith Holstra, Tawn Holstra, Richard Irving, Myrna Isenberg, George Ives, Tracey Jacobs, Cathryn Jaymes, Marsha Jeffer, Janet Joe, Lance Johnson, Kathy Juden, William Kayden, Johanna Kelly, Gary Klopus, Eileen Knight, Viva Knight, Kat Krone, Harvey Laidman, Elna Lawrence, Terry Lichtman, Marci Liroff, Bob Lloyd, Mark Locher, Morgan Lofting, Bruce Logan, Pegge Logefeil, Beverly Long, Judy Lowry, John C. Mahoney, Philip Mandelker, A. Morgan Maree, Sandy Martin, Leslie Martinson, Andrew McCullough, Renee McGill, Mickie McGowan, John Mekrut, Lee Melville, Frank Messineo, Arlin Miller, Pamela-Beth Morris, Rose Morris, Dennis Moss, Mike Muscat, Don Nagle,

Gary Nelson, Patti O'Brien, Fran O'Bryan, Cliff O'Connell, Al Onorato, Tom Ormany, Harry Orzello, Lucy Pegues, Penny Perry, Don Pitts, David Ralphe, John Randolph, Steve Ray, Barbara Remsen, Michael Rhodes, Ruth Robinson, Andrea Romano, Jack Rose, Doris Ross, Brady Rubin, Ira Rubin, Joel Rudnick, Karen Rushfield, Doris Sabbagh, John Sanchez, Sylvia Schneble, Barbara Schultz, Mort Schwartz, Terri Semper, Ralph Senensky, Jerry Shea, Barry Shear, Walter Shenson, Bill Shephard, Tony Shepherd, Marilyn Sherman, Sandra Siegal, Deborah Sills, Kathy Smith, Mary Spencer, Lea Stalmaster, Ron Stephenson, Danny Stewart, Viola Kates Stimpson, Mac St. Johns, Susan Sukman, Arne Sultan, Anne Talltree, Dale Tarter, Judy Taylor, Liz Temkin, Roz Tillman, Melissa Tormé-March, Bob Towers, Howard Trustman, Doug Turner, Renee Valenti, Michael Van Duzer, Colee Viedelle, E. Duke Vincent, Roy Wallack, Polly Warfield, Louise Wein, David Westberg, Howard Wexler, Bob Wollin and Susan Wright.

We'd also like to thank Brandt Aymar who years ago put us on the starting line, Peter H. Karlen for giving us the "get ready," Dan Poynter for giving us the "get set," and Gwen Feldman, Jim Fox and Leon Embry of Samuel French Trade for giving us the "go."

Thanks too to Mark Locher of SAG, Michael C. Donaldson and David Perren for the continuing help, and, of course, Steve Wachsman, Gitte Wilson, Bruce Findley and Terry Madden for being there, and Joe for the inspiration of July 1, 1978.

And finally, to all our students, who over the years have taught us more than we could ever teach them.

AUTHORS' NOTE
FOR THE REVISED EDITION

What's new?

Well, the forest is the same, but the trees are completely different.

Among those changing trees are the titles of former contributors which we've done our best to update. However, it's possible we missed a title change, and, by the time you read this, the custodian at Warners may have become the president of Universal.

In the "some things stay the same" department, we've still chosen to use the "universal he"; we find the use of "she" or "s/he" calls too much attention to the writing. (We still would love it if some genius would take a moment away from $E=mc^2$ and figure out a solution to this problem. "Heshe"? "Sherm"? "Shey"? "Zortplatt"?)

For the record, the role of women continues to expand in this industry, from casting director to studio exec.

Finally, as to addresses, phone numbers, prices etc. In this edition we've opted to put them all in the Appendix. Seems handier.

So what else is new?

Aha. Read the book.

I
PREPARING TO GO AND GOING

A SPECIAL NOTE TO NEW YORKERS

What I've learned is that there are several different definitions of the word "actor." In New York theatre it's what will make the literature work; in Hollywood, it's what sells.

Beth Holmes, Commercial Casting Director

"Culture shock" is about to take on a new meaning.

Strike: bumping into people, "studio" apartments, insanely ridiculous rents, subways, hangouts for actors, galoshes, cattle calls, "youse guys," theatre/theatre/theatre, walking, Nedicks hot dogs, the Russian Tea Room, Goldenberg's Peanut Chews, Macy's Thanksgiving Parade, and pretzel vendors.

Superimpose: bumping into cars, "single" apartments, *sanely* ridiculous rents, buses that come *every* other vernal equinox, skateboards, movies/movies/movies, driving 30 miles to *everything*, "take a meeting," Pink's hot dogs, Spago, sushi, the Rose parade and sheepskin seatcover vendors.

Most important, as to your career, you'll get on the plane and, somewhere over Tucumcari or between the third and fourth peanut, *somebody will change the rules.*

No longer will you be able to indulge in the "starving artist" look so often worn as a badge of distinction in New York; you'll have to clean up your act. You'll have to lose that "edge" so typical of New York actors — it won't play in L.A. You won't be able to make the rounds as openly. You'll be permitted only one agent to rep you for each endeavor (TV, commercials, etc.). You'll be encouraged when your Big Apple credits and training are very well received, and exasperated when you constantly hear, "But do you have any *film* on yourself?" You may be respected by your New York peers, but, unless you're a name, it's back to work proving yourself all over again to the boys in the Universal Tower. Your cold reading technique probably will have to change from theatre-expansive to office-intimate. Those stints as an extra you're so used to doing will now have to be done almost on the sly — if at all. You'll need to drop that theatrical composite and get yourself a good single headshot. The New York sneer at those "non-acting" film actors will have to be replaced by training in, and respect for, acting *for the camera*. And you'll find even more emphasis on your looks.

Everything in this book is as valid for you as any other actor coming from Seattle, Chicago, or West Nowhere. The difference is in the training and experience you may have, not in what you'll need to do.

It's not only the Dodgers who have gotten into a whole new ballgame.

1 MAKING THE DECISION

Before I take on a client, I look for three things: talent, guts, and imagination.

Barbara Best, Publicist

Welcome to the job-getting business...

...That's the *real* business there's no business like.

And if you're in the midst of packing, certain Hollywood had better batten down its hatches because you're the best damn actor this side of John Barrymore, we'd like to shake your hand, pat you on the back — and tell you to stop right there.

There's a fundamental flaw in your thinking. You're confusing being a *good* actor with being a *working* actor.

Working actors know they're good, but they also have come to grips with one very essential fact: If you're thinking of becoming a professional actor, above all understand that you're really thinking of becoming a *door-to-door* salesman — *of yourself.*

An actor's true vocation is selling and job-getting: his avocation is acting. Most would-be actors either fail to understand this or they've never been told it. They spend all their time honing their craft and little or no time on the business of acting. They sit by unrelentingly silent phones, idealistically waiting for someone to "pick up on" their talent. Occasionally this happens, but more often than not they begin to feel like Edgar Allan Poe's famous "Purloined Letter" — there they are, sitting out for all to see, and nobody knows they're there.

Eventually they quit, believing they were failures as actors. They weren't. They were just poor job-getters.

So if you're thinking about becoming a professional actor, put aside your talent for the moment and examine your basic personality. Can you sell? And — equally important — can you live with the idea of being a salesman? Do you have the emotional make-up of a go-getter?

If you can't answer yes to that, we'd honestly recommend you remain a non-pro. You'll probably be a happier man or woman if you don't act for money.

Now don't misunderstand: we're not saying that being an actor is one long toothache. There are many rewards to the profession, not the least of which is being a member of a very exciting, highly creative community.

But that community, to say the least, is overcrowded. There are about 75,000 members of the Screen Actors Guild (SAG), 80 percent of whom earn *less* than $5,000 a year. That doesn't include the other acting and related unions, and it doesn't include you (probably) and the thousands of others who are trying to get into them.

And even being the greatest talent *and* the greatest job-getter won't guarantee success. Consider the following rather daunting little story:

Years ago, we attended a seminar for beginning actors. The guest speaker looked over the sea of eager faces, sighed, and said, "Of all the people in this room, I would say that 75 percent will have quit by next year; 20 percent more will have given up by the following year; and in five years, two — maybe three — of all of you will still be pursuing a career in acting."

Regardless of whether or not he was right, the point is that this is a business for survivors.

"Patience and perseverance are 45 percent; timing and luck are 45 percent; and talent is ten percent, as talent should be a given," says personal manager Melissa Tormé-March. "There are so many people in L.A. who are unbelievably talented, but if they don't have the patience, perseverance, timing and luck, their talent is irrelevant."

Put another way, it's like being in a lifeboat with 75,000 other people — a boat that can accommodate only two or three hundred (that's about how many roles are available in any given week in Hollywood). You're going to have to figure out a way to stay in the boat, to make enough money to keep yourself afloat all the while thinking up ways of pulling yourself out of the crowd so that Hollywood will sit up and take notice of you.

That means this is no business for the meek or anyone whose pride can't stand more than the average quota of bruising. After all, in terms of type, there will always be at least 25 other people who can play the same roles as you. You have the right to think of yourself as special — you are. Now convince everybody else.

You're going to have to be smarter, quicker, and a better hustler than the other guy. (That doesn't mean you'll need to sleep with anybody; let's get that out of the way right now. You're out to make *friends* — not lovers.)

Director/cinematographer Bruce Logan put it this way: "I went to a seminar where all the guest speakers were studio executives, and the buzzword there was '*relationships*.' I mean the word 'relationships' must have come up 150 times in eight hours. That's the way this industry works."

And part of making those "relationships" work involves not only being

ARE YOU MORE IDEALISTIC THAN PRACTICAL?

There's nothing "idealistic" about doing a deodorant commercial, but it beats heck out of waiting tables. Idealism also has nothing to do with writing a good "covering letter," choosing an agent, selecting a play casting directors will come to see, reading and understanding a contract, or battling it out with a producer for an extra 50 bucks a day. As theatrical casting director Paul Bengston put it: "We call it show *business*. We don't call it show-*art*."

That doesn't mean be cynical. You don't have to join the sharks already in the water. Just develop a healthy practical streak; for example, don't always expect to be performing Shakespeare. To paraphrase the old saying, you're going to have to kiss a lot of frog roles before the prince part comes along.

CAN YOU STAND HAVING YOUR LIFE CONSTANTLY UPROOTED?

One day you'll be broke; the next, possibly, a millionaire. You're sitting jobless in your apartment, brooding and ignoring your spouse; a week later you're on location in Oswego aching with loneliness. Your agent never calls, so you decide to quit; inevitably, the phone rings with an offer for a week's work in New York. On the set, you're given a two-page monologue to learn in five minutes, and you do, and everybody tells you Olivier is in deep trouble; the film comes out and the monologue has been cut to one line . . .

Actor, drop one phrase from your vocabulary: "slow and steady."

ARE YOU THINKING ABOUT "BIG BUCKS"? HOW ABOUT GLAMOR?

Just wait until you experience the "glamor" of looking for an agent. Just wait until you experience the thrill of standing in a cold, driving rain for 12 hours waiting to say your one line (alone, because the "stars" won't talk to you). Just wait until all those big bucks pour in from parking cars to pay the rent. If you're thinking about cocktails and limos you're forgetting: nobody is born a star. Every person in this industry has had to endure being treated like a piece of meat, and a glamor fantasy won't be enough to sustain you through the rough years.

As to "big bucks": a few years ago, a major star appeared on a talk show and frankly stated she couldn't afford not to work. Groans of disbelief could be heard in the audience. But she was probably telling the truth.

Yes, get lucky and you can make a lot of money as an actor and appear on *Lifestyles of the Gross and Greedy*. Maybe that's the reason so many believe that the instant a person appears on TV or in a movie, he is "wallowing in the dough."

Well, a working actor makes in the neighborhood of $500 to $1,000 a day. Sound like a lot of money? You may work one day in an entire year.

And, if you do become a "star," you'll probably then have to pay:

- Ten percent to your agent;
- About 15 percent (and possibly up to 50 percent) to your personal manager;
- Five percent to your publicist;
- Five percent to your business manager;
- And, if you're lucky, after deductions, say about 20 percent to the good ole IRS.

That's 50 percent of an income that isn't guaranteed. You may get hot one year and not work for the next three . . . but your house payment will still be due.

Does the star's statement sound plausible now?

Director Andrew McCullough boiled it all down when he said, "There is nothing more frustrating than to be 'in the middle.' To say, 'I want to be an actor, but I also want such and such.' I think there has to be an absolute moral and ethical commitment. God has given you certain talents. Now how you use those talents is the most important question of your life. Be careful not to buy that fantasy of stardom, money, and all the material things that commercials pump into your heads all the time: 'To be really first rate I've got to have a BMW, a house in Brentwood, or be beautiful and have great clothes.' . . . To be an actor means you take a spiritual vow when you say: 'This is the only kind of life I can live.' "

ARE THE PEOPLE YOU'RE EMOTIONALLY INVOLVED WITH ALSO ABLE TO HANDLE THIS PROFESSION?

We're not talking about Mom and Dad; unfortunately, they may never understand. But others who live with and see you every day are going to have to have the understanding of Mother Theresa. Remember, they're on the ride too. They too are going to have to fasten their safety belts for all those bumpy nights. They're going to have to tough it out and be positive psychological influences. If not, sooner or later you're going to have a very serious problem on your hands.

"If I didn't have a super wife, I don't know where I'd be right now because she carried me," says one actor about his first years in the industry. "Talk about guilt complexes. There I was in a one-bedroom apartment in North Hollywood with no air conditioning and a nine-month-old baby, while my wife is in Beverly Hills working. And I *know* she'd *much* rather be with the baby." As theatrical agent David Westberg says, "Acting is not a job, it's a way of life."

ARE YOU GOOD AT GETTING WORK IN THE TOWN IN WHICH YOU LIVE? DO YOU KNOW THE PRODUCTION HOUSES, AGENTS, ETC., IN YOUR TOWN?

Can't answer yes? Better get going. Finding and dealing with people who can hire you to act should be a lot easier in Dallas than New York or L.A. If you can't get an appointment with someone who sees ten actors a week, how are you going to get to talk to someone deluged with 100 actors a day?

ARE YOU A MAN?

Stop the presses! Prospects are *much* brighter for women! Actresses used to get only 25 percent of all roles. Five years later that figure is *way* up: to 33 percent! Rejoice!

ARE YOU YOUNG? ESPECIALLY, ARE YOU A YOUNG WOMAN?

If you're 18, nobody will expect you to have a résumé as long as your arm. But if you're over 30 and still don't have professional credits, better think it over — especially if you're female. "Older" women (by Hollywood standards, any woman over 30) have a rough road to hoe. Here's what personal manager Melissa Tormé-March had to say: "In certain age categories it can be very hard. We had a lady come out from New York who had done a tremendous amount of live theatre and commercials. She's very pretty and very sophisticated and up-scale. She's in her early 40's. Well, I couldn't sell her if my life depended on it. She is competing with Joan Collins, Linda Evans, Diahann Carroll — people who are already established. It's tough. It's very tough." Quote from an over-30 actress: "Since there are so few roles, I can't look at acting as a profession anymore. I have to think of it as a hobby."

ARE YOU NON-ETHNIC-LOOKING?

Things *have* gotten better in Hollywood for ethnic types, especially Hispanics. With the Latin population explosion, and the success of films like *La Bamba*, the corporate commandoes (as actress Elizabeth Ashley calls them) have finally gotten the message that there's a market out there for enchiladas as well as apple pie. But it's still no bed of *empanadas*. Theatrical agent Joel Rudnick pulls no punches: "There's a lot of racism in this industry. And chauvinism. And sexism. For example, there'll be a role for a cop and I'll suggest a black actor and they'll say, 'Oh, . . . yeah . . . I think we can go black on that.' I hate that expression, 'go black.' "

In commercials (from which actors get nearly half their income), there's an expression: "white bread." That's a blandly good-looking person who typifies the cliché Midwestern American. (In this case, it's not a racial term — a black person such as O.J. Simpson can be "white bread.") Most advertisers are looking for "white bread" (see Chapter 21), because they want Orville Krapotnik to remember the *beer*, not the actor. If you're "special," the opportunities to get a decent piece of the commercial pie are limited.

DO YOU HAVE A CAPACITY FOR CONFIDENCE? DO YOU LOOK CONFIDENT EVEN WHEN YOU'RE QUAKING IN YOUR BOOTS?

The actor who doesn't work is scared and shows it. The actor who works is scared but doesn't show it.

DO YOU HAVE AN EASYGOING, BREEZY PERSONALITY, OR ARE YOU CONSTANTLY UPTIGHT, SCARED, UNHAPPY, NON-SELF-RELIANT?

Most of the time you'll be selling your personality, not your talent. Okay, it's not fair. But it sure is Show Biz. "People are always talking about the 'talent' of an actor," says entertainment attorney Michael C. Donaldson. "To me, the 'talent' to be a successful actor involves what I call 'the three A's' of success — they apply to doctors, lawyers and everyone else — they are: affability, availability, and ability — *in that order*."

ARE YOU THOUGHT OF AS "LUCKY"? DO YOU REFUSE TO QUIT, EVEN WHEN YOUR OPPONENT HAS HOTELS ON BOARDWALK AND ALL THE RAILROADS?

"I know you're talented, but are you lucky?" says theatrical agent Jim Gibson. Yes, there is such a thing as pure dumb luck. But, more often, there is *smart* luck — luck created by work, guts and (forgive the cliché), a refusal to quit. Director Andrew McCullough tells this little story: "Jack Lemmon and I started out at Harvard and went to New York where we lived together and tried to get into the theatre. Looking back on it, he worked harder than anyone I've ever known. He would drag me into flea-bitten — I mean *horrible* looking — places that I was embarrassed to be in. And he wore a horrible threadbare raccoon coat . . . And he would go in and con and cajole these secretaries of booking agents, and they hated him. You know, 'Get out! Get out! There's nothing for you today!' And he would say something funny or give them a little present . . . And he had a list of everyone casting in town. He'd write a dozen letters a day. He'd make scores of phone calls every day. And he didn't get parts and he didn't get discouraged. I mean, that was what he did: try. And he did it over and over and over and over again."

Theatrical agent Mary Spencer sums it up: "Don't go around saying 'I never have any luck,' because luck is when *preparation* and *opportunity* meet."

And, finally, as to your talent . . .

WHEN YOU DO COMMUNITY THEATRE, DO YOU FEEL YOU'RE NOT ONLY BETTER THAN YOUR FELLOW ACTORS, BUT YOU KNOW MORE?

You'll be competing with people who have film and Broadway credits. Learn your craft — and the best way is to do play after play. You can go to L.A. to study acting, but, even so, the more training you get before you arrive the better. Theatrical agent Joel Rudnick cautions, "In a lot of ways, if you're 19 or 20, it makes more sense not to go to Hollywood — to go and do regional theatre and do roles that you'd never get to play in L.A.: O'Neill, Miller . . . and develop your craft."

WHEN YOU TRY OUT FOR LOCAL THEATRE, ARE YOU ALMOST ALWAYS CAST? WHEN YOU'RE REVIEWED, DO THE CRITICS ALMOST ALWAYS RAVE?

It's one thing for *you* to think you're good . . .

That's basically it. If you can answer these questions to your satisfaction, and you want to go ahead, we'd say, what the heck, give it a shot. That's better than sitting over a cup of tea at age 65 *wishing* you had.

Maximillian Schell, speaking at a seminar, was asked if he had any regrets. His answer: "I've never regretted anything I've done. It's always the things that I haven't done that I regret the most." Sound like we're encouraging you to be an actor? We hope not. Drama critic John C. Mahoney said it eloquently when we asked, "What advice would you give to actors?":

"Get out of the business. It's the only honest loving thing you can say to an actor because ten percent of your profession will ever work or make a living. If you're interested in the stage, one to three percent of the population gives the slightest damn what it is you do. It's an alien activity . . .

"The effort you put in is largely wasted, except in whatever it gives you. Half the effort would pay off in used car sales, marketing, public relations . . . If you start thinking, 'Wow, is it worth it?' you've already answered your own question. Of course it's not worth it! . . . If you stick with it, it's because you feel you have something to give.

"It is proper that everyone think you are crazy. There's no reason why you should demand that anyone ever understand your commitment or your dedication. And your mother and everyone else is right — you wouldn't have to work that hard, and you could be rich, if you were in any other business . . .

"I'm very fond of actors, but they are *real* stupid to do what they do. There is no good reason to do it unless you approach it like a monk . . . You may always be happy doing it, but you should only have a good job besides . . . The cruelest thing in the world is to encourage an actor. If you can, *in any way*, discourage an actor, you should."

We'll add that we know you could take everything in this book, throw it out — in fact, do *everything* all wrong — and *still* wind up signing autographs on Oscar night. In this industry there's no such thing as no such thing. "The one thing I've found, the longer I'm in the business," says actor John Edwards, "is that there's no general way it happens. Everybody comes through different doors. Which means you have to keep at it in this business, because eventually something weird will happen your way."

This book will give you the business knowledge you need, and a few tricks of the trade to help that "something weird" come your way perhaps a bit faster. But we can't make you into a person who turns this knowledge to his advantage. That's your job. In other words, *we'll* supply the knowledge; *you* supply the talent, guts and imagination.

2. PREPARING TO GO

Be sure you can afford to be an actor.

Vikki Bandlow, Theatrical Agent

Make your plans at least a year in advance. Many things will require that amount of planning, and it's just better for your brain.

GET A CAR

A fuel-efficient one. You can't do justice to your career in L.A. without "wheels" — the distances are too great. If you don't drive consider going to New York instead.

SAVE MONEY

One look at the complete budget in the Appendix and a glance at your personal expenses and you'll see why we say give up the luxuries, and save, save, save. Besides, doing without will be terrific training.

GET INTO THE "RIGHT" UNION(S)

Thousands of aspiring actors go to New York or Los Angeles knowing nothing about the unions. They learn fast.

New York agents tell them, "Sorry, can't help you if you're not Equity." Hollywood casting directors put out casting notices saying, "SAG *only*."

"Well, I'll be dipped!" they say as they realize Equity isn't owning a home, SAG is not a physical condition, and non-union people will starve. So they try to join. And what do they hear? "You can't join until you've got a job," and, "I can't hire you unless you're union." Eventually, this gets old — so old that they quit.

Pity. Getting in isn't impossible — with a little information and ingenuity. If you can, join the unions before you leave home. But if you can't, don't despair. You may find it *easier* to join the unions in L.A. than in your native Cleveland.

Our point? Before you buy that plane ticket, read our chapter on the unions (Chapter 7); it could alter your plans for a year — or more.

NOTE: For a complete budget and prices, fees, addresses, phone numbers of items mentioned throughout the book, see Appendix.

GET FIT

If losing pounds will make you a beautiful leading lady or a handsome leading man, start jogging. Otherwise, you'll constantly hear you're "hard to place" (cast) because your face says one thing, your body another. If you're a character type your weight may be less important and you can pig out longer at the dinner table. Still, remember commercial casting director Pamela Campus' observation: "Fat thighs do not sell peanut butter."

Anything else about your appearance you don't like? Fix it or learn to live with it. Don't go out on interviews feeling bad about yourself — they're tough enough without that added baggage.

You commercial types especially — get your pearly whites pearly white. To paraphrase Ms. Campus, broken teeth do not sell toothpaste.

And, finally, you don't need a wardrobe that would make Gucci go into jealous convulsions, but get yourself at least one good suit/dress and one good casual outfit.

GET RID OF ACCENTS

No, it's not a crime to have an accent — it's just limiting.

If there aren't any dialect coaches where you live (or even if there are), record announcers who don't have an accent, and work to sound like them. "A cheap way to do it is to get yourself a tape recorder and read something — a play, a scene, a newspaper article — into it every day for ten minutes," suggests theatrical agent Pat Doty. If you can't manage this by yourself run, don't walk, to the nearest dialect coach the minute you arrive in L.A.

GET A JOB SKILL

"The longer my old college chums are in the business, the more realistic they become," says one actress.

Don't expect Hollywood to fall into a swoon over your pending arrival. In fact, it's a fairly safe bet that, from the time you get your SAG card, it will be at least a year before you get your first paying acting job.

You can type, wait table, sell wedgies, etc., without the job getting in the way of your career, but these kinds of jobs are only a temporary solution. If you're smart, you'll find something enjoyable (anything from résumé shot photographer to interior decorator) that won't interfere with acting and pays more than a prune danish — an alternate specialty/skill, almost as much fun as acting, that will carry you during those (inevitable) dry spells. True, hit it big and savings and investments can tide you over. But the average working actor needs a supplementary income. Waiting tables when you're 20 is kicky — but when you're 40 it's a kick in the pants.

If you're without an independent income, and unless you're far enough along in your career to chance your savings on the "switchover to L.A." period, at first plan to get (and keep) a *full-time day job*. It's fantasy to leave your days "free for auditions." What auditions?? Unless you get hot fast in commercials (possible, but so is winning the lottery) you'll need your nights free for classes, theatre and showcasing.

Note: we said *and keep* your job. The first time you get an audition, or, holy cow!, an acting job, tell your current employer your Aunt Bertie just died and you've got to go and do some serious mourning. The next time, terminate Uncle Fritz (what the heck, you don't like him anyway). Only when you've gotten enough work to bump off the entire clan should you give serious consideration to part-time work.

Also, pass on getting a job within the industry. You'll make contacts all right, but as what? A go'fer? A bookkeeper? Okay, now try to get them to think of you as an actor. Says television stage manager James Hamilton, "I wouldn't recommend actors getting into production. It's very hard to prove yourself as an actor in that setting."

ESTABLISH CREDIT

Anyone who believes all Californians are 'laid back' hasn't met a banker. Before you leave try to obtain one or two major credit cards (American Express, etc.).

Also, many banks require a recommendation from a depositor before they'll be so kind as to let you open an account. Unless you know someone in Los Angeles, a few weeks before you leave, have your current bank transfer some of your money to a bank of your choice.

TRAVEL LIGHT

Wait until you know where you're going to live. Why add hassles?

WHAT ABOUT PICTURES (RÉSUMÉ SHOTS)?

A photographer in Walla-Walla can't know what Hollywood is looking for. Wait.

SHOULD YOU CHANGE YOUR NAME?

Not if you're thinking of becoming "Rock Granite" or "Jasmine Julep." Those days, thank Arnold Schwarzenegger, are over.

"Iznik Prlrdj" is acceptable in today's Hollywood, if you want to drive people crazy trying to pronounce it. However, if you've got an ethnic name and a non-ethnic face, a nondescript monicker could eliminate your "ethnicity" and increase opportunities.

Before doing anything check with the national offices of SAG, AFTRA and Equity. If another union member has first dibs on your name, you'll have to change it — *even if it's your real name.* If you're "Bob Jones," and any member is Bob Jones, you'll have to become Robert Jones, Robert C. Jones, or maybe even Iznik Prlrdj.

Whatever you do, do it now — before you have résumés and photos printed up and certainly before you get a few roles under your belt. Changing then will be Excedrin Headache #6 for you and your agent.

All done? You're ready to go. Take a deep breath (it'll probably be the last pure air you'll get for a long time), kiss Mama good-bye, and point yourself in a generally westerly direction . . .

3 ARRIVAL IN L.A.

*My biggest hurdle in starting out was taking
care of my personal basics — a place to call
home, a reliable car, some money in my
pocket and, most important, some peace of
mind. Without those I was only getting in my
own way.*

Kevin Michael Brown, Actor

Seasoned travelers admit that moving to a new city can be mind-boggling.
Not some actors: they hit town Monday night, and by Tuesday morning
they're running around on rubbery legs trying to pursue a career, making
mistakes that may take years to repair.

Don't do that. Settle in. The only gun you're under is the one you hold
on yourself. You're starting a career that's supposed to last into the next
century. Spare about six months to get the lay of the land.

Don't get in your way either.

ARRIVAL

- *By air:* There are several airports in L.A., but you'll probably arrive
  at Los Angeles International Airport (LAX), located on the west side
  of town.

  Before getting your luggage, you might stop at the transportation
  information booth outside of your terminal to check options.

  Cheapest way to finish your journey is by city bus — if you like
  suffering. Distances in L.A. are a whole other planet. Take the airport
  shuttle "C" to 98th Street and Vicksburg Avenue, then transfer.

  Better is Airlink, if your destination is a major hotel downtown or
  in Anaheim, or the Van Nuys Flyaway, which takes you to the Valley.
  Both are inexpensive. No reservations necessary; buses depart
  regularly.

  There are also van services which carry you (and others) directly
  home, and flat-rate taxis for splendid isolation. Rates vary by destination.
  Advice from your local paramedic: check costs before jumping in the
  back seat. Of course, you can rent a car. Liberty, Rent-a-Wreck, and
  Ugly Duckling car rental services are among the less expensive, though

---

*NOTE: For prices, fees, addresses, phone number of items mentioned throughout the
book, see Appendix.*

not all these can be rented at the airport. You might want to rent from a "major" overnight, then switch to a cheapie.

- *By bus:* Greyhound-Trailways Bus stations are in downtown L.A., Hollywood, Santa Monica, Glendale and North Hollywood.

- *By train:* AMTRAK's main stop is Union Station in downtown L.A., but trains stop throughout the L.A. Basin.

TAKE A MINI-VACATION

California is just flat-out beautiful. Before you start hitting the career fast-track, ski a mountain or walk a beach. Clears cobwebs.

Locally, you might want to check out Six Flags Magic Mountain, Knotts Berry Farm, Universal Studios Tour, and the venerable Disneyland. Have a drink at the legendary Polo Lounge in the Beverly Hills Hotel — big deals are still cut over scotch and water. For a look at another kind of sabre-toothed tiger, there's the La Brea Tar Pits. Some freebie attractions: Mann's Chinese Theatre (Rita Hayworth's feet couldn't possibly have been that small), Rodeo Drive (nobody's budget can possibly be that large), Greystone Mansion in Beverly Hills (grounds are beautiful, with a spectacular view of the city, so pick a clear day), and Venice and Muscle Beaches (to see the L.A. everyone thinks is L.A.).

BASIC L.A.

"What city, please?" That's the first thing you'll hear when you dial Information. And they're not kidding. Seventy miles wide, the "Big Orange" is just like the cut- open fruit: sections lying all around no obvious core.

Cross a street and you'll find yourself in another city — Santa Monica, say, or Beverly Hills. It's very confusing at first, but later you'll find these divisions helpful. The city or area name immediately pinpoints locations in what is otherwise a sprawling metropolis.

Take downtown — the usual "core" of any city. It exists, but, unless you work there, it'll have as much import in your life as Idaho. Since there are high-rise office buildings, stores, theatres, etc. in every area of town, you could comfortably work and live in one area and never have to leave it except to visit friends, do special shopping, or go to a particular show, museum or restaurant.

The city is fluid, restless, always on the go and changing — fast. Blink twice and you'll miss the construction of a new building. (At a restaurant in any other city, you watch your hat. In L.A., you watch the restaurant.) Anything with ten years on it is a landmark or a tradition.

The people? As a group they're friendly, positive, laid-back yet, paradoxically, career-oriented. You're judged not by your family tree but by how well you cut trees down, how much you're paid to do it, and what kind of car got you to the forest.

Architecture? A zany patchwork quilt of every style importable and imaginable — from English Tudor to Spanish Hacienda to Modern Disneyland — cheek by jowl, connected by a palm tree.

The weather? Gorgeous. Oh, there are a few rainy weeks in winter and foggy ones in spring, but nobody takes them seriously. Sound boring? Take heart. The ground moves. For swimmers, the ocean is often Antarctica; for lovers and philosophers it's Eden. The city's legendary smog has been institutionalized — via the South Coast Air Quality Management District (AQMD), which "manages" what is quaintly called the Pollutant Standards Index (PSI). The index is usually at its lowest in winter, at its highest in summer and early fall. (You want it low. During the worst months you may feel you're coming down with the flu. You're not. The air has merely become unmanageable.)

Food? Anything you want, from fast food to Vietnamese, with a premium on ambiance, chic, novelty, and especially, nifty names. (Thin is "in" anyhow.)

Entertainment? If you want to see it, it's here: everything from female mud wrestling to the Los Angeles Philharmonic. (One day we'd like to see female mud wrestlers *versus* the L.A. Philharmonic.)

And there's no movie you can name that won't be playing somewhere within the year. Same goes for just about any item on the face of planet Earth: if you want to buy it, there's a store waiting eagerly to sell it to you.

Los Angeles was aptly summed up by drama critic John C. Mahoney: "This town is an enormous smorgasbord. You can walk around and create your own city — like a sandwich." It can be one gigantic headache or Christmas present depending on your attitude, how hard you work at making it home, and how energetically you search for people with interests in common with yours.

There's one interest, however, that all Angelenos have in common. They've had a love affair with it long before Isis got the yens for Osiris. It's a status symbol and, according to psychologists, an "extension" of its occupants. They travel in it, eat in it, use it as a baby sitter, make love in it, and even worship in it — the car.

So if you want to know about life in L.A., we must start with . . .

TRANSPORTATION

- *Autos:* One blessing of this car-itis that the city's freeways and streets are usually in good condition and well-marked. There are often special lanes for turning left and blue street signs giving advance notice of the next major avenue. You can pick up street and freeway maps at a gas station, auto club (Automobile Club of Southern California AAA), or bookstore. A favorite is *The Los Angeles County Popular Street Atlas* by Thomas Bros. Maps.

  The curse of L.A. car mania is gridlock. If you want to speed along on the open road, try Texas, because those free-wheeling freeway days are a memory in the Big Orange. The problem gets worse with each word you're reading, so give yourself plenty of travel time. (Figure rush hour from 7 to 10 a.m. and 3 to 7 p.m. Rest of the day is semi-rush. Best time to leave to beat the Friday rush: Tuesday.)

  In some cities, pedestrian crosswalks are there to show drivers where to *aim*. Not here. California is tough about stopping for pedestrians, and, boy, are walkers complacent! They don't confine themselves to crosswalks, and they're not big on looking either. If you see someone at the curb, be prepared to hit your brakes.

  Since it rarely rains, suntan oil builds up on arms and motor oil builds up on roads. Add water and things can get slippery. Be extra careful when it drizzles.

  You probably know you can turn right on a red light, but for more on traffic regulations and car registration information, pick up free copies of the California Driver Handbook and the Vehicle and Vessel Registration Handbook at the nearest office of the State of California Department of Motor Vehicles (DMV).

  Twenty days after you become a resident or get a job you must register your car and obtain a Certificate of Compliance (smog certification). That may mean bringing the old clunker up to snuff. Anyway, look for any gas station sporting a smog check sign.

  Your car is your lifeblood. Keep it in good working condition and expect dents — on your wallet. Everything about automobiles costs more in L.A. — from mandatory insurance to registration, from gas to maintenance.

- *Buses:* Primary system is the Rapid Transit District (RTD). For schedules (including a free route map for your area), mail RTD a self-addressed, stamped envelope.

  Transit-wise Angelenos catch the bus *prior* to the one that's supposed to get them to their destinations on time. In addition to traffic delays, scheduled buses sometimes simply never come. (The schedulers used to write for *The Twilight Zone*.)

Riding buses across this vast city is a time-consuming, exhausting affair. You can't pursue a career effectively leaving the driving to them. Get a car.

- *Cabs:* Hope you're a millionaire.

TEMPORARY HOUSING

If you're only thinking about a stay of a few days to a week or so, the cheapest place we could find was, naturally, the Hollywood YMCA. They rent to men and women.

If you're thinking in terms of a month or longer, you might look into The Oakwood, which is sort of an apartment-hotel. They've got seven locations in L.A. Most centrally located (and among the cheaper rates) are the Hollywood, Mid-Wilshire and Sherman Oaks locations. Call their 800 number and they'll send you a brochure. It won't include prices; for those you'll have to call the specific location you've chosen.

If you prefer motels, shop around. You might find one that's not much more expensive.

FINDING/RENTING AN APARTMENT

Types of apartments:

1. *Efficiency*: One small room, bath and kitchen.

2. *Single*: One larger room, bath and kitchen (equivalent to a studio apartment in other parts of the country).

3. *One bedroom*: Two rooms, bath and kitchen.

Rent will depend on size, location and amenities. Be prepared to be hit up for the first and last month's rent, a security deposit, sometimes a cleaning fee. There may be no lease, a six-month lease or a one-year lease. You'll probably pay gas and/or electricity; they'll pay water. If you use air conditioning, heat up your electric bill. Some areas have rent control, others don't.

You'll find a greater selection if you stick to unfurnished apartments. These almost always include a stove. But often, of late, no fridge. That's right — no fridge.

If you don't mind driving, you can live anywhere you want. However, since most of the studios and casting offices are in the San Fernando

Valley (called simply "the Valley") or the Hollywood area, we recommend the following locations on the basis of proximity:

- *West Hollywood, Hollywood Hills*: Most centrally located; not bad; rents vary, tend toward expensive.

- *Hollywood*: Central location, many seedy areas, but on the upgrade. Wide range of rents.

- *The Valley*: Includes Studio City, North Hollywood, Universal City, Sherman Oaks, Van Nuys, Burbank, Glendale, and others. These areas get hot and smoggy; in summer you'll need an air conditioner. Rents vary.

- *If you don't mind driving and have some money:* anything west of West Hollywood (Beverly Hills, Westwood, Culver City, West Los Angeles, Brentwood). As you move west, the apartments and neighborhoods get nicer, cooler and more expensive. Best chances for bargains are Culver City and West Los Angeles.

- *If you don't mind driving and want to live at the beach*: Santa Monica, Manhattan Beach, Venice, Marina Del Rey. Rents on the high side. Santa Monica, though, has strong rent control. Renting can be cheap but finding an apartment is tough: folks move in and nail the furniture down. Really pricey: Pacific Palisades and Malibu.

- *If you don't mind driving, period*: Pasadena, Montrose, the West Valley, La Crescenta, Flintridge, etc. Generally, the farther out you go, the lower the rents.

Figure out where you'd like to live, then buy a neighborhood newspaper. Unless you want leftovers, find out when these papers hit the stands and be there to catch them in mid-air.

You could check with a real estate agency in the area, perhaps even an "apartment finders" service. The former probably won't charge, the latter will. The value of either is variable, and you can often do better on your own.

In fact, a good way to search for an apartment is just to drive around. Sometimes all the advertising that's done is a sign on a lawn.

When applying for an apartment, identify yourself by your other job: secretary, office manager — even writer if all else fails — rather than actor. Writers are respectable; they smoke pipes. Actors conduct black masses on the bellies of virgins.

Other tips:

- Get an apartment that includes a parking place.

- You want a washer-dryer on the premises. (The "corner" laundry may be a mile away.)

- To avoid air-conditioning, rent a ground-floor apartment. Heat rises.

- If money is tight, consider apartment-managing, house-sitting, and of course, the time-honored roommate. For all three, scan bulletin boards of colleges and the acting unions, the trade paper classifieds, or even take out your own ad. You can try a roommate-finding service, but add a non-refundable fee to your budget.

- L.A.'s Secret Law: there must be a Dragon Lady (of either sex) in every third building. To avoid him/her, size up the manager/owner — whoever lives on the premises — carefully. Lots of rules? Kill the deal. You're not renting a cell in Folsom Prison.

GETTING A PHONE

In L.A., Ma Bell has two daughters: Pacific Telephone and General Telephone. Which daughter you marry depends on the area in which you live.

Neither requires a deposit, you'll pay for installation, and your monthly rate will depend on those little extras, so be careful. You'll probably be surprised at how cheap your monthly rate is; then bam! You get your bill and the "toll calls" would choke a horse. That's because your basic service only extends a certain distance from where you live (they claim it's about ten miles, we swear it's next door), and because L.A. is so big, you're going to place toll calls within the city.

Note your heavy toll-calling areas. Then pour yourself a stiff Perrier and call your phone company. General Telephone has the "Frequent Caller Program"; Pacific Telephone has "Call Bonus," "Community Plan," "Circular Plan," and "Wide Area Plan." "Plan" on asking them to explain these toll-call savings services about six times.

Other services:

- *Call Forwarding*: You're going out. You "program" your phone with the number where you can be reached. When someone calls, their call will be routed to the phone you're near.

- *Call Waiting*: Busy signal prevention. You're adding an additional line onto the same phone number, and can receive two phone calls at the same time.

The two area codes you'll be using most: 213 for most of L.A. county, and 818 for the San Fernando Valley. A close third is 714, for Orange County. (When leaving messages include your area code, and be sure it's on résumés, letters, etc.)

GETTING A JOB

Temporary work is the solution if you need a job quick. Check the no-fee temporary agencies listed in the phone book, trade paper classifieds and union bulletin boards.

But unless your career is already past the early stages or your name is DuPont, ultimately you'll need a full-time job. Don't get one you hate — that's a morale killer. And don't take a job that has you in and out of town or demands a lot of overtime. If there's no time for your career, why are you in Hollywood?

Give your agent your work number and never pass up an audition because you're needed at the word processor. It won't compute and your relationship will crash.

But don't tell any other industry person you do anything but act full time. We once heard a casting director say actors with regular jobs "aren't professional." May all the elastic in his underwear crumble at the Oscars. Most actors work from time to time, and this attitude reveals a terrible (but unfortunately not uncommon) case of the smugs.

FOOD

Eating out is an expensive little pastime, so get a place with a kitchen *pronto*. When grocery shopping, think big — large often equals cheaper.

Distances make it hard for actors to hang out New York-style, but there are spots such as Duke's Coffee Shop on Sunset Boulevard, Dupar's coffee shop and Jerry's Deli (a touch of Manhattan) near CBS Studio Center, Lucy's Cafe El Adobe near Paramount, and most other restaurants near the major studios. Pricier places include Spago's in West Hollywood and 72 Market Street in Venice. Drop by and you'll get an earful of shop talk.

FURNITURE/FURNISHINGS

A newspaper called *The Recycler* is available at most newsstands and contains ads for just about anything people want to sell or swap. You can get some great buys — especially if you can dicker. Same with garage sales and swap meets. Be ready to pay cash.

Adray's, Fedco, The Home Club, Circuit City, and Federated are just a few of the stores that offer name-brand merchandise at low prices.

CLOTHING

Want to dress from head to foot without paying an arm or a leg? Discount clothing stores abound, especially in downtown L.A.'s garment district in the neighborhood of Los Angeles and Ninth Streets.

Others, called "re-sale stores," sell lightly-used clothes, often with designer labels. To actors, one of the most interesting in this category has got to be The Re-Take Room in Studio City. (Don't confuse this with the bar of the same name in Woodland Hills.) This little store sells wardrobes from movie and television shows — some of them incredible bargains and have everyone wondering how you, Paul Oldfellow, can afford to dress like Paul Newman.

ESTABLISHING CREDIT

Whether or not you brought plastic with you, establish credit within the city.

Go to a bank and open a savings account. Let's say you put in $1,000. Then go to the loan officer and tell him you want to make a $1,000 loan, using your savings account as collateral. (You're guaranteeing the loan will be paid back, because if you default, the bank simply grabs the money in your savings account.)

Then, pay it off in about a year. It won't give you the credit rating of a Rockefeller, but it'll help.

INFO LINE

This free service is available 24 hours a day, seven days a week, and gives information or referrals for housing, community services, emergency food, medical treatment, just about you name it. There are nine toll-free numbers in L.A. county.

SIZING UP THE SITUATION

With an apartment, job, and telephone, welcome to L.A.! Now it's time to get that lay of the land, at a leisurely, get-yourself-together pace. Say, three months. You'll know when to get moving; you'll get itchy.

Some places to size up:

- *The unions:* That is, SAG, AFTRA, Equity. Check out their bulletin boards. You'll find all sorts of interesting information, from photographers advertising rates to apartments for sublet, cars for sale, announcements of free seminar or two.

- *Samuel French's Theatre & Film Bookshops and Larry Edmunds Bookshops*: Plays, books and other items on acting and film will beg, "Take me home!" And you will. For scripts, posters, collectables, visit Movie World and The Collector's Bookstore, among others.

- *The American Film Institute*: It's there for the advancement and preservation of motion pictures in general, and for training filmmakers in particular. It's also the home of the SAG Conservatory Program, which we'll talk about later. The Institute has it's own library, with fascinating books and film scripts. Don't be surprised to see actors working for auditions for a student film. Goes on all the time. More on this later, too.

- *Those live TV shows*: Excellent research for an actor. Call the stations and find out how you can get tickets to what's currently in production. When observing, avoid watching the TV sets around you. Watch the actors and what they are doing live.

- *USC, UCLA*: USC's film school is terrific, though the neighborhood isn't. UCLA is a beautiful, sprawling campus adjoining an area called Westwood Village — probably the only true walking area in L.A. The "Village" is relatively safe, clean, with one of the largest collection of first-run movie theatres in town. But the faint of heart should avoid the area on weekends. That's when the dreaded California Teeny-Bopper comes out in force.

- *The studios*: Pass by all the major studio lots (see Map). You'll be auditioning at these places and it'll help you to know where they are. Without a pass, you won't be allowed onto the grounds (unless you've got the chutzpah to take a manila envelope with you, wave knowingly at the guard, and hope he thinks you're delivering something. Less daring individuals can take a studio tour). If you do get on, don't burst into anyone's office hoping to get discovered. These are busy people — with long memories.

- *Theatres, plays*: See play after play. If you're worried about cost, find out when previews are held; they're usually cheaper. Go to enough theatres, see enough plays, read enough reviews and you'll know here you'd eventually like to strut the boards.

- *Acting classes*: No, don't take a class yet — but look around. And, of course, attend all the freebie seminars you can.

- *The trades*: We'll go into these in more detail later, but take a gander at *The Hollywood Reporter, The Daily Variety,* and *Drama-Logue*. They're available at most newsstands and by subscription.

- *Get to know the city*: Get out and around; learn major streets and subdivisions. Try shortcuts. Now's the time to head for Burbank and wind up in Oxnard, not when you're on your way to an audition. Mix. Mingle. Network. Set a schedule. Sitting home doing nothing is the actor's greatest trap; don't fall into it. You're in an exciting city. Add to the excitement.

Studio Map Key
(Map not drawn to scale)

1. ABC Television City, 4151 Prospect Ave., L.A. 90027, (213) 557-7777
2. American Film Institute, 2021 N. Western Ave., L.A. 90027, (213) 856-7600
3. The Burbank Studios, 4000 Warner Bl., Burbank 91522, (818) 954-6000 (includes Warner Bros., same address/phone, and Columbia Pictures/TV, Columbia Plaza, Burbank 91505, same phone)
4. CBS Studio Center, 4024 Radford Ave., Studio City 91604, (818) 760-5000 (also MTM, same address/ phone)
5. CBS Television City, 7800 Beverly Bl., L.A. 90036, (213) 852-2345
6. The Culver Studios, 9336 W. Washington Bl., Culver City 90230, (213) 836-5537
7. Fox Television Center, 5746 Sunset Bl., L.A. 90028, (213) 856-1000
8. Hollywood Center Studios, 1040 N. Las Palmas Ave., L.A. 90038, (213) 469-5000
9. Hollywood National Studios, 6605 Eleanor Ave., L.A. 90038, (213) 467-6272
10. Lions Gate, 1861 S. Bundy Dr., L.A. 90025, (213) 820-7751
11. Lorimar, 3970 Overland Ave., Culver City 90232, (213) 280-8000. Also:
12. Lorimar, 10202 W. Washington Bl., Culver City 90232, (213) 280-8000.
13. MCA-Universal Studios, 100 Universal City Plaza, Universal City 91608, (818) 777-1000
14. NBC Television, 3000 W. Alameda Ave., Burbank 91523, (818) 840-4444
15. Paramount Studios, 5555 Melrose Ave., L.A. 90038, (213) 468-5000
16. Raleigh Studios, 650 N. Bronson St., L.A 90004, (213) 466-3111
17. Ren-Mar Studios, 846 N. Cahuenga Bl., Hwd. 90038, (213) 463-0808
18. Sunset-Gower Studios, 1438 N. Gower St., L.A. 90028, (213) 467-1001
19. 20th Century Fox Studios, 10201 W. Pico Bl., L.A. 90035, (213) 277-2211 (mailing address: P.O. Box 900, Beverly Hills 90213)
20. Walt Disney Studios, 500 S. Buena Vista St., Burbank 91521, (818) 840-1000
21. Warner Hollywood Studios, 1041 N. Formosa Ave., L.A. 90046, (213) 850-2500

II
THE SUPPLIES YOU'LL NEED

SUNGLASSES

TUXEDO

HOME IN BEL AIR

MERCEDES (VINTAGE)

TAN

DESIGNER JEANS

DESIGNER SHOES

DESIGNER PAPER TOWELS

CANNES BUMPER STICKER

BATHROOM TELEPHONE

CAR TELEPHONE

HALL CLOSET TELEPHONE

KIDNEY-SHAPED HOT TUB

CAVIAR ON KIWI FRUIT

4 A LIST OF SUPPLIES

I used to always summarize by saying,
"Persevere." But "perseverance" isn't in my
summary any more. After all, you have to
know what you're persevering at, and you've
got to have the right materials. So, in
summary: Picture, Résumé, Equity-Waiver
Theatre, Cassette, Agent, Producer, and
Casting Director.

Buddy Bregman, Producer-Director

Here's a list of supplies you'll need during your first year. In the Appendix, you'll find a complete budget with dollar amounts for every item mentioned. We've divided your supplies into three categories:

1. *The Musts*: Obviously, items you can't function without.

2. *Other Items*: You can survive without them, but they can help a lot.

3. *Chicken Soup*: You can spend an entire career without ever having any of these items. But, if you've got the money, like chicken soup, they can't hurt.

Take a look at the budget in the Appendix, toss in your personal expenses and you'll have a pretty good idea not only of where to start, but of what you're going to have to/want to do and earn at least for the next year.

A point that bears repeating: Figure you'll earn your first money as an actor about one year after the date you get your SAG card (unless you're fantastically lucky). Don't quit your job and declare that you are "now an actor." Keep (or get) that job; acquire the items you'll need; learn some basics about the business; and save your money.

Except for theatre, showcases and classes (each has a chapter of its own later in the book), the next four chapters will go into detail about all the items below.

• THE MUSTS

Telephone
Headshot session
Headshot printing (500 theatrical, 500 commercial)
Résumés (typing, printing 500)

Union(s) initiation
Union dues
Postage
Envelopes (good-looking manila, some regular)
Academy Players Directory listing
Answering device
Good stationery
Thank-you notes
SAG agency list
Datebook
Theatre, showcases, classes

- **OTHER ITEMS**

Composite session
Composite printing
Card file & notebook
Directories
Working Actors Guide
Trade subscriptions
Postcards
Typewriter
Labels (blank or pre-addressed)
Videocassette (including air-check, stock, editing)
Passport

- **CHICKEN SOUP**

Desk
Computer
VCR
Video camera

5 RÉSUMÉ SHOTS

*Q: When an actor comes into your office and
he doesn't look like his résumé shot, what's
your reaction?*

A: I get furious.

Interview with Judith Holstra, Casting Director

Here's how a contractor we know hires roofers: "Any guy can come into the office and talk a good game about all the wonderful work he's done, but me, *I look at his tools.*"

Your agent (and yourself) uses two tools to sell you: your résumé and your résumé shots. If either is bad, you've tied one hand behind his (your) back.

Photos pour into the offices of casting directors, agents, producers, and directors. Some are good, others, fair. Many are atrocious. There are shots of actors taken with a Polaroid-type camera, half-naked Adonises, figures standing at a distance, waving languidly at the camera... And these are the people who will complain, "You just can't beat the system." Well, as theatrical agent David Westberg says, "We're dealing in a visual business. The first thing you need to get in the door is pictures. If your pictures are lousy you ain't gonna get in the door."

Unfortunately, putting together good pictures is like assembling a toy train on Christmas Eve — it's a pain in the neck. It's involved, time-consuming and filled with wonderful little aggravations and things to remember.

Take the time. Plow through it, step by step. Others will. Don't settle for pictures that are mediocre. Eventually, you'll have pictures you're proud to submit — shots that will pay you back in satisfaction and, more important, in income.

RÉSUMÉ SHOTS: THE CARDINAL RULE

The days of the "Joan Crawford glamor picture" are long gone. Today, casting directors, etc., are turned off by photos of painted goddesses and costumed gods. What they want now is to see *you* — not how you'd *like* to look, but how you honestly *do* look, scars, moles, warts and all.

NOTE: For prices, fees, addresses, phone numbers of items mentioned throughout the book, see Appendix.

We can't emphasize this more strongly. Pictures that don't look like you are worthless. Never forget that.

Now, when starting out, you will need:

- At least one good COMMERCIAL headshot;
- At least one good THEATRICAL headshot.

Before we explain the differences between these two . . .

HEADSHOTS IN GENERAL
(WHETHER "COMMERCIAL" OR "THEATRICAL")

A headshot, sometimes called an "eight-by-ten" (8x10), is a single black-and-white closeup of the actor's face and hair. (Color pictures are a waste of money.) It's eight inches wide by ten inches long, and there is nothing on the back of the photo.

A headshot, again, shows what you honestly look like in street garb. (No sequined evening gowns or Roman togas, and remember, as theatrical casting director Jerry Franks cautions, "Beefcake or cheesecake photos are very offensive.") Women should apply makeup slightly heavier than usual for the shoot, but the result should be a standard daytime look.

In a headshot, look directly at the viewer. Forget cloud-gazing or profile shots (you can get away with a bit of profile — a three-quarters view — but still look straight into the camera).

Don't try for the kind of photo a model would use. Avoid tricky lighting or "mists" around the face, and don't ask the photographer to airbrush out scars and wrinkles.

Be careful of background(s). You are not selling tree trunks.

And, if the headshot is good, it'll capture your special quality. Goldie Hawn bubbles. Robert De Niro smolders. As theatrical agent John Mekrut put it, "The overriding consideration is that the picture has to communicate to whoever is looking at it: this is somebody you want to meet."

THE COMMERCIAL HEADSHOT

. . . Goes to anyone involved with the making of commercials (agents, casting directors, production houses, etc.).

On a commercial headshot, you should look straight out of a musical comedy, showing lots of teeth (they need to know you've got good ones) and gobs of happiness in a "Gosh, it's great to be alive" manner. (No smolder here, please.)

In short, look happy, warm, and perky — very happy, very warm and very perky. Happy, warm, perky people sell soap. And happy, warm, perky pictures sell people to the people who want happy, warm, perky people to sell soap.

THE THEATRICAL HEADSHOT

. . . Goes to people involved with films, television and stage productions (agents, casting directors, producers, directors).

Here's where you sell your special quality as an actor, whether warm and happy or not. If you're a burly, villainous sort, project that. Don't lard it on to the point where you look like Jack the Ripper, but enough to suggest how you might be used. Ask yourself:

- *How am I normally cast?* Do I play a lot of calculating women? Weak little men? Villains? Moody young heroes?

- *What have my friends told me about my acting personality?* Do they talk about my warmth? My wit? My sensuality?

- *Is there a known star I am often compared to?* Comparisons to Burt Reynolds suggest a casual, rugged look; Vincent Price suggests a suit and tie. (We're *not* talking about imitating anybody. The industry already has a Burt Reynolds; it doesn't, however, have you.)

- *What roles on television/movies/stage/commercials could I have done without having to stretch* at all?

The answers will tell you your "type" and what qualities your theatrical headshot(s) should show. Understand this: Hollywood isn't a rep company, it's a business of types. The days of playing Granny (if you're 20) are gone. Sorry.

One other note. Have at least two theatrical headshots — one for dramas, the other for comedies. Your commercial headshot can do double duty for the comedy.

A NOTE ABOUT COMPOSITES

A composite consists of one large photo on the front with three to six — usually four — smaller photos on the back. In Hollywood, composites are mostly limited to commercials.

But save your money. A good commercial headshot will get you interviews with agents. Wait until you sign with an agent — or even get one or two jobs — and then work out your composite with your agent's help.

Do a commercial composite before signing with an agent and we guarantee you'll hear: "We like you, but your composite, well . . ." If it's not the photos, it'll be the layout, and you'll wind up spending more time and money getting a new one. That's why composites are listed farther down on the budget.

PRACTICING

It's one thing to know what you want to project; another to project it — especially if you haven't worked in front of a camera.

Buy a friend a beer and convince him/her to do a mock photo session with you, using any camera capable of taking close-ups. Try different poses, outfits, attitudes, etc., and keep shooting until you get tired or your friend begins to seriously grunt . . .

What you get back from the drug store should tell you quite a bit about how to project yourself. No photographer can pull out "hidden charms" or get silk photos out of a sow's ear of a subject.

FINDING A PHOTOGRAPHER

Q. I've got a friend with a camera. Can he take my résumé shots?

A. We've got a friend with a scalpel. Can he take out your appendix?

In other words, get a pro who knows what the industry is looking for. Finding one is easy. They spend a good deal of time and energy trying to find you. Besides, you can:

- Ask actors. They know who's good.

- Check the trades (see "Trades," Chapter 8). Shooters galore advertise in them.

- Scan bulletin boards of unions, acting schools and other places where actors congregate.

- Pop into photographic print shops. They often have photographers' calling cards, customers you can quiz, and employees with a lead or two.

To get you started, we list a few of the city's many good photographers in the Appendix.

CONTACTING THE PHOTOGRAPHER

First, some "lingo":

- *Headshot session*: It lasts an hour or two. Figure the photographer will take about 70 (sometimes more) shots of your glorious mug.

- *Exposures, shots*: Other words for "photo" (i.e., 72 exposures equals 72 photos).

- *Negatives*: Few photographers will give their clients the actual negatives, as this is the way they protect the copyright on their work. Rather, you'll get:

- *Proofs, proof sheets*: They're little copies of each photo (about the size you get in a video arcade) on sheets of photographic paper, about 16 to a sheet. You then choose the shots you want blown up into:

- *Print(s)*: These are your 8x10's. One to four of these usually are included in the cost of the session. Beyond that, you'll pay a small fee for each additional print.

Now that you know the jargon, ask him:

How does he work?

Very important. "Posing" you is perfect — for wax museums. You want a photographer who snaps away as you move. He should talk to you, coax you, and, yes, stroke your ego a little. (An actress we know went to her session, and the first thing the photographer said to her was, "Gained a little weight, have we?" Guess how her pictures came out.)

How much?

What does he include in his price for a headshot session (i.e., how many exposures and prints; how much for extra prints)?

How many costume changes are permitted?

To a photographer, a "costume change" means a change of street garb-type outfits — not cowboy hats and spurs. Four changes are about the most you'll need, but define terms. Taking off a tie is a "costume change" to some.

How long before you get your proofs?
Minimum: a few days. Maximum: two weeks.

How long before you get your prints?
Same as above.

Does he keep the negatives?

Expect a "yes," but a few will give them up.

What happens if you don't like your proofs?

Sticky question, but ask — before the first click of the shutter. Most photographers will schedule another session at no additional charge. A few give half or all your money back. We wish more would. How do you get good seconds if you tell a guy you don't like his firsts?

FIRST MEETING WITH THE PHOTOGRAPHER

Besides checking to see if you're comfortable with him, you're really there to look at his samples. Don't skim. Scrutinize those shots. Remember, he thinks they show his best work. Notice . . .

Are they clear and bright, or "muddy"? Are the contrasts between light and dark clear and crisp?

The backgrounds: Are subjects in front of brick walls, traffic, spangly paper, etc.? That's distracting and the photographer should know that.

Do the actors jump off the page? Do they excite you? Is there animation in their faces? If it's a commercial headshot, does the actor have life and warmth, or is he just smiling? If it's a theatrical headshot, does the actor look interesting?

Do the subjects look stiff or posed? Do the same poses keep popping up? (Some industry veterans can guess the photographer from the poses.) Nobody's special on an assembly line.

Has the photographer called attention to himself by using tricky lighting, shadows, etc.? *You're* the star, dagnabbit!

Again, and above all, *what is going on in the eyes of the actors?* "The first thing I notice in a picture is the eyes. the eyes sell it," advises theatrical agent Sandra Siegal.

(By the way, use this same criteria when choosing your own photos.)

If delighted with what you see, talk to him a bit. Find out if he basically agrees with how you see yourself, and only give him a go if you think you can work with him. If he makes you feel defensive, irked, or just in the Universe of the Ungood, pass.

SETTING THE PLACE AND "MAGIC" TIME

Outdoor lighting usually gives more depth to a photo — helps to eliminate that flat "high school yearbook" look. (Some photographers can shoot indoors and make it look like it was shot outside.) If you shoot outdoors, avoid midday. Shadows cast by the sun are too harsh. Actually, you'd

DRAMATIC LIGHT, BUT WHO IS IT??

FIND THE ACTOR...

OH, COME ON!

THE CLEAR WINNER

be smart to steal an idea from your own industry. Directors have been known to drive producers up the wall waiting for "magic time" — that special twilight cameras love. Makes the hero look heroic and the *femme* truly *fatale*. Well, though some directors think they're God, they don't own that light. See if you can get the photographer to agree to a shoot around this time.

PRE-SESSION PLANNING

Decision time. How do you want to look? (You might love that spiked hairdo, but will the industry?) Satisfied with your choices? Fine. Now look that way for as long as you use those shots (probably a year or more). Your hair color, length, and curliness may vary only slightly. Your makeup can't change much either. And moustaches and beards cannot be grown/cut off. Want to change? New photos.

Next, raid the closet. Clothing should suit your type and what you want to project. Medium-to-light-colored clothing is best for your commercial headshot (a quiet plaid under a sweater is a highly saleable commercial look); darker colors are okay for your theatrical headshot. But avoid white or black, loud plaids, prints, shiny fabric — anything that distracts from your face. Skip jewelry too. Pick out a dressy and an informal outfit — provided, again, that either doesn't conflict with your type. Don't be shy. Bring a load of clothes and ask the photographer for his opinion.

Finally, go over in your mind what you're going to do. A good photo session is a combination of the actor's ideas and those of the guy with the camera. Photographer Dale Tarter advises, "It's as important for you to be prepared when you come to see a photographer as it is going on a movie set. *Do your homework.* I love it when an actor knows what he wants."

THE SESSION

Do what you planned. Don't be pushed into poses that are wrong for you. Outside of that . . .

- *Nerves:* If you're a bit shaky, say so. A good photographer will do all he can to calm and reinforce you. (We know one photographer who routinely pretends to shoot a nervous actor for about 15 shots. Then, with the actor over the jitters, he really goes to work. Works like a charm.)

- *Lose glasses/contacts:* Specs block the eyes, and contacts reflect light. You can use glasses for a specialty shot, but be careful. "Half the pictures under the category of 'character' in the *Academy Players Directory* show people wearing glasses," says theatrical agent Joel Rudnick, "You know, they do various things with them like putting the glasses at the end of their noses . . . and I don't think it works. It just looks hokey."

- *Don't squint*: Occasionally, between shots, squint as hard as you can. Then relax. Feel the difference?

- *Other tricks*: Moist lips photograph better, so, every once in a while, lick your lips. To avoid glassy eyes, look down to the ground. Set your mood. When the photographer is ready, suddenly look up. If he shoots at that instant, you'll have a lively, animated expression.

And, above all, as personal manager Larry Fonseca puts it, "Look at the camera — that's where your money is. Look at that camera and say 'Buy me.' Think about something. Feel sexy. Feel mean. Do whatever you want, *but think about something.*"

EXAMINING THE PROOFS

In Universe 27-B, everyone's a millionaire, nobody ever hits a red light, and every shot on all proof sheets is fantastic. In our universe (which continually gets mixed reviews), when your proofs are ready, you'll have to be picky.

Using a magnifying glass — ideally one with a light — employ the criteria mentioned earlier under "Choosing a Photographer."

Usually the photographer's choices are dead on, but get other opinions. "Actors should never pick their own pictures," says résumé photographer John Sanchez. "They just don't know the industry." Certainly show your choices to your agent and any other industry-wise person you can pin down. Just remember, we said industry-wise. Mom will fall in love with a mantelpiece shot that's a disaster as a résumé shot.)

Don't narrow your choices to one shot. Why? We're sure it's gremlins, *but no picture ever looks the same blown up as it did on the proof sheet.* Have as many shots blown up as common sense and your pocketbook will allow.

GETTING AND CHECKING YOUR (ORIGINAL) PRINTS

You'll think you're going nuts. On one print, a shadow that "wasn't there" on the proof sheet will now be skiing down your nose. On another, those eyes that "jumped off the proof sheet" now look like Dracula at feeding time.

Like we said, gremlins . . .

With those *Twilight Zone* prints out of the way, examine the rest, again using the criteria under "First Meeting With the Photographer," and add:

- Are there any spots or scratches?
- Is the focus fuzzy or sharp?
- Is the photo too light or dark?

Sometimes these things can be corrected with a little darkroom wizardry, but if the photographer says "no way," forget the picture. You can't look good blurred.

Okay, with at least two good original prints — one commercial, one theatrical — it's time to say "bye" to the photographer and move on to the printer.

PRE-PRINTER DECISIONS

Since printers tend to specialize, before contacting them know:

1. The finish you want.
2. Whether or not to have a border.
3. The location of your name.
4. The appearance of your name.

The finish

There are four in wide use: "glossy," "matte," "gloss-tone," and "pearl." There's no industry standard. Your choice is wide open.

- *Glossy*: Your pictures will look shiny. It's the most- used and usually least expensive.

- *Matte*: (Pronounced "mat.") Your pictures will have a cloth-like look and feel. The preferred finish for composites. (See Chapter 23.)

- *Gloss-tone*: Sort of a toned-down version of glossy. Open a magazine and look at the photographs — that's what gloss-tone looks like.

- *Pearl*: Rather difficult to describe. Looks cloth-like but shiny. Sort of a jazzed-up matte finish.

Note that matte, gloss-tone and pearl finishes don't reproduce as well in newspapers as glossy, and gloss-tone tends to scratch more easily.

Border(s) or "bleeds"

Borders are the white spaces between the photo and the edge of the paper. You're not selling white space so keep borders narrow, say ⅜ of an inch (except for the border containing your name). "Bleeding" means the photo itself fills up (bleeds off) the paper, leaving no border at all. A variation is the "three-sided bleed" — one border (usually at the bottom) onto which your name is printed.

Name location

Horrible thought of the day: A producer sits ruefully staring at your picture. He's dying to use you, but he lost your résumé, and your name isn't on your photo. Skip all other information (agency, stats, etc. This is not true for composites; see Chapter 23) but put your name on your résumé shots.

Name appearance

If you have no border, your name is on the photo itself. You tell the printer where you want it, and he'll use one of three methods: "knock-out," "overprint" (or "overlay") and "reverse."

- *Knock-out*: That's a small block of white space with your name printed in black letters within the block.

- *Overprint or overlay*: There's no white space around your name. It's directly on the photo, in black letters.

- *Reverse*: Same as above, in white letters.

Don't let your name disappear. If you use an overprint, be sure the spot you choose for your name is fairly light. If it's a reverse, the spot should be relatively dark.

Finally, there's the typeface you want (script, block letters, etc.). You'll have to choose from what your printer has available, but give some thought to what will compliment your image. Don't laugh — typefaces make statements. Corporations spend thousands finding just the right "T." (That doesn't mean your name should look like a marquee in heat. The photo's the star.)

IF YOU PIN US DOWN

Okay, okay, let us up . . . We like:

- A *pearl* finish (we just like the look).

- A *four-way bleed* (calls more attention to the subject).

- A *reverse or overprint* (a knock-out tends to draw too much attention on the name).

Remember, that's only an opinion. Like the Valley Girl says, "It's your choice, *totally*."

CHOOSING A PRINTER

Can he do what you want? Okay, now you want to know the:

- *Negative cost*: The printer photographs the photographer's original print, literally taking a picture of a picture, and makes copies from that new negative. (You'll get this negative back.) There's a small fee for doing this, which you can avoid if you have the photographer's original negative — nice if you can get it.

- *Lot cost*: The number of copies made, i.e., 200, 300, etc. If you have an agent, order about 300. If not, start with 200 — a future agent may like you, but not your pictures.

- *Name imprinting/negative*: In his secret dungeon, the printer spells out your name in the type you've chosen and takes a picture of it. He'll use the negative to make copies. (You'll get this negative back, too.)

- *Extras*: Cropping, bleeds, overprints, lightening or darkening a picture, etc., may or may not cost extra.

A NOTE ABOUT "LINES"

This isn't Photography 101, so we'll simply say that if two printers cost about the same and both can do what you want, go with the one who *uses more lines*. Your copies will just look better. (Ask, "How many lines do you use?")

AT THE PRINTER - TEST PRINTS

After telling him all the things you want, order a test print — a sample copy. Some printers include test prints, even test wedges (copies of the picture in various lightnesses and darknesses) in your basic cost. If not, pay the small extra amount to have it done. One bad sample copy is a lot better than 300 bad prints.

He'll want either a deposit or full payment in advance (yeah, we know) and tell you when he'll have your test print (a few days to two weeks). Don't set your watch by any dates a printer gives you. If you're far away, always call first.

CHECKING THE PRINT(S)

Hang in there, you're almost done. Check your test print(s) as carefully as you've checked everything else. Use all the criteria we've mentioned before, and add:

- Is your name spelled right? Is it straight or crooked?
- Is the printing of your name clear or out of focus?
- Are the letters even on all sides?
- Are they "dirty" with white specks or scratches?
- Did the printer do everything you asked for (lightening, additional cropping, etc.)?

Something wrong? Point it out and have another test print done. If you gave the printer a negative (as opposed to a print) and there's a problem, call the photographer. If the negative can't be fixed, choose another picture.

CHECKING THE COPIES

Don't grab 'em and run. After all, this is the last step. From the center of the stack, pull out a copy and examine it, using all the criteria we've mentioned. Unless something very strange occurred, your copies should exactly match the test print.

Satisfied? Go home; take out one of your pictures; pour a drink and toast yourself. You're now way ahead of a lot of aspiring actors. Was it worth it? Here's what casting director Deborah Barylski says: "Every now and then I think 'God, I've got to go through these pictures because I'm going to find a diamond in there.' And I do. It actually happens."

Congrats, now you've got a diamond!

UPDATING YOUR PICTURES

We've already mentioned that, at least every three years or whenever anything about you changes, you've got to have new pictures done. As casting director Kathy Smith says, "Whenever you change your hair, say from long to short, think of it as a $200 haircut." We'd just like to add not to forget weight gain or loss, and getting older.

That last one is a toughie, but it has to be faced. Except for Dick Clark. He's under 40 by contract.

6 RÉSUMÉS

Hand someone a résumé and photo, and you're presenting them a package. Both are your trademarks. Both make a statement about your professionalism. If you're spending hours pouring over your pictures and ten minutes dashing off your résumé, you're wrapping only the top part of your package.

APPEARANCE

Here's the most neglected area of résumés, and it's just as important as what's on it. Some suggestions:

- *Don't use cheap paper*: That'll make you look cheap. Good paper is 20- or 24-weight rag bond, and costs only about two to three cents more than ordinary bond paper. (Just ask the printer to show you a sheet.)

- *Type it on a good typewriter/word processor*: Or have it composed and typed by someone who knows the industry. (Acting résumés are different from business résumés.) The small fee you'll pay will be well worth it. And never submit a résumé with something handwritten on it.

- *Have it nicely copied*: With the advances in photocopying machines, you can photocopy your résumé and it'll look terrific, or have it offset-printed. There's no need to typeset the résumé. Granted, typesetting looks beautiful, but it's expensive and permanent-looking — as if the actor didn't intend to add any more credits. (Still want that look? Check out one of the desk-top publishing services in town — a computer and laser printer can do it.)

- *Try a muted color*: It's eye-catching. We like egg white.

- *Cut the résumé to fit the photo*: You submit a résumé and photo by stapling the résumé to the back of the picture. (No paper clips, glue, spit, bubble gum or tar.) Since the average piece of paper measures 8½" by 11", cut it down to fit your 8" by 10" photo, or ask the printer to do it — before he prints the résumé. Don't forget to allow space for this on all sides when typing the résumé. Sound petty? Might keep your pic around longer. To quote a casting director: "Nothing drives me crazier than résumés that are slightly larger than the photograph. Filing them is a real pain in the neck."

- *Your name*: Is the first thing anyone should notice. If you think that's obvious, you'd be surprised at the number of résumés we've seen that make you hunt for that lil' item. How large should your name be? Make it the most prominent thing on the résumé, but not so big you look like you've got an ego that dwarfs Mount Everest. (See sample.)

  There are four ways to put a name on a résumé:

  1. Have the printer do it. Easiest for you, but expensive.

  2. Have it done on a laser printer.

  3. Cut your name from the border of your photo, glue it onto the original résumé, and make copies.

  4. Go to an art supplies or stationary store and buy rub-on (dry transfer) lettering. It's inexpensive and will give you a professional look that only requires the artistic skill of drawing a straight line with a ruler.

  One other thing. If your agent gives you a blank sheet of paper with his logo at the top, telling you to print your résumé on it, decline unless your agent gets positively peckly. Your résumé should sell you — not your agent.

  Finally, be sure everything is spelled correctly. If not, you'll look awfully stewpid.

WHAT NOT TO PUT ON A RÉSUMÉ

- *Your age or age range*: Don't limit yourself. If your résumé says you're 20, you're opening yourself to some casting director saying, "Oh, no, this part calls for a 22-year-old." (Bureaucrats can pop up even in this creative industry.) An age range doesn't help either. Limits you to the numbers you put on the résumé.

- *Any dates*: All dates do is date you.

- *Your Social Security number, home address or measurements*: Résumés can fall into anyone's hands. When a producer hires you, he can ask you or your agent for this information. Discretion keeps creepy crawlers from entering your woodwork.

- *Emphasis on your singing and dancing*: This may sound like strange advice, but there are people in Hollywood who believe singers and dancers can't act. Dumb? Sure. But the attitude exists. We aren't saying to drop all those musical comedies from your résumé; nor are we saying you can't put singing or dancing, perhaps, under "Special Skills." Just don't make your experience here a prominent part of your résumé. Make up a separate résumé for nightclub, concert or dance work.

- *Your college and/or community theatre credits*: Stop yelling, "That's all I've got!" and calm down. We're only saying there's no need to go out of your way to indicate those credits are from community theatre. For example, put Cambridge Theatre — not Cambridge Community Theatre. Then, as you build up your résumé, drop them.

- *Anything cutesy or autobiographical*: For example, "I was born . . ." A résumé is a list of your credits, not your autobiography or a forum to prove you can write comedy.

WHAT TO PUT ON A RÉSUMÉ AND WHERE TO PUT IT

Here's a typical professional-looking résumé. (Of course, your agent may want modifications.) The little black dots, by the way, are an easy graphic touch you can add by hitting the lower-case "o" on your typewriter and then filling it in with black ink.

- *Your name*: Note it's the most prominent thing you see.

- *The agency name, etc.*: Includes the name of the agency; the name of the actual agent who handles you; their address (including zip code); and their phone number (including area code).

  No agent? Move your phone number over to this spot.

- *Your phone number*: Use your service, if you got. Otherwise, put your home phone number, under the word "Messages." (Creepy crawler avoidance again.)

- *Your four vital statistics (often called Stats or Vitals)*: Height, weight, hair color and eye color.

- *Your unions*: Use the standard abbreviations.

Credits

- *BCF:* Unlike a typical business résumé, always put your best credits first (BCF) unless they are obviously dated. People read from the top down. Since you don't put dates, there's no need to put a bit

Steven Stunning

Messages (213) 333-STAR

REVOLVING DOOR AGENCY
Agent: Slam Gently
#1 Superstar Path
Colossus, CA 99999
(213) 321-BOMB

- *HT:* 11'12"   *EYES:* Red   *UNIONS:* SAG
  WT: 22   *HAIR:* Blue   AFTRA
                                                      AEA

- *TELEVISION:*

NOVA	Celestial Prods.	Guest Star
BIERS	Mortuary Inc.	Guest Body
AS THE STOMACH		
TURNS	Rolaids Inc.	Recurring
I LOVE LOOSELY	Marilyn Chambers Prods.	

- *FEATURES:*

APRIL THE FIFTEENTH	
(PART 1040-A)	MoneyMadd Inc.
IT CAME FROM OUTER	
DA SINK	Hal Roach Prods.
A FAREWELL TO ARMS	DeMilo Prods.
THE CREATURE FROM	
THE BLACK LATRINE	Rotorooter Inc.

- *STAGE:*

100 CLOWNS	Theatre of Reduced Expectations	Clown #99
THE BIG SHOW	Performing Theatre for the Performing Arts	Benito
PERFORMANCE	Performing Theatre for Performing Performers	Performer
LOOK BACK IN ANGER	Theatre for the Angry	Pissy

- *SPECIAL SKILLS:* Fluent Pig Latin, sleeping, Golden Thumbnail in tiddlywinks

part on a soap over a guest starring role in a series, just because
you did the former more recently. Don't bury dynamite under a sea
of trivia.

- *Your television credits:* Start with the name of the show in capital
letters. Then, reading left to right, add the production company followed
by any special billing. (Your agent may want you to substitute or
add the character name and a one- or two-word description of the
character.) No TV credits? Put the next category first.

- *Your motion picture credits, listed under "Features":* Same as above.
In this case the actor had no special billing.

   (Some would disagree with this order, opting to put features first,
followed by television. The arguments on both sides — film has prestige;
TV shows you can work fast — are equally valid. What to do? BCF.)

   If you've only got a few (or no) feature/TV credits, put industrials,
student films, anything that puts your face on film, under the heading:
"Film."

- *Your theatre credits, listed under "Stage":* Reading left to right: The
name of the play in capital letters, the name of the theatre, and the
name of the character. (Add the city if you like — a good idea if
they're New York credits. "Sometimes where you did it is more
important than what you played," says director Noel Black.)

   If you have no TV, motion picture, industrial or student film credits,
your stage credits will, of course, be the only credits on the résumé
and the list should be longer (about 10 of your best credits).

- *Any skills or talents, listed under "Special Skills":* Actors have gotten
auditions because the producer needed someone who could ride a
horse, speak a foreign language, shoot pool, play a musical instrument,
etc. But don't over-do this. We've seen actors list every skill known
to Superman, making themselves look awfully desperate. Also, be
sure it relates to acting. Forget "expert tax consultant" and "black
belt in muffin-making." And most important, *don't bluff* — if you can't
really do it, don't list it. "Chopsticks" doesn't make you a pianist.

- *Training:* (Mr. Stunning doesn't need this, as he's got film credits.)
Only have stage credits? You might list your training — especially
if it deals with the industry (for example, a film technique class); if
the class was in New York or a foreign country, which tends to impress;
or if the instructor is well known.

- *Education:* That is, your college credits — B.A., M.F.A., etc. Unless
these come from outstanding schools of dramatic training (such as

Yale, UCLA, USC, Northwestern, Julliard, NYU), they're — well — nice. Please forgive us if we're sounding blasé about four years or more of your life. It's just that a drama degree by itself isn't going to make Spielberg jump into your lap.

SHOULD YOU PAD A RÉSUMÉ?

Talking about the industry in general, television stage manager James Hamilton says, "Don't ever b.s. someone. These people are experts on b.s. They can spot it a mile away." Excellent advice — especially here. Pad a résumé and you're setting yourself up like the Phantom of the Opera: sooner or later, someone will pull off the mask. But, if you're determined, use your noodle. For example . . .

- *New York credits:* Some terrific theatre is mounted outside the Big Apple, but people in L.A. are often disproportionately impressed with New York credits. Fighting fire with fire, you could take a Dallas community theatre credit (say *The Glass Menagerie*) and move it to a New York off-off Broadway theatre. But, remember, *off-off* Broadway. Saying you played the lead in *Les Miserables* will get you a *miserables* reaction — especially if you also don't belong to Equity. And, if you engage in credit immigration to New York, at least be familiar with that city and the off-off Broadway theatres. Smart is *not* listing New York credits and then telling the interviewer what a lovely strolling area 42nd Street is.

- *Motion picture credits:* Hoo boy. You *might* get away with it if you list an obscure potboiler like *The Bloody Hand with the Greasy Hook That Speared Savannah,* Sharp Productions, Atlanta. Even then, you'll meet someone who knows potboilers or Atlanta production and spots it as a phony. We're not kidding. As one agent puts it, "If you don't have credits, *don't make them up.* You don't know if I was on the set of *'Run Jerry Run'* 14 years ago when I was in production."

- *Television credits:* No way. *Absolutely* no way.

- *Industrials/student films:* Here's your best bet for a little padding, if you must. Many cities have industrial film houses and/or colleges that do student films. Just be sure you know what you're talking about.

- *Stage credits:* Leave them in Podunk and you can pad to your heart's content — provided you at least read the plays. But frankly, if that's where you are, you're about as ready to do battle in professional acting as a baby is ready to do brain surgery. (You 18-year-olds are off the hook here. At your age, nobody expects you to have a résumé as long as your arm.)

One other thing. Drop all mention of commercials on your résumé — including "Commercials on Request." Current industry thinking is that mentioning commercials on a résumé can only hurt. Film/TV people either don't care or might worry about you being "too big" for the camera (commercial acting is different than "straight" acting). And, when it comes to commercials, no sponsor is going to be ecstatic seeing all that experience you've had — advertising other people's products. (For more, see our section on commercials.)

Okay, now go to work, bearing in mind a quote we really like. It was on a sign hanging in the window of a résumé typing service: "When they ask to see it, it better be good."

7 THE UNIONS

Okay. I can't get into the Guild without a job,
and I can't get a job without the Guild.
They're not going to screw my head up. I'm
going to beat them at this.

An Actress

Some actors have been born with silver spoons in their mouths, but no actor was ever born with a union card in his hand. If you think its impossible to get in the unions, we've got some surprises for you. Today, coming up with the initiation fees can be harder than qualifying to join. Stay tuned.

Your main concern as an actor will be to get into AFTRA, SAG, and Equity.

THE AMERICAN FEDERATION OF TELEVISION AND RADIO ARTISTS (AFTRA)

Its jurisdiction is over actors involved in live and taped television shows and commercials, and other TV and radio performers (announcers, disc jockeys and so on; Johnny Carson and Dan Rather are members of AFTRA).

THE SCREEN ACTORS GUILD (SAG)

Actors appearing in motion pictures — whether for use in theatres or on TV — and filmed commercials.

SAG and AFTRA are separate unions, but they now jointly negotiate with producers regarding commercials. All rules (what you're paid, the shoot, residuals, etc.) are the same regardless of whether the commercial is under AFTRA or SAG jurisdiction.

ACTORS EQUITY ASSOCIATION (AEA), CALLED "EQUITY"

Actors and stage managers in live theatre.

However, before we talk about membership...

NOTE: For initiation fees, dues, addresses, phone numbers, see Appendix.

A CAUTION ABOUT JOINING ANY UNION

If you need more experience, and/or want to do community theatre, avoid joining *any* union. Once you do, *you may no longer do any non-union (community) theatre*. All three unions have reciprocal agreements on this.

Exceptions are occasionally granted, but more often union members get around this rule by doing community theatre under phony names. Others, living in North Booneyville, just ignore it because they're outside of major centers like New York or Los Angeles. But any union member doing non-union theatre is subject to a stiff fine the first time he's caught and can even be tossed out of the union(s) if he's caught again. That means bye-bye to his career.

In short, join a union and they'll think of you as a pro. If you're not at that level, avoid the unions and get experience — doing community theatre.

A WORD ABOUT INITIATION FEES, DUES AND THE JOINING RULES

The fees quoted in the Appendix are Los Angeles minimums and can vary depending on the union and where you join. Dues for all increase as your income increases. Also, the rules for getting in any or all of these unions can change. Remember, we wrote this in the morning. You're reading it in the afternoon. Check before you do anything.

THE ONE WAY INTO AFTRA

Got the money? You can join. Anyone can at any time. AFTRA has an "open-door" policy. Obtain an application form from your nearest branch, fill it out, and plunk down the initiation fee and dues in cash, certified check or money order.

It's that simple — for now. However, there's a movement towards merging with SAG which is getting closer with every sunrise. "I think," says Mark Locher, public relations director of SAG, "That SAG and AFTRA will probably merge within five years." If so, AFTRA will probably adopt some SAG rules regarding entry. Getting in won't be as easy.

THE MANY WAYS INTO SAG

At the Hollywood branch (other branches may vary), send a copy of the contract that makes you eligible (see below). They'll check to be sure it qualifies you to join, then schedule an appointment. Bring your initiation fee plus a semi-annual dues payment.

Contrary to myth, there are many "side door" entrances to the Screen Actors Guild, some of which may surprise even experienced old-timers. Again, stay tuned.

The two fast ways into SAG

- *"Taft-Hartley"*: You're not a SAG member, but a producer goes bananas over your face and casts you in his union film, TV show or commercial. You just got "Taft-Hartleyed." Now the fun starts. No union can stop anyone from hiring you, but either the producer or the casting director will have to send a one-page "Taft-Hartley Report" to SAG. Included are the producer's reasons for hiring you instead of a Guild member. If the role calls for an Arabic-speaking midget, no problem. But, if his reasons are "because you're good," SAG will say, "Not good enough. There are, Mr. Producer, at least 74,000 unemployed union members at this moment. Surely one of them is 'good.'" He's then subject to pay "liquidated damages" (basically, a fine) for hiring you, you cur.

  Obviously, getting Taft-Hartleyed depends on how badly the producer wants you. If he doesn't mind the hassle and expense, he'll do it. Most often, this occurs in commercials, low-budget films and network pilots. Occasionally, feature film producers will do it, sometimes even the makers of episodic television shows.

- An *"unscripted line"*: In the middle of shooting *Phantom of the Opry,* the director decides he needs somebody in the crowd to shout, "*Kill that demented yodeler!*" That's an "unscripted line" — a line that didn't appear in the original script.

  Here's what a producer had to say: "I like to tell this to aspiring actors and actresses. If you know a producer or director of a movie, ask him to give you an 'unscripted line.' It can't be in the original script because then SAG will ask why the producer didn't hire a SAG actor to do it. The producer will tell you to be on the set the day he needs someone to yell out a line. He can hire you, on the spot, to do that line, and you automatically have the right to join the Guild." (Be sure to keep the "Day Player" contract you sign on the set — you'll need it to get into SAG.)

  If you don't know a producer or director, you might luck into an un-scripted line doing extra work (for more on extra work, see Chapter 25).

The many slow ways to join SAG: ("Parenting")

Your "parent" union is the union holding jurisdiction over your first job. (If your *first* job is an AFTRA sitcom, AFTRA becomes your parent; if it's a SAG film, SAG becomes your parent; if it's a Broadway show, Equity becomes your parent; if it's singing in a union nightclub, AGVA (see below) becomes your parent; if it's doing a concert at Carnegie Hall, AGMA — see below — becomes your parent. Here's the point: You can join one union *from* another. That is, you can go from your parent union into another union if you meet *two* criteria:

1. *The time criterion*: You must have been a paid-up member of your parent union for a minimum of one year.

And . . .

2. *The work criterion*: You must be able to prove you worked at lest once under that union's jurisdiction (which is what makes it your parent).

Say you join AFTRA on Jan. 1, 1992. Six months later, you get lucky and land a role on that new hit soap, *The Old and the Exhausted*. Since it's taped, it's under AFTRA jurisdiction, and AFTRA becomes your parent union. On Jan. 1, 1993, you will be eligible to join SAG. (You have been a member of AFTRA for a year and have done a job under their jurisdiction.)

And it's not only AFTRA. You can do this from any of the unions mentioned below. (Canadians can parent into SAG through the Alliance of Canadian Cinema, Television and Radio Artists — ACTRA.)

- *Entrance into SAG from AFTRA*: Since you can join AFTRA any time you want, the problem here isn't so much waiting that agonizing year, it's getting that first AFTRA job. Your best shots are commercials, soap operas (they use a lot of new faces) and, possibly, radio work. Also, newcomers often get that first union job in syndicated shows like *Superior Court*.

- *Entrance into SAG from Equity:* Unless you got into Equity via the Membership Candidate Program (see below) you've already got a contract from the show that got you into Equity in the first place. Save that contract. You can join SAG once you've been in Equity for a year.

- *Entrance into SAG from the American Guild of Variety Artists (AGVA):* This union has jurisdiction over singers, magicians, clowns, stand-up comics, etc. — anyone who performs in nightclubs, halls, circuses, even someone's home.

Like AFTRA, AGVA has an open door policy. Just obtain an application, fill it in, plunk down the coin and you're in. Then get the job. How? If you can get anyone to hire you as a singer, dancer, stand-up comic, etc. — repeat, *anyone*, from a nightclub owner to the president of your local Moose or Elks Lodge to your next-door neighbor who hires you, say, to sing at his birthday party — and he's willing to sign an AGVA contract, then call, write or go down to your nearest AGVA Office.

You and he will sign the contract, and, after you warble "Happy Birthday to You" in C minor, your employer/birthday boy should pay you by check.

Photocopy the check, attach it to your contract, put them both in a vault guarded by Dirty Harry, wait a year from the date you joined AGVA, and, yes, you're eligible to join SAG.

- *Entrance into SAG from the American Guild of Musical Artists* (AGMA): Not to be confused with the American Federation of Musicians, AGMA has jurisdiction over "classical" singers and dancers, soloists and choral singers (Luciano Pavarotti, for example, is AGMA), and solo instrumentalists who perform live in concert halls, theatres, etc.

Getting into AGMA and getting that first job occur together. Hypothetically, you could form your own group, hold concerts, rent halls, sell tickets, etc., and ask AGMA to represent you. Otherwise, in Southern California, look for work at the Los Angeles Master Chorale, San Diego Opera Company, Opera Pacific Orange County, or Music Center Opera Association.

Once again, save your AGMA contract(s), wait a year from the day you joined AGMA, and you're eligible to join SAG.

THE SEVERAL WAYS INTO EQUITY

The fast way in

A producer hires you as an actor or stage manager to appear in or work on an Equity show. Bring your contract, along with your initiation fee and dues, to your nearest Equity branch, and you're in. Notice we said this was the "fast" way, not the "easy" way.

The slow way in: Parenting

Like SAG, Equity now permits joining from other affiliated unions. If you've heard differently — or read differently in an earlier edition of this book — it's because a few years ago Equity wouldn't permit this. Equity later reversed itself. As it stands now, you can also parent your way into Equity.

The time criterion is the same (paid-up member of your parent for one year). The work criterion: one principal role, one "under five" (AFTRA) or three days of extra contracts. (If your parent is AFTRA or AGVA you'll also need to provide written proof — a copy of a contract or letter from your parent.)

Also, unlike SAG, Equity permits joining from the Screen Extras Guild (SEG). You'll need proof of three days extra work or a letter from SEG. (We'll talk more about extra work in Chapter 25.)

And the REALLY slow way in: The Equity Membership Candidate Program

If you're a member of SAG or a working member of AFTRA, you're ineligible to join this program. (Exceptions have been granted, but since you can parent your way into Equity, why bother?)

Obtain a list from Equity of theatres participating in this program. Then go job hunting. Once accepted by a participating theatre, send a completed registration form to Equity (there'll be a fee which you can later deduct from your initiation fee, see Appendix). You'll work as an actor, understudy, even a production worker, depending on that particular theatre. Complete 50 weeks of this kind of work and you'll be eligible to join Equity.

Your 50 weeks don't have to be consecutive and can be spent at any number of participating theatres over any length of time. Just keep a record and notify Equity when you reach your goal. Also, you can reduce the number of weeks to 40 if you pass a written exam about AEA.

ON BEING CHOOSY

If you stole a peek at the Appendix, you may have noticed that joining these unions isn't exactly cheap. Ultimately, you should get into the three actors' unions (SAG, AFTRA, Equity — and any others that the shoe fits.) But, if you're short on cash and live in L.A., shoot first for your SAG and AFTRA cards. If you live in New York, get your Equity and AFTRA cards. Los Angeles is a film town; New York is a stage town.

If you've heard (or read in an earlier edition of this book) that the unions give discounts on initiation fees when you join from another union, that policy is now as dead as vaudeville. Today, the only discounts are very minimal reductions in dues. Even these, while not dead, are in very poor health. Sorry.

ANOTHER WORD ABOUT YOUR DUES

Keep your dues up to date. Casting directors notify the unions when they want to cast you. If you're in arrears, that's hassle. So what happens? Bruce Beautiful gets the part.

8 OTHER ITEMS

When I'm casting, I always check "the Book." (i.e., The Academy Players Directory)

Arne Sultan, Producer

You can hammer a nail with a rock. Hammers and the right supplies sure do come in handy, though.

POSTAGE

Send a casting director a photo with postage due and don't be surprised if he refuses more than your mail. If you're uncertain about the postage, wallow in glorious excess.

MANILA ENVELOPES

You'll be using these to mail your résumé and photo(s). Choose sturdy ones. (Cardboard adds protection for the photos. It also adds more glorious excess in postage.)

THE ACADEMY PLAYERS DIRECTORY

"Next to your agent, it's your best agent," says theatrical agent Vikki Bandlow when talking about this powerful opportunity-getter. Published every four months, it's referred to as "the Book" or "the Directory," and is a sort of visual telephone directory of actors: a book of faces with a little information on those faces.

To be listed in the Directory you must pay the fee, be a member of at least one union, or be represented by a franchised agent (who will probably *demand* you be in it).

Choose your best picture and bring it to the Academy of Arts and Sciences building. You'll then select your category: YOUNG LEADING MAN/LADY, LEADING MAN/LADY, CHARACTERS & COMEDIANS/IENNES, and CHILDREN. The Directory will put your name and photo under that category along with: your union(s), agency(cies) and/or personal manager, and their phone numbers. If you don't have an agent or manager, you may list your own phone number.

NOTE: For prices, fees, addresses, phone numbers of items mentioned throughout the book, see Appendix.

If you fall, say, between a leading man and a character actor, give thought to listing under both categories. (Of course, it'll double the cost.)

Naturally, the Directory has a deadline for each edition. They send out notices, but don't hold your breath. Check. (Some agencies call clients to remind them about Directory deadlines — think this isn't important?) If you just miss a deadline, ask your agent to take your picture and check to the Directory, as his deadline is about a week later than yours. He won't fall madly in love with you for asking, but he'll probably do it, because he knows, as producer William Kayden puts it, "It is the Bible." Also, put the Directory on your "To be notified" list if you change agents.

Finally, if you're not convinced about the importance of "the Book," just look through it. Mixed in with "unknowns," you'll see shots of top stars. Time and again, actors get auditions directly from their Directory listing. Theatrical casting director Bob Harbin sums it up: "If you're serious, you should be in there."

Periodically, other services listing actors pop up, some even using computers. As it stands, though, the only one you really must be in is the APD, and, perhaps, the similar New York *Players Guide*.

ANSWERING DEVICE

A rare case of our choosing machines over people. You pay monthly for a service; you shell out once for an answering machine. Today, with features like touch-tone message recall — you can listen to your messages from another phone — the only way to miss a message (barring mechanical or electrical failure) is to fail to check your machine. At least you'll know who deserves the kick in the pants. With a service, finding out who missed your message is like trying to find out who shot Cock Robin.

One plea: keep your message short and identify yourself by your first name. Actors, with their wonderful creativity, try to make those machines less obnoxious by using everything from cartoon voices to Beethoven's *Fifth* — thus making them even more obnoxious. Long, cutesy messages are annoying to people who make 100 calls a day. And it's a serious irk to leave a message for "nameless," wondering if you've reached the right machine. Try, "Hi, this is Mike. I'll be checking for messages shortly, so at the tone please leave your name, number and approximate time of your call."

GOOD STATIONERY

Like your photos, the better your stationery looks, the more responses you'll get.

THANK-YOU NOTES

Sending these every time you get an audition, interview, part or shake of the hand, is not only courteous, it's smart. Puts your name in front of the person one more time.

Now, we've seen the glaze over actors' eyes when we talk about thank-you's, so stop yawning and pay attention: An actress attended a seminar at which one of the speakers was a world-famous producer. She sent him a thank-you and, a little while later, received a letter from him. (He's so well known a friend suggested she frame the letter.) It began: "I just read your note and I want to tell you I was *very touched that you took the time to write to me.*" [Italics ours.]

Dr. Watson, that first sentence tells us three elementary things:

A. Yes, he read her note.

B. He (unfortunately, like everyone else in this industry) isn't exactly inundated with thank-you notes.

C. He won't say "Who?" if she ever auditions for him.

SAG AGENCY LIST

You'll need this list of SAG-franchised agents when it's time for the Great Agent Hunt (see Chapter 11). You can use ours in the back of this book or pick one up at SAG.

DATEBOOK

If you're starting out, you'll find it hard to believe anyone can forget an appointment with a casting director. If you've been at it a while, you know it's possible — especially if you're going out a lot. An appointment book will prevent this dire event from crossing your karma. You'll also see later how vital an appointment book can be come April 15.

By the way, SAG puts out a wonderful datebook which also includes excellent reference material on union rules and regulations in regard to payments, work, etc. It usually comes out in November-December. Order it right away — they go fast.

THEATRE, SHOWCASES AND CLASSES

What you spend on these depends entirely on you, but you will need to be doing *all three.*

COMPOSITES

Important, but wait until you get a commercial agent (see Chapter 23).

CARD FILE

A typical call to a working actor:
Agent: *Have you ever met Slicke Deale, the producer?*
Actor: *Uhm . . .*

Keep a file on every person you meet, the where and why of the encounter, perhaps even your feelings about how it all went.

Also, you don't have to leave information-gathering to the CIA. If, in an article in *Drama-Logue* (see below), a casting director says he likes actors to stand up for a reading, or if an agent at a seminar rails on about actors calling him in the morning, make — and keep — notes. You'd be surprised at the information you can put together. The more you know about preferences and, yes, quirks, the better. Actor/teacher Mike Muscat says, "I have a five-star system for casting directors: If I've met them, they get one star; if they brought me in, they get two; if they gave me a job, they get three; if they bring me in on a regular basis, they get four; and if they've become a friend, they get five."

DIRECTORIES

You can walk out of Los Angeles' several drama bookstores with armloads of material on everything from acting teachers to which agents accept photos from new actors. We're hesitant to name titles here because these directories tend to come and go with the tides, and they change prices faster than you turn pages.

But here are a few highly-regarded ones that have been around for awhile: *The Hollywood Reporter Studio Blu-Book Directory* (similar to *The Working Actors Guide*, see below, but more geared to producers), *Breakdown Services C/D Guide* (helps you find casting directors), *Film Directors — A Complete Guide, Pacific Coast Studio Directory* (a quarterly similar to the *Blu-Book*) and *Ross Reports Television* (a monthly, lists Los Angeles and New York productions and personnel).

So go browse. But be sure to pick up . . .

THE WORKING ACTORS GUIDE

If a Pulitzer Prize were ever to be awarded to a directory for actors, this would win hands down. The *WAG* is a brilliantly comprehensive directory that's worth double its price tag. It's such a gold mine we have to give it special mention. Imagine in one book a list of casting directors, personal managers, agents, publicists, entertainment attorneys, teachers, extra casting agencies, etc., with comments on *each and every one.* Imagine 34 pages of production houses (about 15 to a page) with comments on *each and every one.* Imagine a complete list of theatres with comments on *each and every one.* Imagine all that and you've barely scratched the surface. If you can only afford one directory, this is the one.

TRADES SUBSCRIPTION

There are, basically, four trades:

- *Drama-Logue:* This weekly newspaper is an excellent source of opportunities — who's casting what, etc. — and invaluable if you are trying to get into a play. It also runs interviews, news, casting announcements for student and other films, and ads by photographers, acting workshops, voice coaches and the like. We used to suggest buying *Drama-Logue* only at a newsstand as subscribers tended to get issues too late to audition for some shows. Apparently this late delivery problem has been solved, with most subscribers receiving their issues on time on Thursdays. (Some newsstands do get it on Wednesday evenings.) So we've included a subscription, if for no other reason than it's cheaper if you're reading it *every* week — and you should be.

- *Daily Variety/The Hollywood Reporter:* These are the daily newspapers for anyone involved in show business on the West Coast. Reading them occasionally can be informative, though Show Biz releases should be treated like eggs — better with a grain of salt. You don't need to subscribe to both; perhaps you don't need to subscribe to either. On Thursdays *Variety* prints a rundown of television shows (staffs, producers, directors, casting directors); on Fridays they print the same information regarding films that are in (or about to go into) production. *The Hollywood Reporter* prints both on Tuesdays. You might limit your purchases to those days. However, we've included a subscription.

- *Back Stage:* If you live in L.A., you might want to squeeze in an occasional reading of this weekly to keep abreast of the New York scene. If you're thinking of going to New York, or already live there, read it religiously.

POSTCARDS

You're in a play; you just changed agents; you want to remind people you still breathe; whatever. A postcard is a photo of yourself, reduced to postcard size, with your message on the back.

We used to be more enthusiastic about postcards. They were cheap and effective. However, they're now so prevalent they've lost some impact. "I get so many of these a day," says casting director Ron Stephenson. "You want my honest opinion? It's a waste of a lot of stamps." And they're no longer inexpensive either (right, what is?). Still, postcards remain the most practical, un-pesky reminders of your existence.

TYPEWRITER

Besides eliminating the hassle of finding a way to retype résumé each time you land a job, a typewriter is a darn good investment. Your letters will look more professional and you'll feel better about sending them. If you add in the fact that the cost is tax deductible, you've got a pretty irresistible argument for buying one.

BLANK LABELS/LABEL SETS

Naturally, you can buy blank labels, but you'll save a lot of typing and some research if you purchase them in pre-addressed sets (to casting directors, agents, commercial casting directors etc.) from Breakdown Services Ltd. (for more information on the Breakdown Services, see Chapter 10). Competing companies offering labels tend to come and go; check *Drama-Logue* for ads.

VIDEOCASSETTE

Having a videotape of your work is becoming as important as having a good résumé shot. A casting director or agent can see your work without making an appointment to see you or having the distraction of your presence. So copy everything that can be copied, regardless of the size of the part. Here's how:

- *Have it done professionally:* If you make your initial copy on a home VCR, it'll be on ½″ videotape (that's standard for all home machines whether Beta or VHS). Unfortunately, the industry "standard" is ¾″ tape, which can only be obtained by using professional equipment. (It's true many industry people only have a standard home-type VCR, but others continue to use professional ¾″ equipment. You don't want to lose out if a director is willing to look at your tape, and you can't show it to him because you've only got ½".)

Also, for the sake of safety, you won't be passing around the original tape. You'll want to make two copies, one on ½" tape, the other on ¾" tape. The quality of those copies will be much better if your original is on ¾". Finally, ¾" tape is much easier to edit (see below).

- *"Air-checking" a role:* If it appears on TV, you can "air-check" it (make a copy). Simply notify any company capable of making ¾" videotaped copies, telling them the name of the show, the day, time, and its approximate length. They'll do the rest and give you the tape of the entire show, which you'll then have edited (see below).

- *Copying a movie:* If you don't want to wait the year or so it will take for the picture to become available on videocassette or aired on television, or if you are in something that will never be put onto cassette or TV (industrials, out-of-town commercials, student films, etc.), try to get a copy, at least of your scenes, from the producer or director. Most companies capable of doing air checks are also capable of transferring film onto tape.

  If it's a major motion picture, chances even of borrowing a copy before it's released are virtually non-existent. If it's an industrial or a student film/tape, your chances are much better. Industrial filmmakers are much more open to lending you a copy. Student filmmakers, in our opinion, *owe* you a copy: after all, you worked for free. (For more on industrials/student films, see Chapter 25.)

- *Editing:* Since nobody wants to (or will) wait 20 minutes for you to appear, you'll have your original copy edited down to include only your scenes, the name of the show and your billing (if the billing was special). Once again, only a pro (usually the same person who does the air checks) can do this kind of editing.

  We've included this information just in case you get lucky and win that first job in your first year.

- *Presentation tapes:* Once you've been around long enough to accumulate a number of scenes from different projects, you'll want to re-edit what you have into a ten-minute "presentation tape."

  If you've got a lot to choose from, use the material that shows you off best and, as theatrical casting director Susan Glicksman suggests, "Have your best things first." You won't want to risk somebody turning you off before you ever got "on."

  Don't be too quick to pooh-pooh a bunch of bit parts. Judiciously edited, even they can be surprisingly impressive.

That's why we say *tape everything,* including, "Check your hat, sir?" in a movie and "Where's the beef?" in a commercial. Remember, you don't have to show any particular scene to the industry. If you don't like it, leave it in the can.

And don't be a critic *before* you tape. If you hate the way you played the king, decide not to make a copy, and, when it's aired, come off positively regal, you'll want to shout, "Off with my head!"

- *A word about videotaping prepared scenes*: We know there are companies that will videotape you and another actor doing a scene. We also know you can buy or rent a vid-cam and videotape a scene in a theatre, even at home. Forget it. Any way you do it is too expensive because it's a waste of time. The industry is only interested in seeing tapes of professional work, done under professional conditions (lighting, sets, etc.) — though student films are included here. The quality of the tapes done by companies offering this often leaves a lot to be desired. And a tape on a vid-cam done at home sure won't be better. Besides, if someone wants to see you doing a prepared scene, he can attend a showcase, play, or simply call you in and have you do the scene live.

PASSPORT

Aha! You knew it! Hollywood *is* a foreign country! Well, maybe, but that's not why it's a good idea to have a passport.

First, we're sure you've run into the law requiring proof of citizenship to prospective employers. It's no different in Show Biz. Flashing a passport when you're cast saves a lot of time trying to remember what you need ("Let's see . . . is it my driver's license *and* birth certificate, or . . .")

Second, what happens if you're cast in a project that's shot in Paris, they need you tomorrow, and you don't have a passport? Maybe the producer can pull some strings and get you one in a hurry, but to lose a role and a trip to the City of Lights because you don't have a passport will cut deeply into your *bon appétit.*

You can apply for a passport at some Post Office branches. That's especially helpful during the summer. Avoids waiting in looong lines at federal buildings. Allow about three weeks for the entire process.

DESK

You can work on the kitchen table. It's just good for your attitude to have a specific work area, a place that's designated "Career work done here."

COMPUTER

Imagine making changes in your résumé whenever they occur, quickly and without charge. Imagine writing one covering letter, and, with a few keystrokes, "personalizing" it to each of the 100 people you're mailing to. Imagine . . .

. . .Yep, they're wonderful, time-saving gadgets. And according to *Consumer Reports* you can now outfit yourself with a good computer and printer relatively inexpensively. But, if that would take a megabyte out of your budget, forget it. (Remember, these are under "Chicken Soup.")

VCR

Another "Chicken Soup" item. But it can be of immense help when you're trying to find a scene for a showcase or office scene (see Chapter 18). Also, if you're out a lot, you'll be able to time-shift programs and watch them later. It's important to keep up on the various shows on TV. (We know an actress who was called in to read for a satire of *Hill Street Blues*. She'd never seen it. Think she got the part?)

Actually, having a VCR is becoming more of a necessity every day for actors. (Even the IRS recognizes this — see Appendix.) We'd advise buying VHS. Note: If you're trying to convince Mom and Dad to buy you one, we wrote this so you can put your thumb over the first sentence when you show this to them. That's one you owe us.

VIDEO CAMERA

A *real* luxury item. But, if you get a script in advance and can videotape yourself doing the reading, what you learn from playback could be the difference between getting it or not.

That's it. Now you're ready to get started on your career — except for one other supply item: your attitudes.

9 ATTITUDES:
NEED — THE CAREER KILLER

Have 'screw you' money.

Barry Shear, Producer/Director

Here's the single most important sentence in this book — our best advice:

Don't need the work. If you need the work, you won't get the work.

It's surprising. Time and again, when you boil down all the stories about how actors get jobs, it's due to an absence of desperation; a lack of need; a sense that the job just wasn't all that important at the time.

We know. You understand the concept, but... how can you honestly pretend you don't need something when you do?

By honestly not needing it. And (using a slightly cleaned-up version of Mr. Shear's advice), that starts by...

HAVING "SCREW YOU" MONEY

The industry wants people who can handle pressure. An actor who needs the job to pay his rent has pressures on him that have nothing to do with the "shoot." (Theatrical agent Maxine Arnold calls this kind of an actor a "desperate-ado.") He blows takes and readings — not because he's bad, but because that job is too important to him.

You can't make intelligent decisions when you're hungry. To advance, for example sooner or later, you're going to have to turn down a two- or three-line "day player" part. Keep doing these and you may wake up one morning to discover that's how the industry views you — as a "day player." (Careers, it's said, are made by how many times an actor says no.) But how can you turn down a part if that's all that stands between you and eviction?

Work, beg, or "glumb" it from your parents — but *don't need the money*.

HAVE OTHER INTERESTS

After an informal survey of working actors, we learned that when they got work it was often because the job or audition "got in the way" of something else, usually having nothing to do with acting.

When they auditioned, their minds were partly on that "something else," and they were more relaxed and didn't try as hard. The producer or director saw actors who weren't desperate and hired them, little knowing it was concern over a plot point in a screenplay they were writing or a nagging problem with a sick begonia that kept the actors from being nervous.

We aren't saying don't pursue a career. Sure, make those calls, visit studios, send out photos and résumés, etc. But remember too that life isn't just film running through a camera, and there's a difference between dedication and obsession. "Frankly, the reason I don't handle a lot of actors is because they're too self-involved," says entertainment attorney Michael C. Donaldson. "There's a great line in the movie *To Be Or Not To Be* where one character says to the other, 'Enough about me. Let's talk about you. How did *you* like my last scene?' There's a lot of truth to that. But not so much with successful actors. Successful actors, like successful people everywhere, are involved in the world around them." Or as personal manager Roz Tillman says, "I can't stress enough getting together the basics. I mean the basics of your life. Getting it all together. Don't be a flaky artist."

Have an avocation. Do something that brings in an extra few bucks on the side. Learn a freelance trade that makes you your boss for life. Have a hobby. Smell the begonias.

HAVE COURAGE

"Dare to be hated."   Bette Davis, in a TV interview

We've been to gatherings of actors where the atmosphere was that of a group of desperate, whipped puppies, yapping about their "masters" (producers, etc.).

Well, join the kennel or learn to keep your self-respect.

This industry too has its share of petty, bullying bureaucrats who enjoy "doing a number" on actors. You owe it to yourself not to let them push you around. Someone rude to you? Don't sit there and take it because you're "only an actor" and need the work.

Now, we're not talking about walking around with a chip on your shoulder — then you're the bully. Just don't allow yourself to be somebody's doormat. If you do you'll get frustrated, hurt and angry — exactly the kind of actor who doesn't work.

KNOW YOUR PRODUCT

"Most actors don't know their product."   Mac St. Johns, Publicist

. . . And, even more important, understand that you *are* a product. "You have to define your personality," says theatrical casting director Paul Bengston. "Not, 'I want to be a pirate or a cowboy,' but what you are. What are you selling?"

Know your strong and weak points. Remember, no actor is right for every part. If you look like "Auntie Em," don't try to sell yourself as the next "Dorothy," and then complain about what a rotten business this is when nobody buys.

It's not easy, but try not to take rejections personally. If you were selling a Mercedes, but your customer was in the market for a Cadillac, we doubt you'd take that as a personal affront.

When you don't get that part or agent, it simply means that they weren't in the market for a Mercedes that week.

KNOW YOU KNOW IT

"Know your craft."

Ralph Senensky, Director

There's no way around it. Some dues will have to be paid.

You're going to have to study hard and work at your craft. You're going to have to go through the pain of doing badly before you do well. Make your mistakes before becoming a pro, because, sooner or later, you'll be asked to show what you can do. If you need knowledge and experience, a little voice inside you will scream, "Dear God, I'm not ready for this."

Know you're ready — know it in your gut.

SET DAILY CONCRETE AND ATTAINABLE GOALS

"Try to do at least one thing a day to help your career."

Merritt Blake, Theatrical Agent

Taking off for weekends and holidays, if you do what Mr. Blake suggests, you will have done 250 things to help your career at the end of your first year. That's about 248½ more things than many of your fellow actors will have done. Why?

Well, ask an actor what he really wants, and he'll most likely say, "To be a working actor." Ask him how he intends to achieve that, and his eyes glaze over.

Most actors spend a lot of time spinning their wheels because they don't really know where they're going. Their goals — if they have any — are usually very foggy.

It's a lot smarter to say, "Okay. At the end of my first year, I want to have obtained all the supplies I need; gotten an agent; and gone on one interview."

Personal manager Roz Tillman says, "I encourage my actors to be goal-oriented; to isolate specifically what they want." Then, if you're really smart, you'll break that list down into monthly, weekly and daily goals.

Don't try to set "goals for life." They're not concrete. There are too many unknowns out there that can completely change your life. Make your goals *concrete, attainable,* and *daily.*

We once talked to a recovering alcoholic. This is what he said: "If I thought I could never take another drink for the rest of my life, I'd be back on the booze in a minute. I couldn't deal with that. The only way I can stay sober is to do what Alcoholics Anonymous teaches — *I take it one day at a time.*"

GET OFF YOUR OWN BACK

"Don't worry about it. Alfred Hitchcock always used to say, 'It's only a movie.' "

Angie Dickinson to an actor
who had just blown a take.

It can be therapeutic to take a class. Why? By watching others, you'll learn you're not the only one who ever screwed up.

We actors are amazing. If we're not yelling at our agents, we're screaming at ourselves. Everybody seems to be working better and more.

Try not to get down on yourself. If you do a bad audition/interview/performance, go home, kick a door and forget it. Nothing is life or death. Everybody screws up. As theatrical casting director Bob Harbin says, "Be serious about your work, but don't take this business too seriously. There's just too much craziness that goes on."

Babe Ruth struck out far more than he ever hit the ball — but what's he remembered for? Sooner or later, you'll get "good wood" on the ball.

NON-WORKING ACTORS

"Earlier, I heard you say not to hang around with non-working actors. I'd like to hug you for saying that."

Fran O'Bryan, Commercial Agent

Welcome to Negative City. Population: thousands. Points of interest: none. (After all, it can't be done.)

"If you want to be an unemployed actor for the rest of your life I can tell you exactly how to do it: Spend all of your time with unemployed actors talking about how unhappy you are being an unemployed actor," says entertainment attorney Michael C. Donaldson.

The greatest spur in the butt is to be around people who can do and are doing. They'll inspire you to do more. After all, they're living proof that things can be done.

What do you learn from people who are failing? How to fail. They're magnificent at finding all the ways things can't be done. Worse, stated or not, they don't want you to succeed. They'll commiserate you into doing nothing.

Birds of a feather . . . need together.

ALWAYS ACT SUCCESSFUL

Q: "What mistake do you continually see actors making?"
A: "Being too hungry."

Ruth Robinson, *The Hollywood Reporter*

We don't mean act cocky — that's just a mask for the insecure. And we don't mean you'll have to drive a Mercedes or wear Gucci loafers.

Acting successful means giving those in the position to hire you a feeling that they can be confident in you because you know your value.

Present yourself as a successful working pro, even when times are tough. Act like you've "made it" long before you have.

As actor Edmund Gilbert puts it: "Be there before you get there."

AVOID NEGATIVE BEHAVIOR

"No matter what, try to be positive."   Jack Rose, Jack Rose Agency

A salesman's creed: "To be enthusiastic, act enthusiastic."

If you think that sounds corny, go to a commercial audition. There, you'll find a roomful of actors who know they have to be bright and "up" if they want to get cast. And, because everyone is acting so happy and perky, you'll find it very hard to be negative or "down." Enthusiasm is catching.

Conversely, so is negativity. Be on your guard against it, in yourself or the company you keep.

Consider this quote from an actor friend of ours: "I never read the trades. The trades make me feel that everybody in this town is working but me."

He has a point. If you find yourself getting upset at all that work out there that you're not getting, then don't read the trades. Not until you can read them again for the positive information you can actually do something about. Too often, actors will read something about a film that has been cast, decide that they weren't up for the part, and immediately pick up the phone to chew out their agent. That's one long series of negative behavior.

Here are some other things to be on the lookout for:

- Don't go to see a movie, TV show, play, or even read reviews of a project you were "up for" and didn't get. (Face it — you're being perverse.)

- Don't listen to stories about how a fellow actor didn't get a part or agent. What a downer! (Our favorite way of handling this was in the following overheard conversation: *First Actor*: "I'm really miserable. I was up for a part and I didn't get it because . . ." *Second Actor* (interrupting): "At least you were up for it, baby.")

- Don't listen to anyone who says you'll never make it. (Unless they've shown a remarkable aptitude for walking on water.)

- Don't read bad reviews of a show you are in. (Talk about perversity!)

- Don't fall into "bad mouth" sessions about anyone or any group. (Ever felt better after one of these?)

- Be sure your acting teachers are trying to help you, and not just trying to keep the bucks coming in from a lot of perpetual students, or playing games with your head.

- Don't dwell on the mistakes you made. Dwell on what you learned from them.

- Not a beginner? Stay away from people, groups, or situations that cast you in that light.

- At an audition, don't assume you're wrong for the part. Are you there? Brother, you're right for it.

- Don't get secretly mad at your agent because he has other clients. That's what keeps him in business.

- When criticized, be sure of the other person's motives.

- Don't enjoy someone else's misfortunes.

- Don't listen to doomsayers.

- Don't work for compliments — work for money. That means working to improve your pocketbook, your opportunities or your skills — not merely to get stroked. For example, don't keep working at the same theatre or acting class just because everybody there thinks you're soooo good.

And, above all . . . *don't need the work.*

III
THEATRICAL AGENTS

10 WHAT THEY ARE AND DO

Nobody pays me to keep people out of work.

Jim Gibson, Theatrical Agent

Do you need an agent? Only if you want to be considered a pro, get paid more than union scale, and have a shot at better billing. And only if you want to work.

When casting, the studios, casting directors, producers and directors of Los Angeles hate crowds. (It's hard to be laid back in a mob.) Consequently, they've set up elaborate systems to keep actors *uninformed.* Except for an occasional hot tip from a friend or the trades, without an agent you'll miss out on most jobs simply because *you won't know they're there.*

More important, with an agent you cross a very important psychological barrier. You become a pro; someone (else) in the industry believes in your talent. As voice-over casting director Bob Lloyd put it, "You have to be competitive. Then you have to be able to prove it. And then you need to have someone who believes that and will merchandise you."

And, frankly, one producer said out loud what most industry people feel: "I get leery of actors without agents."

There are about six different kinds of agents, each handling performers in different areas of the business. No matter his special field, he's still a salesman whose product is talent:

- *Theatrical agent:* Television and motion pictures.

- *Commercial agent:* On-camera work in commercials.

- *Legitimate agent:* Theatre.

- *Voice-over agent:* Radio and off-camera work involving only the actor's voice for commercials, cartoons, announcing, and radio drama.

- *Modeling agent:* Modeling and, often, print work (magazine ads, billboards, other print media), although this can be handled separately.

- *Variety agent:* Nightclub work, personal appearances, etc.

As an actor, your main concern will be to obtain a *theatrical* agent and a *commercial* agent — that's where the jobs are.

In Los Angeles, you may sign with *only one agent per category.* (There's no limit in New York.) You may sign with different agents/agencies in different fields, but you may not have several commercial agents, several theatrical agents, etc.

WHAT A THEATRICAL AGENT DOES

The typical theatrical agent has about 50 actors in his "stable." (That's the term. Well, it *is* a horse race.) Each morning, between slurps of coffee, he looks over one of his primary tools for finding his clients work: the "breakdowns" (from the Breakdown Services, Ltd).

Since acquiring and reading entire scripts is time-consuming, this service has become an institution. It provides agents and personal managers with a summary of all roles taken from scripts about to go into production, including the sizes of all parts and a brief description of every character. The Breakdown Service is not available to actors. And there's no guarantee that any role listed hasn't already been cast.

From these descriptions the agent decides which, if any, of his clients are "right" for the various parts. With a typewritten submission sheet, photos and résumés of the actors he's submitting under his arm, the agent then visits the casting director or has his submissions delivered.

The casting director checks the submissions and says yea or nay based on his reading of the script and what the producer and/or director has told him about the part. Most often, the answer is nay: the part's been cast, the casting director thinks the actor is wrong for it ("Some of the things casting directors say about actors is reason enough to have an agent so you won't have to hear it," says theatrical agent Joel Rudnick), or the casting director doesn't know, like, or trust the agent. (Some agents can't even get in to see some casting directors.)

Faced with a turndown, the agent may try to change the casting director's mind; he may submit another client for the part (theatrical agent Colee Viedelle calls this "the Fuller Brush approach to agenting"); or he'll fold his tent and slip away. Rarely will an agent go over a casting director's head to the producer or director — it's not good politics.

If the agent gets a yea, a time is set for the actor to audition. If the actor gets the part, some serious dickering takes place between agent and casting director, primarily over salary and billing. The actor won't take part in these negotiations; the agent will call an actor only to get a thumbs-up or thumbs-down — but, no matter what the offer, he must call.

For doing all this, an agent receives 10 percent of the actor's *gross* earnings when the actor gets paid — *and not a moment before.* He is *never* paid in advance.

The rest of the agent's day is one long series of: phone calls from clients, reading contracts, interviewing potential clients, strategy meetings with fellow workers, etc. And, when the sun sets in the west, he gets to go home, right? Wrong. He's off to see one of his clients in a play.

These dervishes really whirl.

ABOUT LEGITIMATE AGENTS . . .

. . . The agents who handle stage work. The problem is the lack of paying work within the city. "The opportunities to make a living in L.A. theatre are almost nil," says personal manager Larry Fonseca. We know of no agent in L.A. who works stage exclusively. The ones who handle theatre all do it "on the side." Get the picture?

If you want to concentrate on paying theatre, head east. If you ask an L.A. agent to rep you for theatre, be willing to go out of town if you're cast — that's where most of the work will be. But remember, while you're strutting the boards in Birmingham, the rest of your career will be largely on hold. You take the money and make your choice. In any case, the information in this section basically holds true for theatrical and legitimate agents.

A WORD OF ADVICE

Without the right qualifications — good photos, a decent résumé, and a SAG card — unless you're under 21 and look it, *you're wasting your time.* As one agent bluntly put it, "What makes an actor think he qualifies for film work when he's done no films and has few or no theatre credits?"

Postpone the Great Agent Hunt until you've gotten some experience. In the meantime, if you have a good smiling photo, you might try for a commercial agent. Since many commercials don't involve lines, commercial agents are more receptive to a beginner who lacks credits but has a look or personality they think will sell.

Too often, actors in a beginning acting class talk about getting an agent. A one-year-old horse doesn't need a *jockey.* He needs a *trainer.*

11 SEEKING A THEATRICAL AGENT

*The relationship between the actor and the
agent can be summed up in two words: hot
pursuit. It's the actor's job to attack and
attack again until he gets the attention of
someone in the industry who can do him
some good.*

Michael Campus, Producer/Director

Put on a hard hat, 'cause some large chunks of stone wall are about
to bounce off your head. Agents have far more experience turning you
down than you have convincing them to sign you. When you're starting
out, merely getting one to see you will be a time for buttered popcorn
all around.

When you hear the time-honored "Sorry, we're not taking on any new
clients at this time," however, bear in mind that agents are always/never
taking on new clients, and there's no room/plenty of room for you.

"Every agent will tell you, 'I don't need any new people,' and every agent
will tell you privately, 'I'll take someone on if I feel I can make some money
off of him.'" says voice-over casting director Bob Lloyd. And he's right:
let Paul Newman walk into an agent's office, and room will be found for
him.

If you can act, have experience and a SAG card, there is an agent for
you. It just might take many miserable months to find him.

A WORD OF WARNING

To avoid getting ripped off, never sign with any agent who isn't union-
franchised. A franchised agent has agreed to abide by all union regulations,
and you'll be protected from most unethical practices. Once you're union,
in fact, you aren't allowed to sign with a non-franchised agent even if you've
gone too long without a sun hat and want to.

If you are interested in a particular theatrical (movies/TV) agency, check
your list of franchised agents. If its name is not included, call SAG (ask
for "Agencies"); perhaps the agency received its franchise after the list
was published. If the agency you want is legitimate (stage), call Equity.

---

*NOTE: For a list of L.A. agents, as well as prices, fees, addresses, phone numbers of
items mentioned throughout the book, see Appendix.*

Most agents hire additional personnel, called sub-agents. SAG and Equity list them as such, and they need not be franchised as long as the agency for which they work is franchised.

A word of warning: You may run across so-called "agents" or "agency-finder services," with impressive-sounding names like *"Galactic Representatives International."* They prey on the unwary actor. They guarantee jobs; demand money for ads in their "magazines," which, they promise, will be seen by everyone in the industry from Louis B. Mayer (So what if he's dead?) to the washerwoman at William Morris (Who knows? She may be casting something next week); set you up with photos for a mere $500 or so; offer acting classes that teach you to stand in a corner scratching and moaning. The very worst of the lot can even be fronts for prostitution. How can you avoid the sharks in the water?

If an "agent" ever asks you for money, run, don't walk, out of his office. An agent on the up-and-up makes his money from one source only: *ten percent of what you make, after you make it.* Your best protection is that franchise. If the agent isn't franchised, don't sign. Period.

THE SIMPLEST WAY . . .

. . . To get an interview with any agent is to have a producer, director, casting director or even a represented fellow actor put in a good word for you. If you know someone in the industry, ask. Bear in mind, however, that a referral won't guarantee the agent will sign you (or even see you). As theatrical agent Joel Rudnick cautions, "We're always looking at people. But signing and looking are two different things."

THE BEST WAY: PERFORMING YOUR WAY TO AN AGENT

Why the "best" way? Because, even including referrals, there is no stronger introduction to an agent than having him see and like your work. And you can do that by doing (in best to weakest order) . . .

- *A movie or TV show*: Are we kidding? No, actors do luck into these even without agents. Just be sure you've got lines — extra work doesn't count. You may be surprised to find your movie/TV show does you little good before it opens/airs; when it does, however, work hard and fast. Send out letters or postcards, wait a few weeks, then call back.

  To avoid making an agent sit through 50 minutes waiting for your three-minute TV part, include in your letter the day and time of the show and approximately when you appear. (You can get this information from the producer's office. Television books well in advance.) Call *every* agent a day or so before the show airs to remind him. After it airs, call back and ask for an appointment. We know — *aargh*. But don't waste the opportunity — it may be five years before you get another like it. Don't make the romantic (or lazy) mistake of sitting back, waiting for agents to contact you. Go after them.

- *Prepared scene/cold reading showcases*: Non-existent a few years ago, today they are one of the best ways to be seen by an agent (or a casting director). See Chapter 18, "Showcases and Office Scenes."

- *99-seat (Equity-Waiver) theatre*: You may do this kind of theatre whether you are union or not. The theater will seat less than 100, and, if it's a good production and well publicized, your chances of being seen by industry people are fairly decent.

  Understand, it's possible no industry person will come even if the show gets good reaction. Also, the state of 99-seat theatre in general is currently up in the air. (For more see Chapter 26). But no matter what, you can't get seen if you lie around doing your interpretation of a couch potato.

  You "old pros," new only to Hollywood, may balk at this. You may feel you've proven yourselves on stages all over the country, and advice to do more stage work — in small theatres, no less — is insulting and a waste of time. After all, you came to Hollywood for film work!

  Do it anyway. Nobody wants to buy a ham in a poke — unless they see you act, how do they know if you're an experienced, interesting actor or one who's merely left audiences comatose from coast to coast?

- *Equity productions*: In Los Angeles, if you're in an Equity show, there will be industry professionals in at least some of your audiences. Unfortunately, there's little paying theatre in the city, so you've probably got a better chance of getting into a movie or TV show.

- *Community theatre*: Not only off-limits to union members, it's also often difficult to get industry people to come to community theatre. Agents aren't all that interested in seeing a cast composed mostly of insurance executives doing theatre as a hobby; their chances of picking up a client are slim. Still, you might get lucky: someone may come to the show because he's a friend of a cast member. Be sure the theatre keeps a guest book (buy one for them if they don't), and check it *every* night.

When you do any kind of theatre, as opening night approaches, send out letters or postcards to every casting director and agent in town. A sample:

Dear_____:
   This is to invite you and a guest of your choice to the upcoming production of __PLAY__ at __THEATRE & ADDRESS__. We open on __DATE__ and close on __DATE__. Performances times are _____.
   I play __CHARACTER__, and appear __ONLY IN ACT I_,_ THROUGHOUT THE PLAY, ETC__.
   (Please call __(THE THEATRE/ME)__ and make a reservation to insure that we hold two good seats for you.)
   Please come. I believe you'll have a thoroughly enjoyable evening.
                                                                    Sincerely,

If you go over your allotment of complimentary tickets, are doing a major show, or the theatre doesn't give "comps," shell out for them yourself.

THE DIRECT WAY . . .

This method isn't a lot of fun, involves a lot of work, and gets old fast. It's only got one thing going for it: it does work. Take the list of franchised agents, scratch off the top dogs such as William Morris, ICM, Creative Artists, APA, etc., and mail your picture, résumé, and a cover letter to the first ten remaining agencies on the list. A sample:

Dear_____:
   Your agency has been recommended to me a number of times in my search for representation in Los Angeles. A look through *The Academy Players Directory* seems to indicate you have no one quite like me, so I enclose photos and résumé for your consideration.
   I'll call in a week or so, and hope we can get together for a chat.
   Also, do you have a favorite 99-seat theatre?
                                                                    Very truly yours,

The above sample appeared in the first edition of the book, as a *guideline*. We hoped no one would be silly enough to *copy it*. Boing! An agent we know received an exact duplicate, copied *word for word*.

Please, come up with your own letter, keep it brief, and use just about any approach that's comfortable, without getting silly, negative, braggadocios, or out-gushing Ol' Faithful.

As personal manager Melissa Tormé-March observes, "Clever letters attract people." For example, one of the most effective cover letters we've ever seen was sent to commercial agents by a light-skinned black actor:

> Hi! I am seeking commercial representation and would like you to consider me as a client. I am new to Los Angeles, just in from Washington D.C., and am enthusiastic about commercial acting. I have heard wonderful things about your agency, and, although I look more like wheat toast, I think I am the 'white bread' you are looking for.

Need we say he got a lot of replies?

"I think you have to figure out why I'd be interested in you," says director Andrew McCullough. "It really has to be on the basis of 'I have something to contribute.' I mean, so many letters come in, pitched on 'I would like to act.' *Well, so what?* I think that's why so many letters fail."

And one other thing: remember, your letter reveals something about your common sense. "Anyone who can't spell 'Dear Mary Spencer' is out," dryly notes theatrical agent Mary Spencer.

So, send out ten résumés, résumé shots and Pulitzer Prize-winning cover letters in one week. Then, the following week, pick out the next ten agents on the list, repeat the process, and, *in addition*, start calling the *original* ten agents you wrote. For the next six months or so, you'll be calling and mailing to *ten agents a week*. Expect 99 percent rejection. And a few "Can you call us back?" responses. And back . . . and back . . . and back . . .

Sound awful? It is. That's why there are more unrepresented actors than represented ones. Many actors try this approach for a week or so, quit, then wail, "Ya can't get an agent."

A variation is the old dropping-in method. Usually, it doesn't work, but you never know. You may not get to see an agent, but you can leave your photo, résumé and a personal impression — if only on the receptionist. And all that walking is a great way to lose weight.

Whether dropping by or phoning, you're going to be talking to a lot of secretaries. This brings us to . . .

SECRETARIES AND THE BRICK WALL SYNDROME

Today's secretary/casting coordinator/receptionist is tomorrow's agent/casting director/producer. Taking them for granted is like eating ice cream on a diet. You'll be aghast at where it shows up later.

Assistants control access to agents, casting directors, and producers. Whether they throw broken glass or roses in your path is up to you.

When commercial casting director Beth Holmes was a casting coordinator (see what we mean?), she said: "I think actors know to be friendly to me because I have the first waste paper basket."

Because they constantly deal with actors — in person and on the phone — they've developed pretty good defenses. You'll sense that tone of indifference the minute you start talking. Without getting obnoxious, find a way to catch their attention. Learn and use their names. Ask questions. Try to involve them in conversation. Most of the time they'll be too busy to talk and, if they are, leave or hang up.

Every once in awhile, though, you'll catch a secretary during a lull. Then it's time to try to make a friend. What you are striving for is a businesslike amiability — a scaredy-cat, "I'll-just-die-if-you-reject-me" air isn't going to sell you any better than a hotshot approach. As casting coordinator Tawn Holstra put it: "The thing about telephones is that the fears of the people on the other end comes through. I mean, I'm not going to bite you. You can ask me things and you don't have to be afraid of me. There's nothing I can do to you on the phone. *Nothing.*"

And, when you talk to anyone, bear in mind these two tips from theatrical agent Vikki Bandlow: "When the actor calls, he usually calls in slow motion. Get it out." And: "Everything's so heavy in this business. If someone can get me to laugh on the phone, I'll have him in. I love to laugh!"

OTHER METHODS OF GETTING AN AGENT

Classes/seminars

Seminars with agents as speakers can be helpful. Ask questions. Make the speaker notice you. Afterwards, go up and introduce yourself, and see if you can wheedle an appointment. We've seen it work.

If you're well-trained, you might take a class that has "industry nights" when agents, etc., are invited to come and watch/teach/comment. (Don't confuse these with classes that promise jobs or recommendations — avoid those!) Warning: if you're not ready, industry nights can backfire, emphasizing your limitations instead of your strengths.

You could also ask your instructor (especially if he's a casting director), or even a fellow student, for a recommendation. Be aware that the teacher usually is flooded with such requests and has only so many favors he can ask of his connections. (On the whole, however, take classes to learn, to stretch, to take chances in private, away from judgmental industry eyes — not to impress in hopes that someone will do something for you.)

Serendipity

Actually, when seeking an agent you're limited only by your own imagination. Actors have sent flowers (rather obvious) and have taken out billboards on Sunset Boulevard (*very* silly). A fresh approach such as one suggested by publicist Barbara Best can be charming: "To a single agent of your choice, send one genuinely funny greeting card every day for 30 days. When you're done he should certainly be interested at least in meeting you!"

The real key to getting an agent is how hard you try.

INTERVIEW WITH A THEATRICAL AGENT

Lo and behold — an interview! Now, the agent isn't yet ready to sign on the old dotted, but you have at least piqued his interest. There's something about you, your pictures, résumé and/or a performance he saw that is "special" and can possibly fill a gap in his client list. (Unless the agent is merely doing a friend a favor in seeing you.)

Now he wants to size you up. Do you have craft? Intelligence? Knowledge? Common sense? Are you confident without being cocky? Can he send you out on an interview and know you won't make a fool of yourself? Will you come through with poise when the cameras roll or when you meet important people? Are you pleasant to be around? (The last we heard, "Grumpy" still doesn't have an agent.) And, most important of all, can he sell you — will he make money if he represents you?

If he hasn't seen your work and you have no videotape on yourself, he may also want you to do a "cold reading" or an "office scene" for him. (More about interviews, cold readings and office scenes in the next section; they're skills in themselves, and you'll be doing a lot of them for casting directors, producers and directors as well.)

Okay. The interview went smoothly. A few days or a week has passed, the agent has done his thinking and discussed you with his associates, and has decided he wants to take you on. Now the question is: Do you want *him*?

12 CHOOSING A THEATRICAL AGENT

Just because someone shows an interest in you doesn't mean he's necessarily the best person for you.

Jerry Cohn, Personal Manager

It's hard to relate to "Choose your agent carefully" when you're thinking "I'll be glad to, as soon as I can get one to talk to me." And, when an agent shows some interest, it's even harder not to leap into his arms screaming *"Take me!"*

If only one franchised agent is interested in you, sign with him. Still, find out who you're dealing with. A franchise tells you only that the agent is basically on the up and up. It doesn't say that he's any good or that he's right for you. Even if you were buying the last car on earth, you'd still want to know how it runs.

LOOKING HIM OVER

There's no Better Business Bureau for agents; but fellow actors, instructors, and other industry people can be of help. Should you meet a client, ask if he gets out on interviews; if he's treated courteously; if he has easy access to, and is happy with, the agent. Just bear in mind that every agent is hated and loved by someone.

The agent's enthusiasm

The key ingredient in choosing an agent is the excitement factor. His enthusiasm about your potential can cover a multitude of sins. If all his clients hate him, if he doesn't work for anybody else, if he's not very pleasant to be around, but if he's excited about you and works for you — you've got a good agent.

Conflicts/clients

Any actor signed with your agency who would continually go up for the same roles as you is a "conflict." You don't want your agent choosing between you and him for roles. As theatrical agent Joel Rudnick says, "That's a decision that should be made at the casting office, *not* at the agent's office." If you're a direct conflict with one of their clients, a theatrical agent should turn you down.

A little research can save you grief. Find a copy of the *The Academy Players Directory* and leaf through the section that displays your glorious mug. If you spot a conflict, mention it to the agent. That actor may have departed the agency. Or the agent may see you differently. Can you live with that? If not, don't sign — you have enough competition *outside* your agency!

Agency size

To start, you want a small- to mid-sized agency that is excited about and will work for you. Forget the William Morrises and ICM's. If your agent handles Barbara Streisand, who makes millions per movie, and you, who makes scale, who's he going to work for? There's even an expression for this: "Buried in your own agency."

Number of clients

No single theatrical agent can adequately handle more than about 50 people. (If there are two theatrical agents in the agency, they can handle 100 actors; three, 150; and so on.) More than 50 clients means you're signing with a meat market that's hoping you get lucky finding work on your own, and then they'll cash in.

SAG says agents must present their client lists to prospective clients on demand. But, to be diplomatic, pop over to SAG and ask to see the agency's client list. Count the names. (Only those signed theatrically. Some agencies have many different departments. You don't care how many people they've got signed, say, commercially. SAG uses a different code number for each category — ask for the theatrical code.)

One man, one job

If you come across a guy who works alone and claims he's a commercial, theatrical, voice-over, modeling, and kitchen-sink agent, pass on signing with him unless you want your career to go down the drain. No one individual can handle more than one category.

Not across the board

As mentioned above, many agencies have multiple departments with different people handling commercials, theatricals, etc. — and it's possible they may want to sign you in every category (called "across the board"). Well, that's fine, but things can get a bit sticky if you wind up happy with your theatrical agent and miserable with your commercial agent. If that's the only way the agency will sign, and you really want them, go ahead. But it's best to sign with *different* agencies for *each* category.

Clout

"If someone wants you, it doesn't matter who your agent is, says theatrical casting director Marci Liroff. That's absolutely true. But don't let anyone kid you — clout counts, baby. There are such things as "day player agencies" (small agencies a casting director calls when casting bit parts that are shot in one or two days). Most likely that'll be your first agency, and that's fine when starting out. You want to get some small parts under your belt. (It's rare to get bigger roles anyway.) But the agent should intend — and have the drive — to grow beyond this. If he won't, you won't.

Despite any denials you may hear, the size and clout of your agency has a direct effect on how the industry sees you. (An actress we know went up for a three-line bit part. While talking with the casting director, she mentioned that she had just left her "day player" agency for a slightly larger one. The casting director blanched and said, "Oh . . . Oh . . . You're with *them* now? Well, I can't read you for something this small." He then immediately handed her a *guest starring role* to read.) Not convinced? Ask any casting director to pick up the phone and call ICM for an actor to fill a two-line part.

One method of pinpointing clout is to think of all agencies as being "A," "B," "C," or "D" list agencies. An "A" list agency is a giant such as William Morris, CAA or ICM. They handle major directors, writers and, especially, stars (which is what gives them their clout). Whole movies can be, and are, "packaged" almost entirely from within that agency alone. A "B" list agency is almost as big, with mostly name actors and, possibly, directors and writers among their clients as well. A "C" will handle some guest stars and many supporting players. A "D" is your basic day player agency, top-heavy with newcomers.

It won't hurt to ask yourself periodically where you are (are you a "C" list actor yet?) and where your agency is. The twain should meet. But remember, agencies *can* grow with their actors. As theatrical agent Jim Gibson put it, "I'm not a farm club for William Morris."

Office/employees

You can learn a lot by keeping your eyes and ears open when you go for your interview. What does the office look like? Is it one room with paint peeling, giving the feeling the agent doesn't know where his next commission is coming from? What's the general atmosphere of the place?

Dead? Alive with activity? Are the people warm or cold? Polite? Rude? Happy? Miserable? Does the receptionist seem to know what she's doing, and does she treat you with courtesy? How about the agent's stationery — does it show class? All these things are direct reflections on the boss and will tell you a great deal about how the agent views himself as a businessman and how you'll be treated as a client.

INTERVIEWING THE AGENT

Once the agent is finished interviewing you, gently "interview" him by asking . . .

How he sees you

You should both basically agree on how he'll be submitting you. If he's too far off the mark, look elsewhere — but be sure it's *him* who's off. "Be honest," says theatrical agent Pat Doty. "I can't work with people who perceive themselves as Elizabeth Taylor, and I'm seeing Ruth Gordon."

How often he wants to be contacted

One agent answered that question by saying, "My clients are only to call me between 9:10 and 9:30 A.M." Well now, wait a minute — who's working for whom? It's one thing for an agent to ask clients to call him, say, only in the morning; another to give a 20-minute time span. That answer told us he was not only a bureaucrat, but a bully.

Good agents want to hear from you. They welcome ideas. They won't want you to call every day, but will be open to suggestions. Got the feeling the agent "doesn't want to be bothered"? Don't "bother" him by signing.

How much independent seeking of work/auditions/contacts he expects you to do

When you're starting out, your agent will expect a lot. As you move on, perhaps a little less. But neither party should ever be expected to do it all. Some agents will tell you not to seek interviews on your own, as they feel this is "bad form." If so, go along for a few months. If the interviews are coming in, fine. If not, go back to work. You can starve playing by someone else's rules.

After the interview, it's time for a mull. Was the agent straight with you? Did you catch him in any lies? Did he ignore you? (At lunch with a prospective agent and his sub-agent, an actor we know listened as they spent the entire lunch talking about what a great deal they had just gotten for *another* actor.) You don't have to love your agent — perhaps not even like him — but at the very least there should be a little rapport. "It's critical that you have good chemistry with your agent," advises theatrical agent Joel Rudnick. "Your relationship with him or her is very important. If there's someone in town who has good clients and a nice office and irritates the hell out of you, you really should look elsewhere."

And *go with your gut* — agents do. Often, they'll accept or reject an actor strictly on gut instinct. If a small voice tells you something's right or wrong — something's right or wrong.

OTHER SUGGESTIONS

Agencies can get typecast too; some are known for handling character actors, others for "beautiful people," others for ethnic groups, etc. Other agencies mix their talent. It's best to be compatible with your agent's specialty because a casting director in a desperate hurry for your category of actor will call your agency first.

Verbal agreements

If your prospective agent tells you, "We won't have a contract, we'll just have a verbal agreement," bluntly, you don't have an agent. He's waiting: if you fall into a part, he'll be glad to take ten percent. As Samuel Goldwyn is said to have put it, "A verbal agreement ain't worth the paper it's printed on."

But, if that's all you can get, take it — and keep looking for an agent willing to put it in writing. Meantime, write the agent a letter confirming your verbal agreement, send a copy to all the unions, and list him as your agent in the *Academy Players Directory*. This way, potential employers will be able to find your representative, and you'll appear more like a pro.

SAG says a verbal agreement is good for three months, but it's unlikely you'll have problems if you want to sign with another agent within that time. (In practice, the agreement can last as long as you and the agent can stand it.)

THE CONTRACTS

The three contracts you sign with a franchised theatrical agent are standard contracts, hammered out between agents and the unions. There are no "surprise" clauses and all contain an "out" — a provision that, *if you don't get 15 days of work in any 91-day period, you or your agent may terminate the contract*.

This came about because actors didn't want to be saddled with an agent for a year if the agent obviously was not working for them. There's nothing to stop you from signing with an agent you're not crazy about and continuing to look for someone who suits you better, safe in the knowledge that you'll be available in 91 days. It's not the most pleasant thing to do, but neither is looking for an agent when you don't have one.

So, as we said, when you're starting out, sign with any franchised agent who wants you — and, if you're unhappy, keep looking for another, better agent. A cardinal rule of Show Biz psychology is: it's easier to find an agent when you have an agent. (For more on agency contracts, see Appendix.)

13 DEALING WITH/ MOTIVATING AN AGENT

> *Q: When it comes down to it, does the actor work for the agent, or does the agent work for the actor?*
>
> *A: Well, ideally, both.*
>
> Interview with Sandra Siegal, Theatrical Agent

Overheard conversation:

First Actor: "What should I get my agent for Christmas?"

Second Actor: "A cattle prod."

All of us like to think of ourselves as special and tend to get a little bitter when we discover our agent actually has the audacity to sleep at night when we're not working. And when enough sleep-filled nights go by, we start thinking about cattle prods.

Well, that's not the solution — at least, not exactly.

Assume for a moment that your agent has 30 clients. Assume he works ten hours a day. If he treats every client equally, the most he can spend on your career — submitting, talking about, meeting with and negotiating for you — is *20 minutes per day.*

Naturally, the time he spends on your career on any given day will vary. But, if he takes more than 20 minutes, another client loses out completely. In other words, there will be many days when your agent won't be working for you *at all.*

No agent will ever work as hard for you as you'd like him to. He's not your savior. Theatrical agent Mort Schwartz sums it up: "The prime job of an agent is not to help an actor seek work. It is to negotiate contracts and to open doors."

If you're thinking of cattle prods, you'll be a lot happier if you *turn them on yourself.* "You *cannot* sit back and say 'My agent isn't doing anything for me,'" says theatrical agent David Westberg. "What are you doing for your agent? Are you getting out there? Are you hustling?"

WHAT YOUR AGENT LEGITIMATELY SHOULD EXPECT FROM YOU

- *To get work on your own:* Especially when you're new. Frankly, when starting out, think of your agent as the person you call after you've gotten the job — to negotiate the deal. That way you won't be disappointed when he doesn't call and pleasantly surprised when he comes up with an interview or two.

- *To be active and visible:* A life on the beach will net you two things: a tan and no work. Show your talents: do plays, showcases. Stay fresh: take all sorts of classes and seminars. Publicize your activities: if you're in something important enough, take out an ad in the trades (*Hollywood Reporter* and/or *Variety*). If it's a play, send out postcards, résumés, and photos. Theatrical agent Vikki Bandlow says, "I get inspired by someone who's out there doing."

- *Be a fantastic auditioner:* Including cold readings, interviews, showcases, etc. You're only entitled to do badly occasionally.

- *Be on time and don't miss interviews:* "There is nothing worse after you've built up an actor to a casting director for him not to be available for an interview," says agent Doris Ross. Your regular job isn't your agent's concern. He's not going to understand that your boss can't spare you from the typing pool.

- *Be "reachable":* Use answering services, call-forwarding, message machines, etc. Your agent should be able to talk to you in person no later than 30 minutes after his first call. "The first time you don't check your service or machine, as God is my witness, is the day you get the call," says theatrical agent Mary Spencer. If you're out, call your answering service or machine, or the receptionist at your agency, and ask him to check if you're "clear." And be sure to notify your agent when you go out of town. Theatrical agent Pat Doty sums up the feelings of all agents when she says, "When an agent is out there busting his tush to get you roles, you better damn well be where he can find you."

- *Keep your agent well-heeled in résumés and résumé shots:* Periodically check with him to be sure he won't suddenly get caught short.

- *Keep your Academy Players Directory listing current.*

- *Keep in touch:* On the average, no more than once a week; no less than once every two weeks. As personal manager Mel Becker says, "If every client called his agent once a day and spoke to him for five minutes, he'd spend all his time on the phone talking to clients and never get any work done."

- *Come up with ideas:* If a show is casting and you know the producer, remind your agent.

- *Pay him his commission.*

WHAT YOU CAN LEGITIMATELY EXPECT FROM YOUR AGENT

Here's a start from theatrical agent Pat Doty: "My feeling as an agent is that I'm responsible to you as a human being. I'm dealing in your life and your career and I better damn well do a good job for you if I possibly can."

And, to be specific, you should expect . . .

- *To be submitted and talked about:* At the least! If he's not doing that, he doesn't deserve you.

- *To be told the truth:* A lot of smoke is blown at actors, not only about submissions (a very difficult thing to check), but in the entire actor-agent relationship.

- *To be submitted singly:* If an actor from your agency is auditioning for the same part, check to find out if he was called in by someone, or if your agent submitted him along with you. In the latter case, your agent isn't playing fair — not by a long shot.

- *To represent and negotiate for you not only well, but in good faith:* When submitting you, your agent is a salesman. But, when you get a part, he's got to grow fangs and battle for every dime and piece of billing he can get. But he can't negotiate in a vacuum. He knows, sooner or later, that he's going to be back knocking on the casting director's door with résumé shots in hand, acting like a salesman again.

  Further, you're not his only client. Therefore, Truth, Justice and the American Way end at the point where the agent is in danger of getting someone mad at him. He'll be circumspect about going out on a limb for you because, if the bough breaks, his entire tree of clients falls down too. Theatrical agent John Mekrut: "The agent-casting director relationship is funny; subtle; strange . . . you can push them, but you can't push them too far. That's who's going to buy your actors from you and you can't force them to slam the door in your face — which they'll do — ultimately to the detriment of all your clients."

  Don't constantly ask your agent to stick his neck out for you. But he shouldn't be Chicken Little all the time either.

For example, continually asking your agent to go over a casting director's head to producers you know places the agent's entire client list in jeopardy with the casting director. But, if you know a producer will see you for a part and the casting director has refused to call you in, as long as you don't make a habit of it, you'd be right to press your agent to call the producer. If he refuses, he may be too worried about irking people. And this is no business for irk-shirkers.

- *He should keep an office that's decent and organized:* We're leery of an agent operating out of his home. Not professional. If he has pictures scattered all over the place, we'd worry whether we'd get lost in the stack. Yep, neatness counts. In his stationery, too. And in his submissions. Even in the way he dresses.

- *He should return your calls and inquiries:* (But not if you're constantly bugging him.) As one agent put it: "A lot of agents don't want to hear from their clients — ever. That's notorious in this town. Actors say, 'Well, they didn't call me back at William Morris; now they're not calling me back at ICM.' "

- *He should follow up on your suggestions:* Want to climb a wall? Suggest an approach to your career and have your agent greet it with an excited yawn.

- *He should be interested in and see your work:* In a play, movie or TV show? He should be in the audience. When you put together an expensive presentation tape, he should look at it.

MOTIVATING AN AGENT

Start by treating him like he's human — most likely he is. Once with him awhile, take him to lunch, dinner or just coffee and *don't* talk about your career. Try to make not so much a friend, as a *colleague* of him. "It's so important," urges theatrical agent Joel Rudnick, "It's hard to represent somebody you don't know. And knowing a person takes more than just a few meetings in an office." Be honest, but not brutally honest. Try to see his viewpoint. Make him laugh. Give him a hot tip on a good horse in the ninth.

Personal manager Cathryn Jaymes suggests: "Ask your agent 'What can I do to help you help me?'"

Another tip: whenever you visit your agent, wear different outfits. Various looks will generate various submissions.

And another: How about thanking your agent for getting you an interview? As one agent put it, "I almost never get thank-you notes from actors — when I do, I remember them."

However, you may hammer away and still not make a dent in your agent's steel mind. Sylvester Stallone, on a TV talk show, said that whenever he walked into his agent's office (prior to achieving fame) his agent would say, "Oh, we were just talking about you." He'd look down on his agent's desk and, sure enough, there was his picture — *with a coffee ring on his face!*

Your relationship with your agent will be as good or bad as the two of you are willing to make it. It's a kind of wacky marriage. Hopefully, it'll be made in heaven, not in Las Vegas.

Still, don't expect too much. Sure, technically he's your employee. The better agents take that to heart; others merely pay lip service to it. After all, when push comes to shove, you need your employee more than he needs his employer. But even the best agent can only spend those 20 minutes on your career. You can spend 24 hours.

14 CHANGING AGENTS

*Changing agents is like changing chairs on
the deck of the Titanic.*

Olde Hollywoode Saying

"Who's your agent this week?" is a common, if not very happy, joke
in the industry. Some actors change agents like socks.

Agent-hopping is an exercise in futility, can speak poorly of the actor's
judgement, and tends to frighten off prospective agents. After all,
commitment is a two-way street. Establishing a relationship with an agent
helps more than constantly changing cards in a Rolodex.

Agents know you can leave them at the drop of 91 days, and this can
create a lack of drive. When asked if it drove him crazy to work for
a client, only to be suddenly fired, one agent's answer was very telling:
"No. I expect it."

Still, actors do outgrow their agents (and vice versa), and agents can
"cool off" on a client, or not bother from day one. So the trick is to
know...

WHEN?

A tough call. Your agent needs time to get you moving, but it shouldn't
take forever for him to start the car. We'll give a basic time limit, but
take into consideration union strikes, *hiatus* (the slack season — roughly,
April through June), bad economic times and factors particular to you.
(Did it take you six months to get him decent photos to submit?) Also,
if you're *certain* your agent hasn't been working for you, there's no need
to wait for any time limit.

Give him about a year and then ask two questions: *how many interviews
have you gotten,* and *how far up the ladder have you moved?*

If you haven't been out at least a few times, something's wrong. And,
if it's been years and you are still going out on three-line bit parts, it may
be that the agent doesn't have enough "clout."

Is he working?

He keeps telling you he's submitting you — but no interviews. Is that
the truth or is he just "feeding you wolf cookies"? To check, give your
agent photos in relatively small numbers, 25 to 50, and see how long it

takes him to ask for more. If you gave him 50 photos a year ago and there are still 49 on the shelf, some of those "submissions" are phantom.

Is he REALLY working?

There are submissions . . . and then there are *submissions.* "You like to think they're all out there pitching to get you in, but they don't," says theatrical casting director Bob Harbin. "Many of them 'submit' you for a project — they put your picture in an envelope with 40 others, send it in, and hope they get a call. There are a lot of agents in town that I've never talked to. Not because I don't call them back, but because they never call me."

"When an agent says he's put you up for a role, "says casting director Simon Ayer, "Try and find out specifically what that means. Does that mean your agent sent your pictures along with 40 other pictures? Does that mean the agent called the casting director and said, 'What about so-and-so?' Does that mean the casting director didn't know you, but the agent talked to him enough about you to get you a chance to meet him? If you're just starting out and your agent puts you up for the lead in [a series], more than likely it ain't gonna happen. That's one thing that does annoy me about agents. They'll get a breakdown and they'll see [age] 35 to 40, 45 to 50, and you know the guy's gonna be [a well known TV star], and they submit somebody that was just in *the Owl and the Pussycat* in Glendale."

Can he dicker?

Over time, your agent should get you more money and better billing.

Money

At first, you probably won't get paid much more than "scale plus ten" — union scale plus an additional ten percent, which serves as your agent's commission. And, since studios and casting directors keep records of your salaries (called "your quote"), no agent can increase your pay in leaps and bounds. (Any casting director can find out your quote, even from a different studio.) So, when moving from one job to another, expect a maximum increase of about $50 to $100 per day and $100 to $300 per week. If not, your agent may be a lousy dickerer or just too hungry to go out on a limb by saying no to an offer. It's maddening to learn you could have been paid *more* if only the agent had demanded it — and it happens.

Billing is dickered over as fiercely as money. (Better billing is often used in place of higher pay.) If your agent concentrates solely on dollars, he's paying more attention to his commission than your career and he's hurting you.

Does he really know the ropes?

"Come January, a smart agent will try to get an actor in to see me for a general interview because he knows the pilot season will soon be upon us," says one network casting director. (A pilot is the "selling" episode of a proposed new series. Pilots are actually made all year, but the "season" is February to mid-April.) If a network buys the pilot, airs it, and it's a hit, it means years of work, thousands to millions of dollars and possible stardom. Need we say it wouldn't be destructive if you are going up for a few each year?

But it's not just making contacts and selling you. It's his knowledge of contracts, union rules and regulations, and general rules of the game. For example, many agents (and actors) are woefully ignorant of what constitutes a "studio day" or what overtime actors are due under certain circumstances. We're not saying he should be a walking handbook of regulations, but he should know the basics.

As to contracts, he ought to be able to read and understand what he's asking his actors to sign or have someone he contacts for advice. "Frankly, more agents ought to get more guidance than they do," says entertainment attorney Michael C. Donaldson. Actors have literally signed away thousands of dollars because their agents didn't get that guidance.

HOW?

It's not a hot idea to storm out of your agent's office yelling "You're fired!" You might feel better for awhile, and it's certainly dramatic to slam the door and disappear in a cloud of dust — but, when the dust settles, you'll be the one left high and dry. Before you fire that @#!!?$*, have another agent waiting in the wings.

When interviewing with a prospective agent, if you feel the urge to badmouth your old agent, lie down till it passes. All the while you're talking about what a rotter your current agent has been, the new guy is going to be wondering what you'll be saying about *him* in the next few years.

Also, avoid saying you, not your agent, got all of your jobs, even if it's true. The prospective agent has no way of knowing that and might figure you're unwilling to give credit where it's due.

Actually, just say, "Well, my agent is wonderful for many of his clients, but with us, it just doesn't seem to be working out." And drop it. As theatrical agent Bernie Distler put it, "When an actor says 'My agent is terrible,' I think the actor is terrible."

When you're ready to change, write your old agent saying:

Dear_____:

This is to inform you that your services as   TYPE OF   agent are no longer required by me as of this date.

Notice no fireworks? SAG suggests telling the agent specifically why you're firing him, but on this we disagree. (If you've got something nice to say, certainly include a private note.) Not being specific doesn't invalidate the firing, and dropping him is eloquent statement enough of your opinion of his performance.

Sign, date and mail the letter to your old agent, send copies to the unions and your new agent, and keep a copy for yourself.

That's it. Just remember, a bad agent can set your career back; a good one can be a godsend. But no agent will ever be as good a salesman of you as *you*.

IV
SEEKING WORK

15 THE BUYERS OF TALENT

As far as actors are concerned, casting
directors are the keys to the kingdom.

Noel Black, Director

Know a gaffer? Might help. Your dentist's cousin Zelda works in the mailroom at Universal? Ya never know.

Still, your most important contacts are the buyers of talent: network executives, producers, directors, and, especially...

CASTING DIRECTORS

They can be "independents," hired by the job, or studio or network employees. They may or may not be members of the Casting Society of America (CSA). They go to showcases, 99-seat theatres and nightclubs. They hold forth at general interviews and "pre-screening" cold readings. They peer at TV shows, view videotapes, and attend movies from Grades A through Z, all in order to do their one basic job: finding talent.

Using knowledge of the talent pool, they suggest actors to the producer/director/network executives, based on guidelines they're given, the script and agents' submissions. Actors considered "right" are called in.

They negotiate your salary and billing with your agent as the producer's representatives. Rarely do they hire or make final decisions on what to pay or how to bill you. They need the approval of the check writers.

"The only power that the casting director has is to give you the opportunity to come and play," says commercial casting director Beverly Long. "I mean, I invite you to the party. I send out the invitations."

Why not skip the middleman and go right to the host? First, you'll rarely meet a producer or director without being screened by a casting director. Second, "An officer of the DGA told me the majority of working TV directors do only two or three shows a year," says director Andrew McCullough. That means a casting director can cast a half-dozen projects in the time it takes a producer or director to shoot one.

To an actor, a casting director is a walking employment agency.

Note: For prices, fees, addresses, phone numbers of items mentioned throughout the book, see Appendix.

GETTING INTERVIEWS/KEEPING IN TOUCH

We use "interview" as the industry does: an all-inclusive term for:

1. *Auditions:* You perform (usually a cold reading, see Chapter 17).

2. *"Look-sees":* You talk with a producer, director or casting director. You don't cold read, even though they're casting a specific project.

3. *General interviews:* Same as a look-see, but only to meet you for future reference. There's no specific project.

All casting directors hold auditions and look-sees; only some hold general interviews. (Many do showcases too — see Chapter 18.) No matter. The kind of interview counts only when you get one.

That's the key — getting interviews and keeping in touch. And it's tough. After all, your agent is your business partner. You can (and should) occasionally pick up the phone merely to remind him you're around. But try that with a casting director and he'll wrap the cord around your neck. Yet, as one producer put it, "This is an out-of-sight, out-of-mind business." How do you beat this game? Well, first, there's . . .

Your agent

That's his job — getting you interviews and reminding people you're alive. But don't bet on it.

Showcases

Currently *the* way to meet and perform for casting directors. (See Chapter 18.)

Theatre

Especially 99-seat theatre. It's hard for a casting director not to be reminded of you if you're in a play he's watching. Plays beget parts.

Dropping by

In New York, regular rounds by aggressive actors are an accepted practice. In laid-back L.A., rounds must be made with discretion and subtlety — as though you are doing nothing so crass as *making rounds*, but just happened to be in the neighborhood and thought you'd say hello.

To show you how sticky the subject of rounds can be, here's a list of word-for-word answers we got from casting directors when we asked them: "Should actors drop by?"

- "No."

- "I don't mind — if I know the actor."
- "I hate it! Don't drop by. The dialing finger is important."
- "Well . . . no. Except to drop off a résumé shot."
- "I feel terrific about it. But the studio doesn't."
- "Well, it's not too great."
- "Doesn't bother me."
- "N.G."
- "I don't mind, as long as they don't camp out."
- It's the pits!"
- "It works 100 percent better. Not to try to get into the office for an appointment, but to drop a picture, because it's very hard to trust pictures . . . sometimes the 'feeling' of the picture isn't always the 'feeling' of the actor."
- "It's okay, as long as the visit is brief and the actor isn't persistent."

Paralyzing, isn't it? Here's what industrial film producer Don Ciminelli had to say: "There will be times when you'll feel like you're pushing, and maybe you are — but you will find people like me who will understand that that's what you *have* to do. Because if you call me at the right time you get to work for two weeks. You have to keep campaigning."

And personal manager Larry Fonseca: "The difference is, out here we're all 'laid back,' and in New York they go for the jugular vein. That's what I try to instill in my actors — be aggressive. Go for the jugular vein."

Anyway, to find casting directors, use the guides on sale at your local drama bookstore (*The Working Actor's Guide, Breakdown Services' C/D Directory,* etc.).

The offices of most theatrical casting directors are on studio lots, so unless you've got a friend who works there and can get you inside the gates, either wait until you have an audition/job on that lot or try chugging briskly past the guard with a knowing wave and all the chutzpah you can muster.

Once inside, it's visiting time. Since nobody keeps track of how long you stay, bring résumés and photos, and drop in on every casting director. Give the receptionist/casting coordinator/secretary your best "I was in the neighborhood" speech. If he wants to talk, make hay. If not, make tracks. But always ask to leave your résumé and photo. "You could be a little devious and attach a note with it that says, 'My agent asked me to drop this off,'" suggests an agent.

Remember, actually getting to see the casting director will be a bonus — your prime mission is to make that first contact or to jog memories. Stay pleasant, don't be pushy and don't keep turning up like a bad penny.

The mails

Besides résumés and pictures, there are thank-you notes, holiday and birthday greetings and, of course, postcards. Also announcements of your plays, movie and TV appearances. And yes, even an occasional note saying "hello" is okay, especially if it's witty. They don't always get read, but the right reminder at the right time might result in Bank Night. It only takes one.

Phoning

Mostly considered obnoxious, a call is okay if it's about something specific — a play, film or TV show. That's valid business. Expect to leave your message with the assistant.

Other methods

Anything from ads in the trades to asking a pal to say hello can help. For example, every studio has a commissary. Have lunch there when you can (not every week, though; that's too obvious).

Try to keep in touch with every casting director you know, and add several new ones to your list, about every three to six months. If you do, you'll work. Casting directors are the keys to the kingdom.

PRODUCERS/DIRECTORS

Both hire, so once you've worked for either, you'll want to nurture that contact. Use all those "reminders of your existence," and try to spark at least casual friendships. As television stage manager James Hamilton says, "If people like and trust you it's only natural that they'll want to work with you."

Unfortunately, only Jello moves more than producers and directors, so keeping track of them can be tough. Check the production charts in the trades. Producers with "permanent" offices can be located in The Hollywood Reporter Studio Blu-Book or even the telephone book. For directors try a copy of Film Directors — A Complete Guide (see Chapter 8).

It's iffy but possible to contact a director through his agent. Without a prior okay, calling a director at home is more than iffy. It'll get you an audition — at Murder, Incorporated.

While business contacts are the meat and potatoes of getting work, actors have gotten parts through friendships arising from chance meetings at anything from a Lakers game to a fundraiser for The Flat Earth Society. Skip the re-runs of Gilligan's Island and get out there.

But — and it's a big one: if you drop in on the offices of producers and directors you *don't* know, your "rounds" are time-wasting circles. Why? "I can tell you right up front — they *hate* it," says theatrical casting director Ron Stephenson. "It's dumb. If you know that producer as a friend, that's one thing, but please don't go around bugging producers. They really hate it." As one producer put it, "If I'm not casting, what have we got to talk about?" Sure, you might get lucky, but spending your time getting to casting directors pays off more often.

AND NOW A WORD ABOUT THE REAL SPONSOR

Networks get involved in casting, sometimes even to the level of bit parts. While they tend toward "names," newcomers often get their big break in pilots. In fact, that's a major part of a network casting director's job — scouting for new stars. The catch here is, as Susan Glicksman (former Director of Casting for the West Coast, ABC-TV) put it: "We're looking for really unique people — for stars of series. There are always roles for 35-year-old, really gorgeous guys . . . for a young, sexy girl who can do comedy."

Theatrical casting director Paul Bengston: "Television has a look. NBC has a look; ABC has a look; CBS has a look. And I'd advise actors to watch and see what that look is." Absolutely; but, what the heck, no matter what your "look," send your résumés and photos to all network casting directors. Who knows? They may even change "the look" this season.

WELCOME TO THE TEAM

Whenever you meet a producer, call an agent, write a casting director or interview with a director, try to take the long view. Welcome him into your club of contacts. Think of the future rather than that one job. It'll make you a relaxed pro, not an uptight amateur.

In short, you'll probably get to "go" sooner if you think in terms of later.

16 THE GENERAL INTERVIEW/ LOOK-SEE

*Think of it as having a cup of coffee with a
friend.*

Terry Lichtman, Theatrical Agent

You've got five minutes. You've busted your buns to get there, 'cause
that's where the jobs are. Now it's 300 seconds of dynamite or forget
it.

Most actors understand this — when it comes to auditions. But they
treat interviews like spinach — something to get past to the good stuff,
the dessert: the "cold reading" (audition).

Sure, cold readings are vital, but if you think being a "good interview"
isn't important, you don't understand this industry. Jobs often come directly
and *solely* from interviews. Director Noel Black: "That small talk is very
important; in some cases more important than the reading... A lot of
directors don't even read people. They'll talk to an actor for five minutes
and base their decision on whether to cast the actor on what they think
of the actor's personality."

Fortunately, interviewing, like cold reading, is a skill that can be learned
— with practice.

DOING A PERSONALITY INTERVIEW

Hell and bad interviews are paved with good intentions...

"They just want to meet and talk with you," says your agent.

"What the heck does that mean?" you ask yourself. "How do I behave?
What do they want?"

An old high school lecture on "Proper Job Interview Technique" comes
to mind, and, obediently, you take the pinstripe approach: you sit up straight,
answer all questions succinctly, are *very* businesslike, get to the point,
give all your credits, speak only when spoken to...

...And the other guy gets the part.

Want to be a good interview? Tear up those high school notes, drop
any preconceptions you may have had, and start with an attitude that
may startle you: no matter what, *never treat an interview as if you are
applying for a job.*

The purpose of a show business interview is to meet the interviewer and introduce your look, type, voice and — especially — your *personality* to him. That's all.

Forget going to interviews as a job applicant looking for work. Just go to meet and talk with the interviewer, using the techniques we'll describe below, with a friendly and relatively easygoing approach. (We'd like to change the name from general *interview* to general *conversation.*)

In short, don't do a "business" interview — do a "personality" interview — by applying the following five ideas:

1. Be interesting;
2. Be interested;
3. Have a conversation;
4. Control the interview;
5. Be (the better part of) yourself.

- *Be interesting:* When asked what she looked for in an actor, theatrical casting director Sally Dennison replied, "A sense of humor." Notice no talk of business, credits, and so on. Merely being polite will get you a nod of the head. Being fascinating will get callbacks and jobs. Don't confuse this with coming on like gangbusters. If you're naturally quiet, fine — be quietly interesting; as theatrical casting director Ron Stephenson says, "I don't think coming in and bubbling all over the place and bouncing off the walls is the answer."

  At the same time, as theatrical casting director Paul Bengston says, "If an actor just comes in and stares at me it puts me off because I don't know what to do. I really don't." Or, as producer Buddy Bregman puts it, "Don't clam up. The producer or director will think, if you don't have anything to say to him, you won't have anything to 'say' in the picture. If you're shy take a class or something, because shy people just aren't going to make it."

- *Be interested:* Don't talk to the *title* (casting director, producer, etc.), talk to the *person.* As television stage manager James Hamilton says, "If people see you only want something from them, it turns them off fast. They see it all the time and they get so tired of it."

- *Control the interview:* The interviewer may control the questions, but *you* control the answers.

- *Be (the better part of) yourself:* "On an interview, don't try to be something you're not," advises theatrical casting director Jerry Franks. If you're up for the role of a villain, and apply for the job by trying to behave like Boris Karloff, the interview will be a disaster. You'll come off phony and affected. If you're a brooding Nicholas Cage type, don't try to act like Robin Williams; if you're a bubbly Goldie Hawn type, don't try to be a cool, aloof Faye Dunaway — no matter what you think they want. "I think you get in to trouble when you try to second-guess what I'm looking for," says one casting director. "All you can do is to give us you and be true to that."

"But what's me?" we often hear. Stop worrying about it. You don't have to try to be yourself. You already *are*. The trouble only starts when you actively try to be anyone else.

However, notice we added "be the *better* part of yourself." If you're a miserable rotter, we'd suggest behaving as you did last August, on that one day you were fun to be around. Being a spoiled child because you've decided "that's me" is not being yourself, it's being self-indulgent — at your own expense.

Shortly, we'll show you how to put these ideas to work. First . . .

BEFORE THE INTERVIEW

There's no dress code for an interview. Clean and neat is good. And, as theatrical agent Miriam Baum says, "Lay low on the jewelry."

Also note: come-ons are turn-offs. If the interview is with an agent there's no reason for you to be wearing an outfit that makes people wonder if you're out trying to get in or vice-versa. Even if it's a look-see for the role of a hooker or gigolo stay within the bounds of good taste.

ARRIVAL

Always, always bring a résumé and photo with you, even if you're sure your agent has already sent them ahead. But offer them only if asked, so you won't seem too eager. (Keep them discreetly tucked in a purse or briefcase.) Don't bring your book (a book of photos, used by models). Booooring. Besides, acting is not modeling. (You might bring your book to an interview with an agent, but only offer it if asked.)

Arrive early or forget it. "I never hire people who are late for readings," says director Andrew McCullough. "They often have brilliant excuses, but I'm afraid they'll be late to the set, so I don't hire them." Give yourself plenty of "get lost" and "get set" time. "Get lost" time is for getting stuck in traffic or running all over the lot, looking for the right office. (We've yet to understand the directions given us by those friendly, helpful guards at the gates. We're sure they write tax forms in their spare time.) "Get set" time is for catching breath and thinking about what you're going to do.

(By the way, if you drive onto the lot, here's some good advice from theatrical agent Pat Doty: "When you arrive at the studio and get out of that car, switch on 5,000 watts, 'cause when you're walking across the lots you never know who's going to see you. And keep up the energy and don't drop it until you have returned to the car.")

Don't make the mistake of going around glad-handing fellow actors. Focus your energy. Sit down and think about . . .

THE MOST-ASKED QUESTIONS AND HOW TO HANDLE THEM — AND YOURSELF

The following questions are only a shorthand method to get you to talk. They're formula stuff, more boring to the interviewer than you. And he'll ask more than one or two of them only if you make him feel like a dentist who has to pull things out of you. Thus, the more of these questions you're asked, *the worse the interview is going.*

"Tell me about yourself"

The dreaded question. And you can bet it will be asked. (Or a variation — "What've you been doing?", "What's been happening?", etc.) The usual bad reply: "What do you want to know?" (Terrible. Answering a question with a question is obnoxious.) Or the actor responds by becoming the fearsome Incredible Walking Résumé, reeling off credits to an increasingly glassy-eyed interviewer. Imagine listening to that litany actor after actor? If the interviewer wants to know your credits, he can read your résumé. If you're ever tempted to "talk business," remember producer William Kayden's statement, "I look for that undefinable quality called 'uniqueness.' I'm not interested in credits." Credit talk only makes you as serious as a tax auditor on a bad day. Director Noel Black: "Don't give your credits. A lot of time you'll look too eager, as if you're distressed merchandise."

So how do you answer the question? *Any way you want.* Translated, "Tell me about yourself" means: "Talk — and *please* be interesting."

That's why you need "get set" time — to think of something entertaining, interesting, memorable and/or funny. Then, you'll be ready for THAT question. You can talk about your recipe for nut soup, how you spent your childhood in a lighthouse, or even, as theatrical casting director Paul Bengston suggests, "Find something that happened that day." The point? The topic literally doesn't matter as long as *it's interesting and leads to conversation.* "We're interested in what you're interested in," says commercial casting director Pamela Campus, "And, if we're bored, we'll change the subject, don't worry."

Remember, it's a *personality* interview. Talk about something you're genuinely interested in and your personality automatically comes shining through. We've seen it. Try to be "businesslike," and you hide your personality. We've seen that too.

One other little bonus. With an interesting enough topic, there's a good chance the interviewer (if a casting director; an agent eventually needs to talk turkey) won't get around to any more of these by-rote questions. If so, you just had a super interview!

"What have you done recently?"

The one time you discuss your career. But it too requires planning. During your "get set" time, pick one or two of your best credits and find something specific and interesting to say about them. (Rambling on about finding motivations for Hamlet is dull; talking about how the technical crew conjured up Hamlet's Ghost could be fascinating.)

Notice we said your *best* credits — *not* your most recent. With no dates on your résumé, no one knows if your best credit isn't your most recent unless it's obviously dated (*Leave It to Beaver*, for example).

Idle times come to all actors — times when recent credits are getting slightly dusty. When (not if) that happens to you, and the interview is with a casting director, producer or director, it's frankly time to bend the truth a little. We hate telling actors to fib, but saying you haven't done anything for six months (or longer) makes you look a little yellow around the gills. "In my opinion," advises director Noel Black, "Its a lot better to say you're in a play at some little theatre than to say 'I did something eight months ago.'"

On those occasions, pick a credit that's undated (maybe an out-of-town play) and say you just "recently" finished it. If, however, the interview is with an agent, tell the truth. Never lie to an agent. If you haven't done anything recently, whimper so.

"How old are you?"

Answer the question and drop it. "How old do I look?" or "Well, I can play between ages 20 and 30," or "How old do you want me to be?" etc., all sound like you're embarrassed. Should you lie about your age? Up to you, but pick one realistic number and stick to it. Don't go around giving different ages in order to qualify for particular parts. The age you say will be remembered — we promise.

Two other points. First, if you lie about your age remember (at least as it is now) your employer is going to see the awful truth on your I-9 form. Second, if you're under 18, don't age yourself up. When the truth comes out — and it will — the legal problems will be enormous. Besides, adding numbers to your age is foolish. Eventually it'll haunt you like Amityville.

"What brought you to L.A.?"

A good answer: something like "This is where the action/business/work is." A bad answer: "This is where my boyfriend lives."

"Do you have any film on yourself?"

They mean a videotaped record of a film or TV appearance. If you don't, simply say, "Not yet."

"Do you have an agent?"

With a casting director, producer or director: if you've got one, say whom but don't proceed to bad-mouth him if you're unhappy. You may be talking to the agent's best friend, and (supposedly) only non-working actors are unhappy with their agents. Either say something nice or *nada*.

If you are interviewing with an agent, simply say you have no agent if that's the case. And try to avoid crying hysterically.

Questions about your résumé

Once again, that "get set" time is invaluable here. Use it to go over your résumé. Be prepared to say something positive and interesting about every item on it. And be sure you know who produced, directed and cast every production mentioned. We know one casting director who said she'd never cast any actor who didn't know this. That's extreme, but knowing who you worked for avoids a lot of stammering.

Can you (do a skill: ride a horse, affect an accent)?

Say "yes" only if you can do it. That builds trust. If asked about an accent, however, don't fall into the trap of replying in that accent. Looks too eager, and you'll invariably blow it.

Other questions can include:

- *"Where are you from originally?"*
- *"What made you decide to become an actor?"*
- *"Who have you studied with?"*
- *"Are you studying with anyone now?"*

- *"Have you done any theatre in L.A.?"*
- *"Have you worked only on stage?"*

Naturally, your answers to these depend on your personal circumstances. But be ready to handle them. Only Mortimer Snerd goes to an interview not knowing what he's going to say ("I don't know, yup, yup"). This doesn't mean having a set spiel, by the way; just know basically what you want to say.

Okay, now you're ready. When called, put out the smokes, get rid of the gum, and remember the interview starts when you walk in the door. That first impression is vital. With your hand on the doorknob, take a deep breath, mentally say "Action" — *and be ready for anything.* For example, most interviews are one-on-one (you and the casting director, director or producer), but be prepared to talk to a roomful of people if that's the case. Or, as theatrical agent Miriam Baum cautions: "Even when you go on a general interview, you'd better be ready to do a cold reading."

OTHER RULES OF THE GAME

Don't be negative

Laugh and the world laughs with you; cry and the other guy gets cast. Each negative remark lessens your chances; each positive word increases them. Be especially aware of how you talk about yourself. We've seen actors with credits as long as their arms talk as if they're total greenhorns. Question: "What have you done recently?" Answer, from an actor who has just finished a guest-starring role on a major TV show: "Oh . . . not much." Or "Well, I just did a small/nothing/tiny/silly little/non-existent role on Broadway." Think we're kidding? Those are word-for-word answers we've heard.

You'll be treated exactly as you tell people to treat you, and they'll look on your previous work exactly in the manner in which you explain it. We're not talking about "hype." We're talking about pride.

Don't be hostile

It's surprisingly common. If you've got a temporary mad on, go kick a garbage can. If it's permanent, go yell at a psychiatrist or take up linebacking for the Chicago Bears. As theatrical casting director Susan Sukman observes, "Negative vibes will come out whether you know it or not."

Don't talk in a vacuum

It's a conversation, not a monologue. Some actors give the impression the interviewer could leave the room and they would just go on yapping. *Listen to what the interviewer says and ask questions.* For example: it's the start of the interview and your topic is skiing. As you talk, the interviewer says "Oh, I love to ski." The foolish actor drones on. The smart actor zooms in: "You do? Do you have a favorite spot?" Bang! A conversation. The more you involve the interviewer, the more involved he'll be with you.

Don't try to be Henny Youngman

There's a difference between having a sense of humor and having an *act*. Also, never make yourself the butt of a joke; like Rodney Dangerfield, you'll get no respect. Be sure your sense of humor isn't negative, cruel or so off-the-wall that people will think you're weird. And don't get glad-handy or act like an Uncle Tom. All of these things hide you as much as sitting there like a sphinx. In fact, they're worse. At least sphinxes don't land on you like a ton of bricks.

Know when to leave

When you hear "Thank you for coming in," it's curtain. Skip the exit speech. Split.

SPECIAL NOTES

The techniques we've talked about will work with anyone, with the following minor differences:

If the interview is with an agent

There really are two possible kinds of interview, depending on:

1. Whether he only wants to talk business.
2. Whether he likes to schmooz first, with business later.

Since you can't know in advance which it's going to be, start with your topic. He'll either play along or abruptly change the topic to business. Either way, you'll be ready.

If the interview is with a producer/director (a "look-see")

Try making your topic *his project.* If you've read the script, ask a question about it. If not, you could always say, "I'm curious, how did you come across the script?" or "Will you be shooting on location?"

There's also a chance he may start talking about the project on his own. When that happens, bad interviewees sit stonefaced, as if to say, "But what about ME?" Good interviewees are fascinated. Not only are you conversing on a subject dear to his heart, but the talk is almost always interesting.

In short, show an interest in his project (but not an overt interest in putting yourself in it).

Also, as theatrical casting director Marci Liroff points out, "Some directors love you to say 'I liked your last movie'; others hate it." We'd advise not saying anything. Makes you look too much like a fan or that you're applying heavy butter.

A word about nerves

General interviews/look-sees can be rattling, but most industry people will go out of their way to relax you. Theatrical casting director Sharon Himes is an example: "When I see an actor is nervous, I'll tell him, 'I just did two loads of diapers this morning.'"

Granted, it's hard to be blasé, especially if you walk in, and there, seated on a sofa, is your all-time favorite star. Unfortunately, you just can't come off as a Nervous Nelly; they'll worry that if you can't handle the pressure of a simple interview, you sure won't be able to handle the pressure on a set. "If you go in very shy and inhibited and very insecure about what you're doing there in that office, they're not going to feel very respectful of your talent, unfortunately," says theatrical agent Maxine Arnold.

Remembering not to "apply for a job" can help. So can remembering to treat anyone you meet as a fellow professional, not as some god whom you can't wait to worship. Nobody hires fans.

Practice

If you can't afford a class, set up a tape recorder (or vid-cam) and do a mock interview. Enlist a friend to ask the questions and listen to (or watch) the playback of your answers. Videotape can be invaluable — gets rid of tics.

And a word about listening

Oh don't be silly. Of *course*, when the interviewer opens his mouth you'll listen. Theatrical casting director Mike Fenton:

"We were casting a film with Claude LeLouch. LeLouch speaks English but he doesn't think he speaks it very well . . . We were having interviews. An actor would come in and sit in a chair, and I would say — per Mr.

LeLouch's instructions — 'Mr. LeLouch is very pleased that you've come to see him today. He is hesitant about his English. He doesn't feel comfortable speaking it, so he probably will not say a word. But what he would like to know, first of all, is: What did you have for dinner last night?'

"Well, that stumped a lot of actors. I mean they were totally thrown. They didn't know what to do. And then, *there would be a further instruction*: 'Say it as if you were very angry' or 'Say it as if you were very joyous'; 'Say it in a sensual way'; 'Say it as if you were mad at the world.' So there were different instructions on how to say what you had for dinner last night. Well, it was bizarre. An overwhelming number of actors *never heard* the second instruction. They just went off saying what they had for dinner without adding to it the inflection he was looking for. So that, at least 65 percent of the actors who came in for that motion picture never had a chance at it because they never heard what was said to them. They never heard the instructions. It's real important to listen."

'Nuff said.

AFTER THE INTERVIEW

How'd it go? What worked? What laid an egg? Did you control the interview? Did you do and say the things you wanted? How'd they react? Any negativity on your part? Did you fall into the trap of bad-mouthing yourself? Was it a conversation or an interrogation? A joy or a bore?

If it worked, know why. If it didn't, know that too, and treat it as a learning experience, not the end of the world — or your career. Which brings us to our last point.

You were great? Enjoy it. Fair? Okay, work on it, but remember, nobody does a *perfect* interview. Bombed? Try not to get down on yourself. As theatrical casting director Judith Holstra puts it, "You're not doing cancer research, y'know." No matter how badly it went . . .

. . . Life will go on, phones will continue to ring when you're in the bathtub, that flick you've wanted to see will still be playing at the Bijou, your income tax will still be due on April 15 — and other interviews will come your way. And Fido, God bless him, will wag his tail just as frantically when you walk in the door.

Ultimately, that's far more important.

17 THE (ALMOST) COLD READING

*The most distressing thing is when an actor
feels the people he's going to read for are
enemies. If I'm bringing you in, I'm rooting for
you. The producer and director are wide
open. They've got to have someone in their
show and they want someone good. So you
walk into a room full of people who are
pulling for you. It's a room full of friendliness.
We all want you to be terrific. So come on in
and be wonderful.*

Ron Stephenson, Theatrical Casting Director

"Oh, I'm terrible at auditions," blathers the famous actor. If you believe that, we've got a condo we'd like to sell you — on Venus.

In rare cases, an actor will be seen in one show and cast in another without ever auditioning. If that happens often enough, he becomes famous without ever having to read for a part. Still, how did he get the first part? By osmosis? And do you want to bet a career on that kind of luck?

Cold readings are the crux of an actor's career — make-it-or-break-it time. Read poorly often enough, and you'll find yourself back in Sweetwater, Nebraska, being a plumber like papa wanted in the first place. Read well often enough and you might become just famous enough to demur, "Oh, I audition terribly."

UNDERSTANDING COLD READINGS

The confusion starts with the name. Nobody "reads." It's an audition with script in hand. And only an idiot does it "cold."

But that's just the tip of an iceberg that sinks an awful lot of actors. Far too many otherwise competent people blow jobs — sometimes careers — because they don't know what's expected of them at a reading.

Start here: Cold reading is not an art. *It's a skill.*

You cannot go about it in the same way you perform a rehearsed role. Your preparation will be different, and your goals are different. Why?

1. You don't have the time.
2. You'll be acting with a script in your hand.
3. Nobody wants a full-blown performance anyway.

Don't take that to heart, *take it to bone*. First, though...

FOR WHOM THE PHONE RINGS

When your agent (or, in rare cases, a casting director) calls, get the particulars: when, where, and for whom, and repeat them back to make sure you've got them right.

Then find out as much about the character as possible. Your agent can read you the description from the Breakdown Service, or pass on any other particulars obtained from the casting director. (Sometimes nobody knows nuttin'.) Scripts are *supposed* to be available 24 hours in advance of the reading. If so, go get one. If not, see if you can't at least get the pages you'll be reading, called "sides."

Now, to the closet. On a theatrical cold reading, dress to *suggest* the part. If you're up for a construction worker try jeans and a workshirt. But don't wear a hard hat, carry a lunch pail or rent a pneumatic drill.

ARRIVAL/PREPARATORY WORK

Be at least 30 minutes early — you've got some homework to do.

First, be sure you get the right script and the right part. We're not kidding. We've seen the deflation that comes with walking into the producer's office, ready to read "Spag," only to find you were supposed to do "Hetti." (We know they'll give you more time, but somehow it's just never the same.)

So, if you're not positive, check. In fact, if there's anything you don't understand, including the pronunciation of a single word, don't be a scared rabbit, talk to the casting coordinator. "That casting coordinator is a resource," says theatrical casting director Deborah Barylski. "If you have a question about the material, ask."

Now before you go to work, here's . . .

WHAT NOT TO DO

Don't memorize

Ever been to a first rehearsal "off book"? It's a disaster. Why? Because you can't act and worry about lines at the same time. Don't try to memorize in the hope you'll impress somebody. You won't. *Cold readings are not line memorization contests.* It's assumed you can memorize, and you're only setting yourself up to fail. "As a matter of fact," says casting director Susan Glicksman, "We discourage actors from memorizing lines because they get too involved with remembering the lines."

(Some say memorizing guarantees you'll keep your nose out of the script. Gorilla pucky! Staring out with glassy eyes, trying to remember your next line just looks like there ought to be a "Vacancy" sign on your head.

If you have only a couple of lines, or you're one of those rare individuals with photographic memories, go ahead. Otherwise, forget it.)

Skip "business"

Every time you decide to do something in a reading (a cross, a way of reading the line, etc.) you've got another job to do. The more jobs, the worse the reading will go. We call that "assigning yourself too many tasks." Lewis' Law: under the stress of a cold reading, the human mind can handle only so many tasks before it blows a gasket.

If you see "*demurely*" in parenthesis, that doesn't mean you have to interpret it that way (as long as you're not changing the writers' intent) and if the script says "He lights a cigarette," forget it. In fact, ignore all stage directions — including your own. Skip props, pantomime, or nifty ideas for blocking.

Remember, your strongest selling point is your eyes. So, if you want to be effective, sit. Uncomfortable sitting? Then stand. Still. Movement distracts.

(Speaking of all this, theatrical agent Joel Rudnick tells the following hilarious story: "Never use props at an audition. I mean you learn that in Acting 101. At our agency we had an actor who was going up for the role of a bad guy in a very important movie. And he decided that he would be shaving the other person in the scene. You know, holding the knife at the other person's throat. And he went out and bought a straight razor. And the person who was reading the part opposite him turned out to be the casting director. And it wasn't just a casting director, but the head of talent of a major studio — an executive. And I can still remember when he called us back to tell us how it had gone, the voice of the agent yelling into the phone, 'You what?!? You *what*?!? *YOU-KNOW-WHO-THAT-WAS?!?* . . . .   *YOU-HELD-A-RAZOR-TO-HER-THROAT???!!!???*' ")

Don't get cute

First, rehearse and play what's on the page. Don't read a love scene and decide he secretly hates her. He doesn't. As theatrical casting director Judith Holstra put it, "Don't look for hidden meanings . . . they just ain't there, folks." Second, don't start "improving" the script by purposely changing the lines. The "help" won't be appreciated. "I put no limitations on an interpretation or how a scene should go," says director Leslie Martinson, "But never ever change the lines. That's a no-no. An *extreme* no-no."

Don't create a "character"

Whenever an actor asks theatrical casting director Judith Holstra, "How old is my character?" she replies, "How old are *you*?" In theatre, you merge and adapt yourself to the character; in film, you merge and adapt the character to you. In other words, *play yourself.* (That's a lot of people. "You" can be a doctor, lawyer or Indian chief. "You" can be angry, loving, murderous, shy.) Forget limps, aging yourself up or down, nifty speech patterns, accents, etc., unless the role specifically calls for that. "I look for naturalness, not 'acting.' Don't hide behind a character," says director Gary Nelson. "When an actor comes in and acts and talks one way and then, when he picks up a script, acts and talks differently, I get scared."

Immunize against the "I'm not right for this" syndrome

Like silly mistakes? Here's a lulu: You're a brunette, who's, well . . . pretty, and you look around, seeing nothing but gorgeous blondes. What do you do? You become your own (negative) casting director. You decide you're not right for the part, and give up before you start.

Well, Dummy, as theatrical casting director Bobby Hoffman says, "A part isn't born till an actor gives birth to it," and you have no way of knowing how they see the part. Maybe they're vacillating between a Farah Fawcett type and a Jo-Beth Williams type. Maybe they're positive they want the next Marilyn Monroe until just lil' ole kinda-pretty you walks in, blows them away with your reading and they, in Hollywood terms, "Change the concept." Or maybe they only cast you in a different and bigger part.

If you've been called in, *assume you're right for it — period.* (Besides, the worst thing that can happen is you get called in later for another part.)

Don't overwork the scene

There's an expression: "Being too good at a reading." That's when an actor comes in with a full-blown performance. A reading is not a house, it's a blueprint for a house. It's a way of saying, "Okay, guys, here's an idea — but, if you don't like it, it can change." Don't try to do too much with it. (Actors especially get into trouble with bit parts. They try to make "Telegram, ma'am" into a devastatingly dramatic, Oscar-winning Moment. As casting director Barbara Remsen put it, "Don't make two lines more than they are.")

Don't "work on" being nervous

Telling you "Don't be nervous" is like saying, "Try not to breathe." Besides, a certain degree of nervousness is good. Gets your energy up. (There's an old radio saying: "When you're not nervous, it's time to get nervous.") But deal with the nerves — don't fixate on them. Don't sit there thinking, "I'm scared . . . I'm SCARED . . . GOD, AM I SCARED!!" Don't give nerves the "mental time." Channel your mind away from them by concentrating on what you're trying to do with the reading. Rehearse. Go over objectives. Re-read the script for new insights. When nerves attack, fight back by . . .

WORKING ON THE SCENE — IT'S YOUR STAGE

Before going to work, we want to pass on to you the best seven words we've ever heard about cold readings. They came from director Noel Black and should color your entire outlook: "Its your stage — do what you want."

Okay, find a place to rehearse, even if you have to leave the building. If your rehearsal area — which includes the sidewalk, if that's all you can find — is out of calling range, tell the assistant where you'll be and periodically pop in to let them know you're still nearby.

If they call you in early and you haven't finished rehearsing, ask for more time. Never read before you're ready. (Unless you arrived late — tough luck, bro'.)

On the other hand, if you finish and they're not ready for you, sit quietly and keep your mind on your reading. Don't clown around with your fellow actors. Save your energy. You're there to get a job, not to make friends.

Now, to work — step by step:

- *Read your script:* Sound obvious? Hand an actor a script and he acts like a thoroughbred chomping at the bit. Bang! He starts saying the lines, bolting the starting gate before he even knows what race he's in. And where does he wind up? Dead last. So we'll repeat, READ it. As if you were reading a book. Ask yourself:

  1. *What type of show is this?* (Soap opera means an intimate, underplayed delivery. Sitcom means a bright, zesty reading with lots of energy. A standard TV show or film is more energetic than soap opera, but not as zesty as comedy; be energetically real.)

  2. *What's going on?* What are these people talking about? Anything you're not clear on? Again, ASK.

- *Memorize the first and last lines:* That insures being out of the script at the very beginning and the very end of your reading. Makes a strong first and last impression.

- *Say your lines out loud:* That's why you need a rehearsal area — a place where you can talk out loud without disturbing some secretary's typing. Inevitably, the first time you say a line it doesn't come out "right." The way it comes out may even throw you. Have that shock come when you're by yourself and can fix it.

- *Get your eyes out of the script:* The sure way not to get cast is to read with your nose stuck in the script. If they can't see you — especially your eyes — forget it.

  Look up and out to an imaginary actor. Work especially on being out of the script when he would be speaking. Watch out for the "reading trap": looking down, reading the other person's lines as he speaks.

  If you're worried about losing your place, run your thumb down the page as you go along, but, with a little work and trust in yourself, you'll find your *eyes* automatically will go to the right place. Anyway, no one is going to jump down your throat if you get lost for a second and take an extra beat to locate your line.

- *Pick a "direction":* That's a way to play it — which consists of two things:

    1. *Specifically, how does the character feel?*
    2. *Specifically, what does he want?*

    Period. Nothing else. And don't worry about being "wrong." As long as you play what's on the page, you're right. Better an interesting reading than a safe one — even if it misses the mark. That can be corrected. Being tepid is too boring to fix. "Too many people try to please instead of doing what they want to do," says director Andrew McCullough. "There's something impressive about an actor who comes in and says 'This is the way I want to play it.'"

- *Practice going out on a limb:* Once you make your two choices, *commit to them.* If you've decided your character is angry, be Angry, not just irked. If "She" wants to keep "Him" there, fight to keep him there. Take chances. Go for it — *really* go for it. Director Harvey Laidman: "I look for intelligence, good choices. Even if you're wrong, be interesting. I'm looking for people to keep me awake."

- *Work on playing to, listening and reacting to an imaginary partner:* A solid direction makes the reading interesting. Adding listening and reacting will get you *cast.* "You have to remember that sometimes the camera's on you when you're not doing lines," says producer William Kayden. "Reactive readings are very important." (Nobody means "mugging" — exaggerated facial expressions — or "indicating" — making sure your audience "gets it." Think it and feel it — they'll see it.)

    Doing this with no one there to look at might feel odd, but it'll get your mind on listening and reacting — and that's vital. When we asked theatrical casting director Doris Sabbagh what she looked for in actors, she answered typically: "Listeners. Don't stand there waiting for your next line."

    That's it. Nothing more. You don't have the time. Even if you did, anything else would gum up the works.

    If you want the part: *eyes up, "feel," "want,"* and above all, *listen.*

INTO THE BREACH

"I was involved in casting for a major studio with the executives, etc., and the person who generally got the pilot or that role on an episodic show was the guy who came in and sold us *before* he started reading. You've got the job when you walk in the door — if you walk in *right*," says theatrical casting director Paul Bengston. "I look for three things," says theatrical casting director Deborah Barylski. "First, when you walk in the room, what do I get from you as a person. Second, what do I get from you as an actor during the reading. And third, do I like you as a person."

So, when you're called, take that proverbial deep breath, put on your pleasant face, walk in oozing confidence, and. . . .

. . . *Expect the unexpected.* There may be a roomful of people or one lone, slightly embarrassed-looking director. You may have to sit in a chair smack in the middle of the room or on a sofa in the far corner. Two seconds into the room someone may say, "Ready?" or you might hear, "Let's not read, let's just talk." The atmosphere may be funereal or "Hey, Joe, you got gum?"

No matter — don't alter your reading because of the atmosphere. Remember, as theatrical agent Pat Doty puts it, "The minute they say 'Are you ready?', you're in command. Take command."

THE READING: ANSWERS TO TYPICAL QUESTIONS

Should I try to get more information before reading?

We've come around to "No." Creates more problems than it solves. Sometimes, though, the producer/director/casting director will launch into a dissertation. Let 'em talk. The more said, the more you know. If what you're hearing is completely different from the way you rehearsed it, switch gears and get as close to that as possible. Yep, you've got to be a chameleon in this business.

Should I ask "How do you want this done?"

"That's amateur night," says director Ralph Senensky. Why? Is it wrong for a chef to ask if you want your eggs scrambled or sunny-side up? Four (typical) views:

Commercial casting director Pamela Campus: "For years I thought, 'Gee, I'll just tell every actor who comes in, 'this is what we want, and this is how we want it.' And the actors would look at me as if to say, 'Oh, O.K.' And then they'd still deliver it their way. I learned the hard way. You let them deliver and see what they do, and you either like it or you don't. And if you don't like it, but you think they have potential, then you offer a suggestion — once. And if they're really good, they'll get it."

Producer William Kayden: "What we want is what you give us. We don't want to sit around and intellectualize the role."

Director Leslie Martinson: "I never pre-channel an actor's thinking. [Besides] we're hearing the lines for the first time too."

Director Noel Black: "Some great actor may come in and have an inspiration, and for me to tell him something might be unfair . . . insulting."

Should I say anything about the script?

Not worth it. Compliments are nice but tend in this situation to turn your nose brown. Anything negative will end it for you. If they didn't write it, they chose it. "In all the years I've worked," says one veteran director, "I've only had one producer ever say to me, 'This is a piece of crap. Do the best you can. Dazzle them with footwork.'" Remember that and dazzle them with footwork.

Should I ask to sit or stand?

Nope. Sit or stand *without asking permission* (assuming you're not directed to do otherwise). You're not a child, you're a pro. "Come in and take charge of the room," says theatrical casting director Deborah Barylski. "Not in a jerky way, but as a professional. That's where your power is. Take it."

How long before I start?

A beat. During which, you collect yourself and get in the scene. Nobody ever got cast by breaking the record for the fastest start. But, remember, we said a beat. Don't stand off in a corner "preparing" for five minutes. That's artsy-craftsy, wastes people's time and will lose it for you right there. "When someone does that in my office," says personal manager Larry Fonseca, I'll give them about five seconds and then I'll say 'Next!'"

Who do I play to?

To the person reading opposite you. Don't include the others — they want to watch. Just make sure they can. Position yourself so they can see your face. And get the hair out of your eyes.

What if the other person is bad?

Play it as if he's Laurence Olivier. If the other person (often the casting director) can't act his way out of a paper script, and you commit to what you rehearsed, it really won't matter — provided you go at your own pace. If you feel rushed or can't hear your cues, ask him (nicely) to slow down, speak up, or whatever.

What if I get lost, blow or accidently change a line?

Nobody cares. They know the difference between that and an "improvement." But you care. So, until the very end, if something goes awry: start over. Nobody will get mad. Trying to muddle on with your mind still going over that mistake will destroy your reading. "Stop if you're doing badly," says producer Philip Mandelker. "After all, you've only got one chance. If you can, try to do it humorously. What have you got to lose?"

What if I'm not sure it worked?

Try saying something like "Was that the general ballpark?" (Not "Was I good?") And don't be negative. They may have loved it. If you (or they) are unhappy, ask to do it again — once. You can't keep doing it over and over. Two tries and rack your cue. "When a reading is over, it's over," says producer Michael Rhodes.

Did they hate it if they directed me?

"Even if the reading was right on the money I'm almost always going to give you a second direction, just to see how quickly you adjust and whether you resist the direction," says theatrical casting director Deborah Barylski. That happens a lot — but only if they like you. So, don't get upset, rejoice! They almost never stop an actor who can't act. They let him read straight through and say goodbye. "One of the things I always do when I read actors is to direct them," says director Andrew McCullough. "Even if I like what you're doing I will ask you to do something else."

Why? Are they just playing games?

Director/cinematographer Bruce Logan answers: "I never read an actor once, because I want to know if I can change what they did or if they can only give me one thing. Usually, what they brought in is a lot better than what I give them, but it's just a way of finding out how flexible they are."

What if they just cut me off?

Not a bad sign either. It probably means they liked you and your reading and they don't need to hear any more. (This is decidedly different from a New York stage audition, where being cut off is almost always curtains.)

What if I'm asked to read a different scene or character?

Ask for time. Never read anything cold — it's the surest road to failure. You *must* work on it. And unless they get sticky about it — which we seriously doubt — leave the room. This shouldn't upset anybody, if for no other reason than it's a sign of your professionalism. That's not a bromide. It's the absolute truth.

Should I ask if I got the part?

Only if you don't want it.

What if I was terrible because my salamander died?

Make no apologies or excuses. No matter how justified, excuses always sound like excuses. Besides, you probably don't need an apology: most actors feel they did far worse than was the case. Say thanks and go.

Isn't "they're on your side" just a lot of bull?

Honestly, no. They really do want you to be successful. Theatrical casting director Tony Shepherd put it all into perspective: "We all want you to be good, if for no other reason than once we get the role cast, we all get to go home."

AFTER THE AUDITION

Always call your agent, and, unless you're positive the audition was a disaster, simply say it all "went well." Don't worry your agent with a lot of yammer about all the mistakes you think you made.

Then, if you're upset, go home and kick a door. And forget it. Your reading is only a part of the casting process. You may have read beautifully but be too tall or too short; the role may have been all but cast before you read; the producer's wife may want the part; the part may be cut; the budget may demand an actor who will work for less. "Quite often it has to do with pairings." says commercial producer Bob Wollin. "The best people aren't always cast."

"If you don't get it, it could be for a million different reasons, sometimes very subtle," says director/cinematographer Bruce Logan. "For example, I'll say I like what this actress is doing and I like what that actress is doing, but the character is supposed to be genetically related to this other actor whom I've already cast, and the first actress doesn't look like his daughter."

Not enough for you? How about this one from theatrical agent David Westberg: "It may be a 'pay-back show.' When they get down to the end of the season, and there are 21 or 22 episodes of a show in the can, with only one or two episodes left, there are favors all over this town that are owed to friends, relatives, the brother-in-law of the guy who put up the money to back the show . . . It's the pay-back show where all those roles go to pay back favors done throughout the year."

It's hard to generalize, but, in television, you often know within days if you "got it." However, that painful time span can vary from five minutes to five months depending on the project.

Don't expect your agent to call when you don't get a part. Nobody has the time. The casting director only calls the agent if you're cast or (rarely) if you were absolutely embarrassing. If the role is special, you can ask your agent to inquire, but don't make this request every time you read. If you miss this "bus," eventually there'll be another.

CALLBACKS/SCREEN TESTS

If your reading was for the producer or director and was only a few lines or speeches, you won't be called back. But don't be surprised if you're called back half a dozen times for a major part or a continuing role in a series. (Call-backs, even for one word, are very common in commercials.)

If you read for a casting director (as a screening process) he'll either call you back or take you to meet the producer/director on the spot.

Regardless, remember: you did something right. Do the second reading just like you did the first. Don't outsmart yourself by changing things (that's called "improving your way right out of a part"). We'd even wear the same clothes.

Unless you're up for a major role, you'll almost never be asked to do a screen test. If you are, though, check the material in Chapter 20, "On the Set," and again, make as few changes as possible.

FINALLY . . .

We promise you'll never learn to cold read just by studying a chapter in a book. You're going to have to practice, at best in a good class, at least with fellow actors at home. And the time to start is not when you get "the call."

And never forget that everyone involved in casting is on your side. "The greatest moment for us," says theatrical casting director Jane Feinberg, "is when the director says 'Him.' "

18 SHOWCASES AND OFFICE SCENES

*I had two people in to do one, and they set
up a place setting, and candles, and real
food... and by the time they were through
setting up I was so bored...*

Susan Glicksman, Theatrical Casting Director

In addition to the traditional office scene, new and very important ways of being seen have cropped up. So, first...

THE KINDS OF SHOWCASES

Today, when someone says he just did a "showcase," he might mean any of three different things:

1. *99-seat theatre:* Often referred to as a "showcase production," a "showcase," or an "Equity Waiver" production, this is a play produced in a theatre that seats 99 people or less. The only money involved may be pocket-change salaries. (For more, see Chapter 26.)

2. *The prepared scene showcase:* You and a partner prepare a scene and perform it in front of an audience of one or more casting directors, agents, producers or directors — and you pay for the privilege.

3. *The cold reading workshop:* The newest (and most potent) wrinkle, it's now *the* way to be seen in Hollywood. It's a standard cold reading, usually done for a casting director or agent, and — yes — you pay for these too.

SHOWCASES — SHOULD YOU DO THEM?

That involves two questions — readiness and ethics.

- *Readiness:* "The readiness is all," says William Shakespeare. The purpose of a showcase is not to show how bad you are. If you're not a good actor, don't do a prepared scene showcase. And if your cold reading technique is anything less than terrific, don't do a cold reading showcase. Not only will the competition kill you, but agents and casting directors have very good memories.

NOTE: For some showcases, see Appendix.

- *Ethics:* Actor Steve Ray (who has done well over 100 of these) summed up showcases like this: "I can think of no other way to describe a showcase other than an audition that you pay to do. That's really what it comes down to, no matter how many nice little colors the casting directors or the people who run them try to put on them, it's basically an audition that you pay for."

Should you pay to be seen? Fact of the matter is a lot of people are making a lot of money running these things or doing what they ought to be doing as part of their job: seeing who's out there. (According to *The Los Angeles Times,* in one year one casting director made $16,000 in fees attending showcases.) But: showcases work. Actors do get roles from doing showcases. *Lots* of roles. Actress Terri Semper says, "I look at each showcase as a small investment in my future. Many times actors get called in for an audition up to a year or more after they've done a showcase. It's a great opportunity to publicize yourself."

And actor/teacher Mike Muscat (who has also done hundreds of showcases) sums it up: "Small theatre just doesn't pay off as fast as showcases. It takes three months to get a show up once you cast, and unless you get in a play in which all the elements mesh — unless it's one of the hottest plays in town — it's hard to get industry people to the show. I hate to pay to be auditioned, but it's the lesser of two evils: I pay my fee, and I know just who I'm going to see and what shows he casts."

SHOWCASES — WHEN YOU DO THEM

A few hints:

Pick your shot carefully

Doing showcases willy-nilly wastes time and money. If you don't have an agent, do one for an agent. If you have representation, do one for a casting director who casts shows you have a chance to do. "When you're picking showcases, go to the ones that can do you the most good," says one casting director. "For example, if you're starting out, try a soap opera casting director. Or, say it might be better to do a showcase for the casting director who does a large cast series simply because there are more small parts that they need to cast." And bear in mind your type. The *Cosby* show doesn't use a lot of gangsters.

Each showcase gives a list in advance of the casting director or agent in attendance for each session. (Some places have more than one room, and will offer more than one showcase per night.)

Forget learning anything

Some places call their showcases "classes" or "workshops," but no matter the label, learning ain't why you're there. You're there to be seen. Yes, we've heard of people lucking out by getting someone who knows acting and can teach. But, frankly, a lot of industry people think a "super-objective" is an objective that's just peachy. "My experience," says theatrical agent Joel Rudnick, "Has been that most casting directors don't know what they're doing. Casting directors should teach casting directing, not cold reading. Actors should teach acting. Not agents, not casting directors, but people who have done it themselves."

Don't let somebody with a title next to his name ruin years of solid training. When you're critiqued, you may need to purposely ignore what you're told. (Some of the things actors are told during these showcases range from the silly to the absolutely bizarre. One example: With his voice dripping in venom, one agent told two excellent actors, "You're *obviously* of the 'less is more' school. Well, let me tell you, *stillness is for stars.*")

Don't volunteer

In our chapter on cold reading, we say to give yourself at least 20 minutes to go over the script. In many of these showcases, the person will hand out a script and give the first couple up five minutes to go over it. *Five.*

Insane? You bet. (One casting director said he just wants "to see what the actors will do with it." So did Pavlov.) Remember, directors and producers in a real casting session could care less if you've had five minutes or five days with the script. They just want to see a good reading. Nobody hands out gold stars to the actor who gets it down fastest. They hand out *parts* to the actors who do it *best.* Trying to do a cold reading for anyone in five minutes is just plain dumb. The casting director may think of it as a bogus casting session, but it isn't to you. What he winds up thinking of you is very, very real. So, if you can take longer by hanging back, hang *way* back.

If no one is given more than five minutes, read the script over once, decide what strikes you the most about the scene based on that first reading and then *go for it!* Don't second-guess yourself. Trust your instincts and go out on a limb. Better to be interesting and totally off than to be "correct" and dull. Bear in mind a five-minute reading is pure and simple a form of gambling. Enjoy the roll of the dice. Your odds of doing well if you trust yourself are far greater than hitting sevens at Las Vegas.

Follow-up/be patient

Once you've met the person, go after him. Don't expect him to run all over town looking for you. And be patient. The showcase you do next week may not pay off until next year. As Mike Muscat put it, "Follow-ups are crucially important. So many actors do 30 showcases, don't follow-up, don't get anything and then are ready to quit. I did 50 before I got cast, 150 before I really started working — but now I figure I've made 20 to 30 times the amount of money I put into showcases."

PREPARED SCENE SHOWCASES AND OFFICE SCENES

A "prepared" or "office" scene is exactly that — a scene (no monologues, please — they want to see you relating to your fellow actor) performed by two actors, preferably each of the opposite sex.

The rules of the game for prepared and office scenes are virtually identical. Really, the only difference will be where you are performing it. You'll perform the former on a stage and the casting director or agent will come to see you. For the latter, you'll go to their offices.

The Cardinal Rule

Maximum: five minutes. Strong preference: three minutes.

Sound like acting for a stopwatch? When you work in TV, that's exactly what you do anyway. Don't try to cheat the time limit. We know of actors who were cut off in the middle of a scene long before, as they put it, "we even got to the good part."

If the scene doesn't fit into that three-minute time span, cut it or find another scene. When you begin working on the material, read it aloud with your partner and time it. Since blocking and business adds time, when it's ready to be seen, time it again. Longer than four to five minutes? Pull a "Jason": chop without mercy. If you err, be short. As theatrical agent Miriam Baum put it, "Too short is fine — if you make an impression."

Choosing A Scene

The source doesn't matter. You can cull your scenes from television and movie scripts, plays and books. (You can even write your own — if you can write and are shrewd enough to keep your authorship to yourself so your audience doesn't judge that instead.)

If you've got a VCR, videotape television shows and films regularly — especially ones that are not all that famous and/or seen by the general public. (Your local video store is a treasure house of obscure movies.) Or try soap opera: the intimacy and intense actor-to-actor relationships make them perfect.

Beyond that . . .

- *Cast yourself close to the grain:* Don't stretch. Perform roles you would play. Forget accents, roles calling for you to be older or younger than you are, and character pieces — they're not looking for a new Dracula. Says actor Steve Ray, "One thing I hear all the time from casting directors is 'The person miscast himself.' Pick something that you would get cast in."

- *"Who's that other guy?":* If an agent has you in to do an office scene, choose one that shows you off — not your partner. If it's a showcase — where both actors are paying equally — both parts naturally will have equal weight.)

- *Res ipso loquitor:* That's a Latin expression, used in law, meaning "the thing speaks for itself." Make sure the scene is self-explanatory. "Intros" are boring and they won't help.

- *Make sure it "translates" well:* You're going to be doing the scene in someone's (probably cramped) office. The more activity, the "bigger" you have to be to make the scene work, the worse your choice. The aim of the scene, remember, is to show you relating and reacting to your fellow actor; a lot of running around defeats that. And scenes requiring emotional fireworks can be embarrassing around typewriters at 9 A.M. (You can be slightly bigger in a showcase — you'll be on stage.) The best scenes are usually two people sitting, talking and reacting in a relatively quiet way.

- *Forget English Lit 101:* Shakespeare, Ionesco, Pinter and the other masters may speak well of your knowledge of theatre, but not of your knowledge of what's needed on television.

- *Find something fresh:* As one casting director put it, "If I see one more version of a scene from *Barefoot in the Park*, I'll scream."

- *"Who's doing Brando in this one?":* The only person who gets anywhere doing famous scenes, pitting himself against legendary performances, is Rich Little.

- *A good laugh . . .:* Some food for thought from Steve Ray: "There's a theory that anybody can do drama but not everyone can do comedy

— comedy is special. So, if you do a comedy well, they will assume you can do drama. But if you do a drama they will not assume you can do comedy."

He has a point. So, if you're good at it, give serious consideration to comedy — but only if you're good at it. "I prefer comedy," says theatrical casting director Paul Bengston. "I'm there for a long day's work and I don't want to cry. Also, comedy sticks in the mind."

- *Don't have set- and prop-itis*: When choosing (or working on) a scene be sure your concentration is on acting. If it'll take longer than 30 seconds to set up, it's wrong. The best scenes require nothing in terms of props or set. And choose one that keeps blocking and business to a minimum.

Bottom line, the scene should only ask you to do four things: *sit, talk, listen,* and *react.*

Choosing A Partner

If you're not in an acting class, or have no actor friends who are "right," you can tack up a notice in one of the many workshops around town. Or ask an instructor for a recommendation. Or simply place an ad in *Drama-Logue.*

Just be sure your partner understands it's your scene if it's an office scene and a *shared* scene if it's a showcase — not a chance for him to upstage you. And don't choose a partner who is a bad actor in the hope that he'll make you look good. He won't. On the other hand, thinking of choosing a partner vastly better than you? Razor blades are quicker.

Above all, be careful. "Most actors choose friends," says Steve Ray. "Your friends are not always the best people to do a scene with."

And, once again and most important of all, don't ever EVER do a showcase or office scene if you're not ready.

V
WORKING

19 MAKING A DEAL

Your money indicates your value. You don't
want a hungry agent who just wants to make
a deal.

Jack Rose, President, Jack Rose Agency

With respect to Charles Dickens, the period between your audition and the closing of a deal is "the best of times and the worst of times." You know they want you, but how much? And your participation is usually limited to saying yes or no to a deal that has been worked out between your agent and the casting director.

Just remember: billing is at least as important as salary. From the top down:

- *Star:* Name usually above the title.

- *Also Starring:* Name after the title.

- *Guest Starring:* Most often used in TV. Name usually will appear before the story, after the above.

- *Co-Starring:* Name after the above, usually at the beginning, sometimes at the end, of the show.

- *Featured; also called "end titles" in film:* Name appears at end of story, in the "crawl" — the names move upwards from bottom of screen.

- *Separate card:* Name appears by itself on the screen regardless of type of billing. Naturally, "Star" and "Also Starring" are almost always separate card. "Guest Star" and "Co-Star" separate card billing may require some dickering. "Featured" is almost never put on separate card.

There are all sorts of variations ("Extra-Special Super Whoopy-Doopy Guest Star," etc.) including type sizes, name in a special box, and so forth. Your concern will be to move up from "Featured" to "Co-Star" to "Guest Star." Beyond that, you no longer need this book.

Regarding money, you'll be hired on a daily basis (called "day player"); on a special three-day contract (television only); or on a weekly basis (called "freelance"). Most likely, if you're working for "scale" (minimum union

---

NOTE: For fees and other contract regulations, see Appendix.

salary), an additional ten percent for your agent, called "scale plus ten," will be added to your paycheck.

As you move up, your salary will increase. But be careful. As theatrical casting director Ron Stephenson puts it, "An actor should get a raise periodically, but an agent shouldn't price an actor out of the business." And bear in mind producer William Kayden's comment: "Usually that part is budgeted. Sometimes we'll 'steal' money from another role, but generally, if you can't get one actor for your price, you get another." Sticky, isn't it?

If you're hired as a day player to work for two days on, say, *Space Sluts in the Slammer* (that's a real movie, by the way!) and the producer sees he's going to need you to work longer (say, four days), obviously he must pay you for the extra time. However, he can convert you from day player to weekly contract player (called "weekly conversion") to save money. Assume you're making $500 per day. Four days would be $2,000. He might convert you to a week at, say, $1,800.

However, the reverse is *not* true. If you're contracted for a week and work only one day, he's still on the hook for a week's salary.

According to SAG, you've got a firm engagement if: the studio or producer gives you written acceptance; you're given a contract signed by the producer; you're given a script with intent to hire you; you're fitted (other than wardrobe tests); or when you're called and agree to report.

However, once your agent calls the casting director to confirm you said yes, for all practical purposes, you've got a deal. The speed of this industry requires a telephone conversation to be considered a contract; sometimes you'll be working the next day.

If there's no time to assemble a full-fledged contract, as further protection you're supposed to get a "booking slip." It's messengered to you along with the script, or sent to your agent, or given to you on the set, and is a memorandum briefly outlining your length of employment, what you'll be paid, how you'll be billed, and your start date. Don't bet your inheritance you'll get it.

If you're hired but not given a specific date, and another job offer comes along (jobs come in clusters — for reasons, see your local guru), you or your agent must give the producer 24 hours' notice. If he gets back to you and gives you a specific start date, that date and job become binding to you both. If he doesn't get back to you, you're free to accept the other job.

To further clarify the negotiating process, here's what agent Jack Rose had to say. Pay special attention to what he says at the end:

"There are many types of negotiations, so I'm going to give you a very simple one . . . They call for an actor to work for a period of time to do a film. They tell us how many days they want the actor, and how much they want to pay. At that point, we say, 'Well, that's not enough money.'

They say, 'Of course that's enough money.' And then we say, 'Well, on the last film the actor got X numbers of dollars per week.' Now, some casting directors already have that information in front of them, so you can't lie to them. Once you lie to those people forget it; forget about dealing with these people again. And you know which ones work that way, so you say, 'Yes, *but* the actor has another project that we're probably going to have to sign him for, unless you offer him more money.' Or, 'You want him for a week; your film's going for three weeks, let's make it a two-week guarantee.' And you come to some kind of compromise that way.

"Then you get into billing — if they're going to give billing or not and the position of the billing. Those are the simple terms of a basic negotiation . . . Unless your agent is a good negotiator, you're going to wind up making very little money, and just working as a day player."

20 ON THE SET

Q: How much direction do actors get on a set?

A: Well, let's be honest — you're not going to get a whole lot.

Interview with Harvey Laidman, Director

Big cities, move over. There's no lonelier time or place than a first day on a set. It's kind of a combination opening night/first day on a ("regular") job. If you feel a sense of alienation, you're not alone. You'll sense a curious arm's-length between you and everyone else on the set — until you work. Then you become one of the family.

PRE-SET DOINGS

Costumes/scripts

Once you're hired, the producer will have a complete script (assuming there is one) delivered to your door by messenger, or you'll be asked to pick one up.

Next comes the call from the costumer. When he calls depends on how soon you'll be working.

Now prepare yourself for an unglamorous shock: If the show is modern dress, you'll be asked to raid your closet and provide your own wardrobe. Yep — just like back in South Patooie Community Theatre. You'll be paid a fee, though.

On the phone, the costumer and you will decide on what you will wear on the show, and you will be expected to bring your "costume(s)" with you to the first day of work. (If you don't want to drive the sound man crazy, avoid polyester and leather. They're too noisy.)

Even if you provide your own wardrobe, however, the costumer will want to know your sizes in case the clothes you show up with aren't "right."

- *Sizes men should know:* Shoe, hat, glove, shirt (small, medium, large, extra large), sleeve length, collar size, pants (waist and length), jacket and/or coat.

- *Sizes women should know:* Shoe, hat, glove, blouse, dress, pants, jacket and/or coat.

NOTE: For on-set rules, regulations, fees, etc., see Appendix.

If the show is a period piece, you'll need a fitting. After getting your sizes, the costumer will set a day and time for you to come to the studio. (You may or may not be paid for this, depending on your contract.)

Preparing

First, when rehearsing, stay with the basic interpretation you had when you auditioned. That's what got you hired.

Next, understand that anything can happen, and that it's a lead-pipe cinch your scene won't take place the way you envision it. Positive you'll be behind a desk? There won't be a desk in sight. Rehearse the scene in as many ways as possible: standing (looking left, then right); walking; and yes, even behind a desk.

Know your lines, but be ready to see them (drastically) changed. And don't bet on getting the right cues. Besides error, many actors — especially stars — can't resist "improving" the writing.

As "opening day" approaches, your agent or the second (A.D.) will phone to give you your "call" — the day and time you're expected on the set. You'll get as much sleep as a rat on catnip.

ARRIVAL

Don't run up to the producer or director chirping "I'm here!" They've got other things on their minds. Report to the second assistant director (A.D.). He'll show you to your dressing room (it should be private) and give you your contract or booking slip. Bear in mind it's his job to have you ready to go. If he makes a mistake he's going to have you ready too early. There's a lot of "hurry up and wait" on movie sets.

Settle into your dressing room, perhaps get a cup of that brown iodine they pass off as coffee, get into costume and then report to the makeup artist. (Unless you're highly experienced, leave makeup to the experts. Street makeup is one thing; stage makeup is another; camera makeup is yet another.)

With those chores squared away, sit down in your dressing room and prepare to wait . . . and wait . . . and wait . . .

THE CONTRACT

While waiting, read your contract. Check to be sure your name is spelled correctly, that your Social Security number, address, phone number, and salary are correct, that your billing and any other special deal is as agreed. If everything is okay, be sure to sign all copies (usually three). Then fill out your tax forms. And then . . . more waiting.

SAVING ENERGY/BEING READY

Eight hours rehearsing is less tiring than four hours sitting around on a set. You're bored. You're antsy. You're *very* bored. You're *very* antsy. You just can't relax. Try. Don't go running around. Lie down in your dressing room; read, do crossword puzzles, vegetate. You may wait 30 minutes or eight hours. Save it for "Action."

About 732 years later, the second A.D. will come a-knocking at your dressing room door, saying "We're ready for you." It's rehearsal time.

When you arrive on the set itself, the second A.D. will introduce you to your fellow actors; you'll "re-meet" the director, and, if he's there, the producer.

What you do next will depend on the project . . .

FEATURE FILMS/FILMS FOR TV

Films for television include almost any drama made for TV except a "three-camera show" (see below). Feature films are movies. For you, the only real working difference between these two will be the number of takes you do. Feature film directors tend to shoot scenes over and over until they're happy with what they've got. TV Films — figure three takes and out.

We'll assume you've landed your first job on the hit new series about Beverly Hills dentists: *L.A. Jaw.* What will "the shoot" be like? It'll all start with what is laughingly referred to as . . .

THE REHEARSAL

You'll go through the entire scene. Your fellow actor — if he's the star — may be carrying a script, mumbling his lines as he goes. Sooner or later you'll realize that unless you want to look like a statue, you'd better move. So you do — totally on your own. And when you stop, somebody rushes in and puts a piece of masking tape at your feet. The scene ends. The second A.D. comes onto the set, says "Thank you," and yells, "Second team please!" That's it. "Rehearsal" is over.

In a state of shock you go and sit. Where's all the talk about motivations and stuff? Where's the struggle to get it right? What's going on here?

A typical shoot.

Want direction? Go back to the stage. In TV and film, you're expected to come up with the ideas. Blocking will be vague, usually of the "play it over there" variety. And forget discussions about character motivation. Directors expect you to be ready to perform when you arrive on the set. (As one director expressed it, "I don't have time to play schoolmaster.")

Some directors feel giving direction to actors is "insulting." Others are camera nuts who wouldn't know how to direct an actor if their lives depended on it. But all are fighting one relentless enemy — the clock.

A director shooting a one-hour TV show has a week to ten days to get it all "in the can." Why? Time is money. If he "goes over" without a darn good reason, *he's* either gone over or just plain gone. So, if at all possible, he'll want to rehearse the scene once, light it, and shoot it in *one take*. (Yes, feature film directors have longer schedules, but still, as director Noel Black says, "You'd better assume you're going to do your great work on take one.")

Okay, while you've been sitting there, people have been moving back and forth, lighting and "dressing" the set (putting in props, drapes, books in bookshelves, etc.).

Now, it's time for . . .

THE SHOOT

You stand where you started when you rehearsed. (Called "first position." "Second position" is your next "stopping point"; "third position" your next and so on.) Often they'll strap a hidden microphone on you — this is "being miked" — and the following (in order) will occur:

- *"Roll camera!" or "Turn over!"*: Is called out by the first A.D. Either term means the cameraman is to start running the film through the camera.

(When it does, you'll then hear: "We're rolling!")

- *"Speed!"*: Is called out by the sound man to let the director know his tape recorder is running and recording properly.

- *"Marker"*: Standing a few feet away, the man with the legendary clapboard (called "the sticks") will snap it (sometimes in your face if they're doing a close-up) to synchronize sound with picture.

(Somebody always then quietly says, "Settle, please." Who *is* that guy??)

- *"Action!"*: Is said by the director. That's your cue to start.

And what are you shooting? A *take* called . . .

THE "MASTER" SHOT — WHAT TO CONCENTRATE ON

The "master" is the "scene setting" shot. It tells the audience where the scene is taking place, and who's in it. It's always the first take, includes all the actors involved, and lasts for the entire scene. It's also almost always the first part of the scene you see in the actual final movie, and the director may cut back and forth to the master as the scene goes on.

When shooting the master (or any shot) concentrate on . . .

- *Marks:* Remember those pieces of masking tape they put at your feet? Not decoration. When you move, the cameraman has to know in advance where you'll be stopping so he'll stop with you. Those stopping/standing points are "marked," and it's your job to hit those marks — *dead on.* "Marks are of the essence," says director/cinematographer Bruce Logan. "If you don't hit them, you won't be in the light; you won't be in focus; and you won't be in the shot."

    Mostly, masking tape is used; sometimes chalk. With either, they want your toes directly on the mark. (If you're standing on grass they'll use a wooden "T." Each foot is on either side of the stem, with the toes immediately behind the bar of the "T.")

    "Marks are critical," says commercial producer Bob Wollin. "You're dealing with very sophisticated lenses." Miss a mark and the cameraman will have to stop the shoot — he's aiming for one spot and you're in another. Keep missing? 'Bye now.

    Unfortunately, if you're inexperienced at hitting marks they'll really get in the way of your acting. If you can't afford a film technique class, practice with masking tape at home. Pros hit their marks, amateurs don't — and they're not paying you to be an amateur. From an article in *PEOPLE Weekly:*

    ". . . Robert Conrad is taping a scene for his new CBS adventure series, *High Mountain Rangers.* The afternoon is cold and the crew is tired when, suddenly, a scream loud enough to roust a bear out of hibernation rings through the wintry air. It is Conrad, and he is enraged. 'We had a chopper in the scene, and there was a storm, but the skiers on the back side of the mountain could still hear him,' marvels Joan Conrad, the show's producer and the star's daughter. The reason for his fury? 'One of the actors,' says Joan, '*missed his mark.*'" [Italics ours.]

- *Matching:* Remember last night when you were watching *Attack of the Slima Beans?* An actor lit a cigarette. The camera cut away from him for a moment. When it returned, no cigarette. That's an extreme example of a bad match.

    Whose fault? The actor's. Yep, matching is your responsibility. There is a script supervisor and/or a continuity person to check on the general continuity of a scene, but you're still expected to match.

"Continuity mistakes from an actor are really unforgivable," says cinematographer Howard Wexler.

If you shout "Get out!", pointing on the word "out" in one shot, point on that same word every shot. Match all movement (when and how you rise, sit down, turn, gesture, pick something up, etc.), and also be certain to look the same (costume, hair, general makeup). You should also match the emotional intensity of the scene from one shot to the next. If you're furious in one shot, and merely angry in another, you're not matching.

Unless the mistake is blatant (like the cigarette mentioned above), it's possible no one will tell you you're not matching. But it will be spotted later. Where? You got it. "If it's not matched, it won't go together and it will wind up on the cutting-room floor," says director/cinematographer Bruce Logan.

They'll use other shots of the scene and you'll lose screen time (most likely close-ups). Ouch.

- *"Cheating towards the camera"*: Always be aware of where the camera is located, and position yourself accordingly; it's your audience. If the camera can't see it — face, prop or whatever — it doesn't exist. "Actors," says director/cinematographer Bruce Logan, "Make two mistakes: not being aware of the camera; and being overly aware of the camera."

- *Overlap(ping):* In theatre, cues need to be fast and stepping on another actor's line can often add excitement. But film actors shouldn't do this. It makes editing the scene difficult. Often, if you overlap, the take will have to be re-shot. Exceptions are allowed (a "violent" argument or Altmanesque film), but in general, let your fellow actor finish his line before you speak.

- *Scaling down your acting:* In a feature film, everything you do will be "blown up" about 35 times. The TV screen may be smaller, but it hates overacting. Be careful not to be too "big." "Step back" from the camera. Don't "show" the camera what you're thinking or doing; allow the camera to "discover" it.

- *Stillness:* That is, feeling comfortable moving less, and more economically. Director Leslie Martinson: "Actors will sometimes move for the sake of moving, which is deadly. If you have a head-to-head scene, play it. Many times the actor will say, 'I'm glued here,' and I say, 'Where would you like to move in the middle of a line like that?'"

- *Staying in it:* For as long as the camera is running. You can't break concentration for a second. As TV newsman Dan Rather phrased it in the title of his book: the camera never blinks.

  And you *absitively, posolutely* cannot break character until you hear . . .

- *"Cut!":* This is when you stop acting — not a moment before. There will be times you'll feel the camera has been on you forever, but never break character until the director says "Cut." He will need this extra footage later when editing.

  If he didn't like it, or he wants to see what else he can get, he'll re-shoot it — as many times as he can — which in TV isn't a lot.

  If he liked (or because of time had to settle for) that take, he'll say, "Print," or "Print that." Essentially, he's saying, "Okay. Good. Save that shot. That's one I'll (probably) use."

  When you hear the director say "Print," that's the shot you'll need to match — all through the many and various kinds of additional shots of the scene that will be taken.

OTHER SHOTS — "COVERAGE"

A cardinal rule: Time is money, but film is cheap. In other words, a director will try to "cover" a scene using as many different shots as the clock will allow. His least concern is "wasting film."

Here's a brief list of the most common shots that'll involve you. Remember, each one requires the camera to be placed differently, the lighting to be changed, etc. (called "a new deal.") That's why filming is so time-consuming.

- *Two-shots/three-shots, etc:* A two-shot has two actors in it; a three-shot, three actors, and so on.
- *Long shot:* Takes in your whole body.
- *Medium shot:* From the waist up.
- *Close-up:* (Usually) head and shoulders.
- *Choker close-up:* The top of your head to your chin.
- *Extreme close-up:* Anything from an eyeball to a pore.

Since you can't always tell by the location of the camera which is being shot, *"Where are you cutting me?"* is the question of the day, for two reasons:

1. *To scale to the shot:* The closer in they go, the smaller you must get — both in movement and acting.

2. *To always have things "in frame":* Important props such as letters, books, etc. must be held at the right height to be seen.

SEMPER READY

Does all this sound tough? You betcha. To illustrate how tough, here's an example of what can happen to you on one line:

You've shot the master and they're ready to shoot your close-up. As the final seconds tick off, the cameraman says, "Listen, you're slightly off your mark and, when you say that line, cheat over a little into the light." You nod. (Now you're thinking, "Let's see: mark, cheat over, I'm angry in this scene . . .").

The sound man approaches. "Listen," he says, "try not to drop your voice so low on that line; I'm not getting you." "Right," you reply. (Now it's "Mark, cheat over, voice up, angry . . .").

The director passes by and says, "Don't do that line quite so angry." "Gotcha, " you say. ("Mark, cheat over, voice up, less intensity . . .").

The makeup artist slips in and pads the perspiration off with a Kleenex as the cameraman adds, "And be sure to hold that cup up high enough so we can see it." "Uh huh," you reply. ("Mark, cheat over, voice up, less intensity, hold up cup . . .").

The assistant director says "Stand by."

Your costume begins to itch.

You hear "Roll camera," "Speed," a man snaps a clapboard in your face, saying "Marker," the director says "Action" . . .

. . . And the star changes your cue.

The next time you're watching television and you think the actors are "phoning it in," remember this example. And get training. Lots of it.

And one other word about keeping up your energy. If you're working on a feature film, and the director keeps re-shooting the scene, after the fifteenth take it's easy to stop caring about what you're doing. Care. Inevitably, the take you got sloppy on will be the one they use — because the rain was just perfect.

THE LINGO

As you're shooting, here's some other terms you'll be hearing:

- *Wild track:* To prevent calling you back another day because of sound problems, you'll occasionally do a "wild track." You'll stand at the microphone saying your line(s) as the sound man tapes it/them.

- *Looping:* Is done in one of two ways. Let's say you're looping one line. You hear that line on a "looped" tape that plays over and over like a short version of your home answering machine. You listen to the way you said it during filming, then try to duplicate the line reading so your words will match the way your lips move.

  The other method is done in a projection room, with the scene shown on a screen. Wearing a headset, you'll hear four "beeps." You start after the fourth, matching your words to the movement of your mouth as you see it on the screen.

- *Key light:* That's your own personal "spotlight." (Daytime, outdoors, it's the sun.) If you don't know where you're key light is, ask, and try to make sure you're in it when shooting.

- *Hot set:* When shooting is suspended the set will be labeled "hot." This means nothing is to be moved, so that everything will match when shooting resumes.

- *Honeywagon:* The trailer(s) containing dressing rooms.

- *Call sheet:* Given out toward the end of the day, it's the list of actors, their calls, and other crew and items needed the next day.

THREE-CAMERA SHOWS

At the beginning of a half-hour sitcom such as *The Bill Cosby Show*, the announcer says, "Taped in Hollywood before a live audience." That's a three-camera show.

Three cameras are used simultaneously and the show is taped in sequence, just like a one-act play. There's no stopping to change camera setups (that's why they use three), and breaks occur only when actors move from set to set. Made a mistake? Keep going unless it's drastic.

Like a play, rehearsals start with a read-through, with the cast seated at a table, and proceed to blocking and business. The rehearsal period is usually four days, followed by taping on the fifth. On the day or night of performance, you'll probably do the entire show twice, in front of two different audiences.

With the exception of the re-writes that constantly come up, stage actors love this. It's as close to doing a one-act play as you can get without actually doing one. Directors work more with you and the audience adds to that ole theatre feeling. Also, the level of your performance is close to that of a comedy or musical done in a small or medium-sized theatre.

SOAP OPERA

These, too, are three-camera shows, but they're usually rehearsed in the morning and shot in the afternoon of the same day. Short of summer stock, there's no better training ground for learning lines, business, and delivery of a believable performance in a short period of time. "Soap operas are one of the best ways to learn your craft," says producer William Kayden. "They're marvelous training."

Once again, even though there's no audience, you only stop to move from set to set. The standard rule is: keep going. And the acting level is extremely understated. The audience should feel as though they're observing you in your living room through a keyhole. That's why one producer cautions: "Soaps are wonderful training because you are forced to very quickly make transitions, build up to a certain emotional result, etc. But, I don't think, if you possibly can avoid it, that you should stay on a soap too long because there is the danger of becoming too facile."

THE WE-HATE-TO-MENTION-IT DEPARTMENT

We wish we could promise you a grand ole time on every set, but, if the truth be known, there will be times you'll think you walked into a scene out of Dante's *Inferno* — and, if you're not careful, you could get burnt.

Understand first of all that a caste system does exist on a set — unspoken, but there in spades. At the bottom of the heap are the extras; at the top, the stars. Extras are served last at lunch. Day players would be wise not to sit in the star's chair. Stars get the best dressing rooms; other actors get smaller but still private rooms; extras of the same sex dress in one room together. "I've worked on sets where a principal comes up and we'll start talking," says one SAG actor who also does extra work, "And as soon as they find out I'm an extra there's a whole change in attitude. And they make you feel kind of . . . really crummy. And it's not just them — it's everybody." You'll see plenty of top dog/underdog manifestations of human behavior, and you'd be smart to take note of how much of it is taking place on any given set.

On some sets, this behavior is kept to a minimum, with everyone sharing in a joyful, generous camaraderie. On others, it's best to keep to yourself and not try to become "one of the boys," as you'll be at grave risk of being humiliated.

If your spouse joins you on location (there's usually no objection), be circumspect about inviting your sweetie to the set itself. On a good set, visitors are treated with the utmost respect and charm. On a bad set, they're made to feel like they just walked in on a very private conversation.

Even on a good set, be discreet. Don't run up to the star to introduce yourself or — great holy amateur night! — to ask for an autograph. Have the second A.D. introduce you at the right time. Don't even start a conversation with a star; let him take the lead.

Sound like Chicken Little? Two stories:

On one set, a *veteran* actor (a you-know-his-face-but-not-his-name type) sat next to a major star. Silence. Hours of it. Finally, the actor turned to the star and ventured, "Hi, I'm ———. I just can't sit next to someone and not talk to them." The star slowly turned to the actor and replied, "I can."

A highly-talented actress got a part on a show when the star was having a contract dispute with the producer. At the start of rehearsal the actress said her first line, and immediately, the star threw up his hands, saying, "I'm not going to work with such an incompetent actress!" and he walked off the set. Naturally, her stomach knotted up as tight as a fist. Fortunately, the director knew her and took the time to tell her not to worry, the star was just using her as an excuse not to work.

Using her.

"I think there ought to be a class at every institution about temperamentalism," says theatrical agent Joel Rudnick. "I call it 'star-itis.' It's an occupational disease that people get that can exist on the star level and on the amateur level. And it's important to know about it for two reasons: first, to know how to work with people like that, and second to know how to deal with it when it happens to you."

We're not saying that your on-set experiences need be bad. Just be on your guard. As producer Michael Rhodes jokingly put it, "You already know you have to be crazy to be in this business, so, on the set, treat everybody as if they're potential ax murderers, and you'll be all right."

WRAP

If you're working the next day, the second A.D. will hand you your "call sheet." If you're not working the next day, but are still on salary, next to your name will be the word "Hold."

When you're ready to leave the set, the second A.D. will ask you to sign out. Note carefully the arrival and departure times he has recorded. This is what they will base any overtime on. Be sure the times are accurate and in ink.

Don't expect anyone to come rushing up to you telling you how wonderful you were, especially not the producer or director. They may have loved your work, but right now their minds are on the next scene.

Then you're on your way back to your hotel, or home. You won't be very good company that night. You'll feel as though you've just come back from another world — and you have.

VI
COMMERCIALS

21 COMMERCIALS: THE WONDERFUL WORLD OF HAPPY

What do they want? What plays in Disneyland.

Pamela Campus, Commercial Casting Director

THE COMMERCIAL TYPE

"We're not in the entertainment industry. We're in the business of selling widgets. And, if you sell a lot of widgets other people will hire you to sell a lot of their widgets," says voice-over casting director Bob Lloyd.

Want to know how much work you can expect to get in commercials? Or how to look? Or how you should act? Sit down in front of a TV set. Mostly, you'll see "white bread" — an industry expression describing actors (of whatever race) with rather bland, wholesome, all-American looks. You'll see "P&G housewives with perk" — another industry expression meaning idealized Midwestern mother types oozing perkiness and cheer. (P&G stands for Proctor and Gamble — purportedly the inventors of what is now a standard look.) You'll see warm, loving dads with short hair and conservative clothing, adorably cute children, teens who never saw a pimple (unless they're selling zits removers), grandmothers still dressed like they did back in 1926. Clean streets. Musical comedy. Happy endings. Energy. Brightness. Warmth...

"Most calls, they want Midwestern," says agent Karen DiCenzo. In short, you gotta think Iowa.

You'll have to look harder for character faces, and many nights may go by between "ethnic" faces or actors with accents... unless you're tuned to an "ethnic" station, where "ethnics" will predominate. Only a limited number of high-fashion products will use women in low-cut, sexy dresses, heavy rouge, or orange eyeshadow. Men will almost never sport mustaches or beards.

In short, you'll see the look the makers of commercials want. The closer you come to that, the more you'll work.

Which brings us to...

ARE COMMERCIALS WORTH IT?

Are they worth shaving off that beard you love so much, or changing your hairstyle and makeup from "*Zoweena of Hollywood*" to "*Mary Smith from Peoria*" just to please some faceless corporate executive who's decided (based on millions of dollars of research) that his customers relate to "Middle America"? Should you hassle finding an agent or go to the expense of putting together a composite to work in an area that makes the *product* the star? (The script designation for a product is the word "hero"!) Is attending commercial workshops, learning to convince America it can't live without Uncle Georgie's Better Mousetraps worth the time of a serious actor? Three points . . .

Money

Don't want to do them? Okay. Cut your wallet in two. According to SAG, nearly half the income of actors comes directly from commercials. A commercial is almost always shot in one day and can pay thousands of dollars in residuals. Not too shabby for eight hours' work. Beats slinging hash in a diner.

Career

We could fill these pages with the names of stars discovered doing commercials, as commercial casting director Pamela Campus testifies: "A few years ago I walked through Columbia Pictures Studios, and I saw up on their wall all these pictures of [TV stars] . . . people I had hired five years ago. And I said to myself, 'Wait a minute, I'm training these people for sitcoms, mini-series and television.' Let me tell you something. The top people you see in commercials today, especially if they're comedic, will be the top people you later see in a series. If you stand out in a commercial, usually you'll be picked up in a series. I've seen it."

Entrée

If you're a middle-aged housewife from Peoria who's thinking of fast bucks or doing commercials on a lark, we'd advise skipping it. Getting an agent will be rough, and even if you luck into a commercial or two, the sparse work won't be worth it. Regular work in commercials requires you to be experienced and highly trained. Sorry.

However, if you're a newcomer with some theatre and/or commercial training, commercials (along with industrials and low-budget films) can be the way to that first break. Casting for commercials is far more cut-and-dried than theatricals. When you're called in for an audition, they know exactly what look they want — fit that and you've got a good shot. As one agent put it, "Commercial agents sometimes sign non-SAG people because they know that if the advertising agency loves your face and loves the way you sell their product, they have enough clout — money — to get you into SAG via Taft-Hartley." (See Chapter 7.)

Further, as theatrical agent Mary Spencer points out, "Many times, if you're new, you can get into an agency 'across the board.' If you have a great commercial look, and are saleable, they'll take you on in all fields."

Just remember: newcomers yes, untrained, no.

Are they worth it? If you're not convinced, better stay out. If you're contemptuous of commercials it'll show, you'll annoy people, and wind up not working anyway.

If you want to do them:

- Get *commercial* training.
- Make yourself as "white bread" as possible.
- Find the one person you simply can't do without: a commercial agent.

22 COMMERCIAL AGENTS

You can eat your way to a fortune
in this industry.

John Fisher, Commercial Agent

Two kinds of people spend their lives on the phone — bookies and commercial agents. Here's why:

Each commercial agency puts together a "book" (a three-ring binder containing pictures of all their clients). When casting, the commercial casting director looks through them, chooses the "right" actors, and calls the agent. The agents phone those people and give them information regarding the audition.

Get the part and the casting director will phone your agent to tell him when you'll be shooting. (Unless you're a celebrity, there are no salary or billing negotiations — more later.) The agent then calls you with that info.

A fairly set routine? Couldn't get much setter. In the fast, furious world of commercials, you're either right for the part or you're not. Your agent doesn't sell you — your pictures (and, later, you) do. "We're really order takers," says one commercial agent. Naturally, if the agent is smart, he'll make friends of all commercial casting directors. He wants them to go to his "book" first.

Sometimes the casting director gives casting information to the Breakdown Service and the agents submit your pictures for a specific part. But don't expect the kind of personal attention from your commercial agent you should be getting from your theatrical agent. Your commercial agent serves as a kind of clearinghouse of commercial types *before* you're cast, a messenger of information *when* you're cast, and a guardian of your financial interests (straight pay and residuals) *after* you're cast.

Further, in Los Angeles you can't survive in commercials without an agent because there's little opportunity to submit yourself directly for a commercial. Most casting directors freelance; besides, commercial casting is a speedy business, often going from first audition to "in the can" within a week. You can search the trades from now till Elsie the Cow comes home and never know what's casting.

NOTE: For more on commercial agency contracts as well as agency addresses and phone numbers, see Appendix.

Voice-over agent Don Pitts: "In New York you can make the rounds to the ad agencies and production houses. Out here, there's nobody there to talk to, and, at the ad agencies, nobody wants to talk to you. You really have to rely on your agent."

SEEKING/CHOOSING AN AGENT

Since you won't need the personal attention so necessary in theatricals, there's nothing wrong with your commercial agency having a client list that numbers in the hundreds. In fact, the larger the better. Big agencies tend to be more trusted by casting directors and, consequently, receive the bulk of the calls. "The others get the crumbs," said one commercial casting director. Some of the best known:

Abrams, Rubaloff & Lawrence
Nina Blanchard Enterprises Inc. (Be seriously beautiful)
Sonjia Warren Brandon's Talent Agency (AKA Commercials Unlimited)
Iris Burton Agency (kids only)
Cunningham-Escott-Dipene Agency
Joseph, Heldfond & Rix
Tyler Kjar Agency
MGA Agency (Mary Grady) (kids)
Susan Nathe & Associates/CPC
Jack Rose Agency
Special Artists Agency
Sutton, Barth & Vennari, Inc.
Talent Group Inc.
Herb Tannen & Associates Inc.
Wilhelmina Artists Representatives

How do you interest a commercial agent? Compared to finding a theatrical agent, it's refreshingly simple. Just send a *good* commercial headshot (with résumé and covering letter). Recommendations can help, but one good pic will do the trick — if the agency is looking for your type.

When called in, use all the techniques found in "The General Interview/ Look-See" and add a good helping of "perk."

DEALING WITH/MOTIVATING THE COMMERCIAL AGENT

Taking your agent to lunch and making a colleague of him is a given — even in commercials. Beyond that . . .

What he'll expect of you

Obviously, he won't expect you to get commercials on your own. He won't care that much if you do plays and showcases except as a way for you to keep fresh and promote your general value as an actor. (And don't expect him to come and see you — that's like asking a baseball manager to come watch you play quarterback.)

And he won't expect you to be calling him with suggestions regarding submissions.

He will expect you: to be a fantastic auditioner; to be on time and not to miss interviews; to pay him his commission; and to keep track of your residuals and, especially, your conflicts (see Chapter 24). He'll also want you to keep him well-heeled in composites (see next chapter).

(Some commercial agents will hand you a list of commercial casting directors and ask you to drop off a photo to them for their agency books. They'll say it's a great way for you to make contacts, but the fact is they're being lazy and you'll mostly contact receptionists. Do it anyway.)

Above all, be reachable! Commercial auditions pop up fast. Do all in your power to be sure your agent can reach you on a moment's notice. You're out to lunch. You call your commercial agent at noon. You're "clear." Ten minutes later, he gets a call telling him they need you *now*. You don't call back until two P.M. You're *really* out to lunch.

He may not mention it, but he'll probably want you to take as many workshops taught by commercial casting directors as possible. The reason? Contacts.

What you should expect of him

Assuming you've given him good pictures, and you're "white bread," you should go out on commercial auditions far more often than for movies and TV shows. It may take a little while, but once you get rolling, expect to go out at least twice a week.

"The most I ever went out on," says one good commercial type, "was ten in two days." Lower that number if: you're not "white bread," your agency is small, you haven't got good pictures, or you suddenly "cool off" (hang in there; things will eventually pick up again).

Beyond this, your agent's most important function is to keep track of your residuals and conflicts, and to help you put together your strongest selling tool: a *super* composite.

CHANGING COMMERCIAL AGENTS

You change commercial agents in the same way as theatrical agents (See Chapters 12 and 14), but there's one important difference. In a theatrical contract, if you don't get 15 days' work in a 91-day period you may fire your agent. Since most commercials are shot in one day, that's asking your commercial agent to come up with 15 different commercials every three months. So a dollar figure is substituted: if you don't earn $2,000 or more in any 91-day period, you may fire your commercial agent.

If you have signed with an agency "across the board" (commercially and theatrically), the theatrical contracts take precedence. You may fire him if you didn't get 15 days' work in 91 days.

23 COMPOSITES

*I look for saleability, sparkle, and an
expressive "grabber"- type shot.*

Tracey Jacobs, Commercial Agent

A smiling headshot will do, but a composite will do better...
...A bakery owner and a commercial casting director are thumbing
through photos. First, there's a headshot of a man in a business suit.
Next, a composite, including a shot of a friendly fellow in a chef's hat,
holding a tray of rolls.

Which actor gets called in?

Don't hock the wedding ring. Your agent can use your commercial head
shot(s) until you: can afford a composite, are sure you're happy with him,
and are convinced you'll be going out enough to warrant the investment.

THE "USUAL" SPECIFICATIONS

A composite measures 8½ by 11 inches, slightly larger than your headshot.
There's one large close-up on the front and from three to six other photos
on the back. (Four, usually.) It's printed in a matte finish, with three holes
punched out on the left for easy insertion in agency books. Unlike headshots,
in addition to your name your stats are included, as is your agent's logo,
address and phone number (see illustration).

GETTING STARTED

Shooting a composite can be three hours of Disneyland or dental
appointment, depending on how much planning you do. Start by re-reading
our chapter on headshots. Then...

Talk with your agent

First, ask him to show you some composites he likes. Note the layout,
how many photos, etc. He may direct you to a printer familiar with this
look, maybe even one who already has a negative of the agency logo.
That's legit — even if he suggests a photographer or two — provided
all rates are reasonable and he doesn't insist on any one person/shop.
(If so, he might be getting a kickback.)

Next, find out what he thinks will sell you. Are you the classic "P&G
housewife with perk"? Are you too young for a "loving daddy" shot? Do

you look like you belong in an office? A supermarket? A kitchen? A baseball diamond? Would you look silly holding a monkey wrench? If so, how about a bookkeeper's shade? Does your agent see you selling dishwasher detergent or shampoo? Trucks or computers? Try to agree on the "must" photos. Remember, it's your composite, but his agency's name will be on it too.

Then go and get . . .

A good photographer

One who's good at commercial composites — not just headshots. He'll be willing to go "on location" to a park, a supermarket, etc., and will work with a child if needed. He'll have ideas, but will respect yours. Don't depend on him, or let him push you into agreeing on all his ideas — not unless you want recycled poses. Decide who provides the props and costumes (bring many of your own — his are already in other composites), set the time (avoid high noon — the light is too harsh), and go home and think about . . .

WHAT'S ON A GOOD COMPOSITE

A good composite includes:

- At least one (smiling!) close-up for the front of the composite;
- One shot of you from head to foot;
- Probably, one shot of you in a business suit, jacket or dress;
- At least one shot in casual dress (can be most shots);
- At least one "costume" shot (meaning anything from a pair of glasses, whether you wear them or not, to an apron and chef's hat, a football uniform, tennis togs, nurse's uniform, etc.)
- For women, at least one variation on hairstyle if possible;
- One shot in full- or three-quarters profile.

Mix and match the above with a variety of your own ideas and the following suggestions:

- *The "loving mommy/daddy shot":* Vital, if you're the type, even if it's rent-a-kid time. Be sure you're relating warmly to the child, but keep the focus of the picture on you. He steals your heart — not your scene.
- *The "consumer shot":* Chomp a burger, sip a shake, push a cart full of groceries, pump gas into your car, etc. (Keep brand names

out of sight — if you're up for an M&M's commercial you don't want to be seen unwrapping Lifesavers.)

- *"At work shot"*: That's white- or blue-collar, and includes housework. Make these shots active and full of fun. Look like you might work in a supermarket? Deck out in cap and apron and "rescue" a teetering stack of apples.

- *"Outdoorsy/sports shot"*: You jog, fish, play baseball, go camping, jump over the net with a racquet in your hand, and so forth. Your entire composite could be outdoorsy if that's "you." Important note: show only activities you can do.

FRONT (ABOVE) AND BACK OF A TYPICAL COMPOSITE...

A FINAL WORD

Above all, know your type and shoot it. A terrific example of this is the composite of an actor named Edward Ashley, who's got an upper-class air, indeed even a slight English accent. His composite consists of five photos:

On the front, Mr. Ashley in a jacket and turtleneck, hair neatly in place, a warm smile on his face: your basic commercial headshot.

Picture two, on the back, is a full body shot of Mr. Ashley in a suit, a small briefcase in his hand, leaning against a Rolls-Royce with a mansion in the background (his "at work" shot).

Picture three is Mr. Ashley in an expensive tux, menu in one hand, warmly beckoning the viewer to sit down. In the foreground, an expensive-looking bottle of wine is barely discernable (a mixture of "costume/at work" shot).

Picture four shows Mr. Ashley in a shirt and hat suggesting an African safari guide, looking very handsome and elegant (a mixture of "costume/outdoorsy" shot).

Picture five features Mr. Ashley on a boat, wearing a casual jacket and open-necked shirt. Yachts are seen in the background ("outdoorsy" shot).

Each picture, everything you see, proclaims "upper class," "expensive," "cultured," exactly the aura the actor exudes when he walks into a room.

Now that's a composite!

24 FROM AUDITION TO PAYOFF

*We actors often tend to over-analyze
things... I don't want to complicate it. When
it comes to commercials, it's selling. There's
no other way to put it. It's selling the product.*

John Edwards, Actor

Depressed? Skip the pills and go out on a commercial audition. There you'll find a roomful of people who are up, bright and happy. (If they want to work, they'd better be.) Just being around all that enthusiasm will brighten your day. "In commercials," says commercial casting director Beverly Long, "You have to be willing to make a fool of yourself. To jump in and say, 'Oh, I get it. This is all a game. Okay, I can be a fool too and have a good time doing it." Or, as commercial casting director Estelle Tepper says, "Just go out and have some fun."

And sell.

BEFORE THE INTERVIEW

Unlike movie/TV auditions, where you "dress to suggest," in commercials, dress as close to the part as you can without visiting a costumer. Cowboy hats, jeans and boots are perfect for a Western commercial, but not six-shooters and spurs — that's *too* eager. As one commercial actor put it, "I once went up for a commercial in which there was a writer. I've never seen such a profusion of pipes in one room in all my life."

When your agent calls with the usual *when, where,* and *for whom* information, press him to be specific about how you should look. "Don't let him blow you off," urges Beverly Long. "Just say, 'I'm really not clear about that. Could you call them and find out what I'm supposed to wear and then call me back?' They [sponsors, etc.] can't see beyond what you are wearing. If you come in for a truck driver in a suit and tie, that's it. Goodbye. You're history."

Many commercial actors keep these "audition clothes" in their car, along with a box of probable props (boots, sneakers, eyeglasses, and — yes — pipes, etc.), in case they're out of the house when the call comes in. Their portable equipment also includes photos, résumés and a clipboard

---

NOTE: For more on commercial regulations, on-set work rules, holding fees, exclusivity, residuals, etc., see Appendix.

(you'll learn why later). And they keep their cars gassed up. Casting director Kathy Smith advises, "Always have at least one casual and one 'up-scale' outfit in your closet. When the call comes in, that's no time to try to run to the dry cleaners." And Beverly Long adds, "All the guys should have a sweatshirt in the back of their car because a sweatshirt goes with a lot of things — a jock, a guy playing softball, an auto mechanic, a jogger. Or a plaid shirt. Or a tie in the glove compartment just for emergencies."

Once again, arrive early to the audition with composite in hand. Then find the table with the "sign-in" sheet which requests your name, Social Security number, agent, the time you were told to arrive (called "Player's Actual Call") and the time you actually got there. Leave blank, for the moment, the next box that says "Player's Time Out"; put your initials in the next box and circle the number that corresponds with whether it is your first, second, third or fourth audition for that commercial. In commercials it's very possible to be called in three to four times. (They must pay you for the third and fourth.) These sheets are sent to the unions, so if you don't want to inconvenience the casting director, don't forget to sign in *and* out.

In addition to your composite/head shot, they'll often want to take a photo of you with an instant camera.

What you do next depends on the kind of audition you'll be doing, but it's almost certain you'll be videotaped. After screening out inappropriate candidates, the casting director sends these tapes to the advertiser, often in another city. He chooses what actors he wants to cast or call back. "Remember," says Beverly Long, "There are fast-forward buttons on those videotape machines. You don't want to be a 'fast forward.'"

PREPARATION

Preparing for the general interview audition

You'll rarely do a general interview with a commercial casting director. In commercials, a "general interview" is a form of audition. If you're faced with this, you'll need to be proficient in the techniques described in our chapter on "The General Interview/Look-See," especially regarding the art of choosing a topic. And be more upbeat than *Little Mary Sunshine*.

The improvisation audition

There's no script — you're given a situation and asked to improvise it. And that's where the problems start. The unions are concerned because there's nothing to stop the commercial-maker from stealing a good idea from you. Therefore, if you do an "improv audition" you're supposed to be paid a "creative fee." Since it's typical to audition over 100 actors for *each role* in a commercial, that means producers would be writing hundreds of checks for "creative fees." So, you'll see that fee about as often as you dance with a dinosaur. Instead, improv auditions are simply held without paying the actors, most of whom know nothing of the fee anyway. Then a little birdie informs the unions. Then that same little birdie flies back to the producer and tells him the unions are about to clamp down. End of improv auditions. Eventually the atmosphere relaxes a bit and improv auditions, to mix a whole bunch of metaphors, start rising from the ashes like Phoenixes. Then the little birdie flies again and . . . In any case, if you're asked and choose to do one, the best approach is to be alert and alive, have fun, not stand there like a lump. Classes in improvisation and pantomime can be a big help here.

The scene audition

There's a script and you'll need time to work on it. First, ask yourself: what's the tone of the scene? Intimate? Yahoo? Slice of life? If the script itself isn't in storyboard form (a shot-by-shot illustration of the commercial), ask the casting director if there's a storyboard nearby to look at. The more you know about how to approach the commercial, the better.

If you're going to audition with a partner, ask who the actor will be and work with him. The scene may call for you to be a part of a large group, or to be mommy, daddy, sister or brother in a "family unit" that includes a child. Don't be swamped by the others, especially the young-un'. Make a friend of the little bugger, then control him.

If you've got only a line or two in the scene, go ahead and memorize. Otherwise, it's not necessary.

As you work on it, bear in mind that even the most realistic slice-of-life commercial should be kept relatively light. If you're doing a commercial for Dr. Zhivago's Wonder Elixir and your character has a headache, be mildly in pain — not ambulance agony.

You'll probably find the dialogue horrendously stilted. After all, it's a sales pitch, not a play. It's your job to make those words sound as if you just thought of them, as if you naturally say, "Man, that's coffee!"

At the same time, your acting will usually be broader than for most movie/TV work. A good approximation is sitcom level.

The spokesman audition

The most difficult. It's just you and the camera. You'd better be well-trained before you go out on one of these. And be vocally trained, and know how to enunciate (*comin'* and *goin'* will not get you workin').

You're given 23 seconds of copy and, if hired, will have to be able to take tenths of a second off your reading, stretch a word here, emphasize a word there, all the while looking into the camera (without blinking) being absolutely warm and genuine. Without solid training, we doubt you'll be able to hold up to the stress. Be ready or pass.

Spokesman commercials — indeed, all commercials — present a *problem*, followed by a *solution*, followed by a *resolution*. In pencil (so you can erase it later), break down the copy into these three sections. Your approach to each will be slightly different. You *present* the problem, *emphasize* the solution, *sum up* with the resolution.

Often, these sections are preceded by "transition words": "so," "but," etc. Punch these words slightly harder, take a beat, then continue — that lets the viewer in on the fact that the solution/resolution is coming.

Also look for "billboard words" — words to be emphasized. These can include: "only," "delicious," "bigger," "better," "safer," "new," "superb," etc., as well as a price — if that's there, the advertiser thinks it's a selling point. Ask yourself, "If I owned this product, what part of the copy would I want to stress?" "The successful performer, says voice-over agent Don Pitts, "Will go through the copy sentence by sentence, and look for the key words — look for the 'hooks' in the copy. That's what separates the successful performer from the one who's just good."

Next, say the speech out loud, working to create the "golden triangle" of spokesman commercials: you to the viewer to the product. A common error beginners make is to treat the copy like a speech to an audience. It isn't. It's a *conversation* between you and one other person, seated in his living room, and you talk to him about the product. "Don't make them feel that you're trying to sell something," says Don Pitts. "Rather, make them feel that you're sharing some information with a friend."

For maximum effect, be sure you're out of the script at the beginning and end. Memorize (only) the first and last lines. Give some authority to your voice; make the viewer feel you know what you're talking about. But don't be a bully. And don't point. Make all gestures, even facial gestures, "soft" and restrained. Do it standing. And *love your product*.

Finally, find a way to "tag" your reading. Smile, nod knowingly, do something that puts an ending on the ending. Acting shtick is usually stomach-turning, but in commercials it works. We saw an actress wink at the end of her reading — *wink!* — and it played.

Above all, you'd be wise to heed Beverly Long's advice for any kind of commercial audition: "A lot of actors miss out because they don't understand commercials. They think, 'Oh, I might screw up all the rest of the copy, but that last line will be brilliant.' Or, 'They'll be able to see that all I need is time. I can get all this down by next Thursday. I'm going to be great when they give me the part.' Wrong. They are only going to hire the person who does *exactly* what they want *at the audition.* Not tomorrow, and not next week, but *this instant.*"

THE AUDITION

When you walk in, you may see one lone person standing behind a videotape camera or any combination of producer, director, advertising agency representative, product rep, or casting director.

First, you'll be given a mark on which you stand or sit (if possible, stand — it's easier to be energetic). Next, they'll ask you to "slate" — give your name — into the lens. Treat the "slate" as part of your scene. As Beverly Long puts it, "From the moment you hit the door, by God, you'd better sparkle — including the way you say your name."

You may see an "idiot card" next to, above or immediately beneath the camera lens. Don't use it — you'll look like you're reading. If you have a lot of lines, put the copy on that clipboard we mentioned and hold it up at eye level, just out of camera range. Glance at the copy as needed. (You could hold the copy without the clipboard, but even the slightest case of nerves will cause the paper to shake, rattle and roll.)

If anyone says anything, *listen.* As commercial casting director Pamela Campus says, "Listen for the key word whenever you're being given direction. For example, someone says to you 'You're looking out the window. It's raining. It's a Sunday afternoon and it's cozy and intimate with your spouse.' 'Cozy' and 'intimate' are your key words." A common complaint is that actors don't listen. "You don't have to have a lot to say. More important is to listen to what's said to you." says commercial producer Bob Wollin.

If you don't like your reading, you can ask to do it again. But don't be surprised if they say no. As mentioned, they're often seeing more than 100 people. Also, don't assume a "no" answer means they didn't like what you did — they may have loved it.

Whatever you do, don't make negative comments on your reading — especially on camera. Before anyone says "cut," we've seen beaming actors suddenly break, grimace and say "Aaargh." That's the last thing anyone watching those tapes will see — the actor with a contorted, ugly face, being negative. Aaaargh.

AFTER THE AUDITION

Be sure to sign out. If you are kept longer than an hour, you're supposed to be paid. But as one commercial casting director says, "If it's only five or ten minutes, to keep relations with the casting director, I'd advise you to be kind and sign out under that one hour." It's that old penny-wise, pound-foolish thing again.

Then go home, feed your goldfish, and don't give the audition another thought. The advertiser and the producer are back at the studio, arguing over the length of your eyebrows — We're *not* kidding.

After screening the original tape, the advertiser will want to call back (often several times) the people he likes. If that's you, remember you didn't get there by doing something wrong. Match your original reading as close as memory allows — unless instructed otherwise — and wear exactly what you wore the first time. "If the ribbon was on the right side of your hair the first time, I'd advise it not be on the left the second time," says Pamela Campus.

A FINAL WORD ABOUT AUDITIONING

It's one thing to read about doing commercial auditions, another to do them. There's also the added problem of dealing with the camera. We've seen that little collection of wires make jelly of even the most experienced. So, if you want to do commercials, take commercial workshops. Be sure the class uses videotape, that you get plenty of turns on camera, and that it's taught by someone (usually a casting director) who works in the field — that's who's best equipped to teach you how to be a "P&G housewife with perk." "Every one of my clients had taken at least one commercial workshop with a commercial casting director," says casting director and former commercial agent Kathy Smith. "Schools can teach but commercial casting directors can relate experiences." Sometimes it's good to take a class just to find out how the casting director works.

And watch commercials — lots of them. Notice the "spokesman" style, what trends are current, how various products are advertised. Those "messages from our sponsor" are your own personal school bells.

THE DEAL

You're paid union scale for the day (called your "session fee"). "Scale" commercials make up the bulk of all commercials produced. Unless you're a celebrity, stuntman, or established model, you'll rarely get more than scale.

WAITING TO SHOOT

You'll get a wardrobe call, and most likely have to go to a fitting. Since most commercials are shot off the lots, you'll also be given a map to the location. And don't change a thing about your appearance. That dynamite suntan can wait.

ON THE SET

The only real difference will probably be the number of takes and the number of possible "advisers" hovering around the director.

Anyone from the account executive to the product owner himself may be intently watching. After each take, you'll see numerous huddles. Everybody worries a lot. Somebody doesn't like the way your hair looks. Somebody notices the product was at the wrong angle. Somebody thinks the direction is getting too serious. And, yes, somebody doesn't like the way you said, "Goshums Martha, this stuff is great." Try not to let all this throw you, or take any of it personally, even if some joker says something incredibly tactless (such as "That was lousy!"). Could be he's not a show-biz type and isn't used to working with actors. Throughout the day, have a "Hey, no sweat" attitude.

Since they've got you for eight hours and have only 30 seconds of film to put together, you'll probably say "So eat Munchies!" enough times to dream about those little crackers for weeks. (We know an actor who had to dive into a swimming pool 200 times in one day.) As commercial producer Bob Wollin put it, "Even if the very first take is good, they may pick at it for hours."

Afterwards, go home and, again, forget it. Don't hold your breath waiting for all those residuals to come rolling in. Even if everything went beautifully, they may never use the commercial.

EXCLUSIVITY/CONFLICTS

What is the advertiser buying for what he pays you, besides your services as an actor on the day of shooting?

As your contract states, he's buying the right to keep you "exclusive" to his product — *whether or not he ever airs the commercial.*

Do a commercial for Maxwell House Coffee, and you can't do another for a competing product such as Yuban. That's called a "conflict."

If you do the second commercial, both companies will become perturbed — but Maxwell House can become perturbed enough to sue your agent *and* you, and force the two of you to rob your piggy banks to pay for a new commercial sans your presence. Figure, oh, about $100,000 or so. Plus the loss of your agent. Plus trouble with the unions.

Never try to get away with doing a conflict, even if your commercial for the competing product is only being shown in Dry Prong, Nebraska. Keep careful records. If your agent calls with an audition for a conflicting product, remind him and pass. Voice-over agent Don Pitts says, "It's very important to keep records of conflicts, and not to assume it's the agent's responsibility."

If it's a gray area (is a cereal commercial a conflict with a bread commercial?) and if you're both not sure, have him call the casting director. Don't fool around with nitroglycerin or conflicts.

How long does this exclusivity last? As long as the advertiser sends you a repayment of what he paid you for your session (called a "holding fee") every 13 weeks, it can continue for 21 months — called the "maximum use period." Again, the advertiser doesn't have to air the commercial.

Four months to 30 days prior to the end of the 21 months, you/your agent must notify the advertiser that your commercial is coming up for renegotiation. Fail to do this and, if the advertiser wants, he can start a brand new 21-month period. If you do notify the advertiser and he wants to continue to use the commercial, he negotiates a new deal with your agent. You're not obligated to agree. If you say no, his rights to that commercial end at 21 months.

USE FEES (COMMONLY CALLED "RESIDUALS")

"Don't ask me about residuals," says a commercial agent, "I've been in the business for 13 years and I still don't understand them."

Yep, they're complicated. Mighty. To avoid turning your brain into Grey Poupon, we'll only take a look at the basics.

First, understand that what you're paid for the use of a commercial has long ago been dickered over down to the last nickel. And it's based on a combination of two factors:

- Where it's shown
- How it's used — what kind of commercial it is.

Where it's shown: In a sense, you don't do commercials — you do "units." Obviously, a commercial can air in one or many cities, so each city is assigned a number of *units* depending on its population. (Houston is five units; San Diego/Tijuana is three units . . .) When your commercial airs — in one city or many — the units for those cities are added together and . . .

. . . We're halfway there. Next, we have to know *how the commercial was used* — that is, the *kind* of commercial it is. This will govern not only how much you're paid for those units, but whether you're paid for those units in a flat fee (once every 13 weeks) or each time the commercial airs.

The kinds of commercials:

Network commercials

(Technically called "Program Usage Commercials.") If you're lucky, here's the down payment on that Porsche. A list of cities in which the commercial airs is made and the units for all those cities are added together. Then, how much you should be paid for a network commercial with that amount of units is looked up. And that's what you're paid. And, when it airs again, the process is repeated. (It's possible on the next airing that Pittsburgh was dropped and Cleveland was picked up.) This happens over and over and over again, because *you're paid every time this kind of commercial airs*. We can't give you dollar amounts, because we don't know what cities your commercial will air in, or how often it will air. But we can tell you it can mean big bucks.

Wild spots

Remember watching *Witch Women of Azuza* on your local late show and, in between evil spells, you kept seeing the same commercial (an evil spell itself)?

That's probably a wild spot. This kind of commercial cannot air on a network show (unless they cut to a local station). You're paid a flat fee, based on the city or cities in which it will be shown (the "unit" system). For that fee, the advertiser can show the commercial as many times as he likes, without paying you anything more. He does, however, have to pay that fee every 13 weeks. There's a bit of controversy over these commercials, specifically because the advertiser can air them time and time again without additional compensation to you.

Dealer commercials

A local Toyota dealer, say, wants to run a national Toyota commercial, at his own expense. In this case you'll get a flat fee (again based on the unit system) and he'll get unlimited use of the commercial for six months. Don't get too distressed, since few dealers can afford to run a commercial over and over again.

Seasonal commercials

Santa Claus selling "Ralph's Reindeer Vitamin Supplements" is a "seasonal." Again, you'll be paid a flat fee based on the unit system, but the advertiser can use the commercial for only *13 to 15 weeks*. (Santa Claus in May wouldn't work anyway.) The advertiser can, however, bring back that commercial for another run a year later.

Test commercials

Sometimes an advertiser wants to see if a given commercial will work, so he airs it only in a limited market in order to see what reaction it gets. That's a "test." Since by definition the commercial will run only in a few cities at most, thus earning you only a few units, there's obviously very little money in test commercials — unless the advertiser gets great response and decides to go national with it. Then the commercial is converted to "program usage." (This is called a "roll-out," perhaps because, as far as you're concerned, it means "roll out the money.") Nice — if it ever happens.

AGENTS' COMMISSIONS

Your agent gets ten percent of every dime you make, regardless of the kind of commercial you do, what use fees you are paid, and including your session and holding fees, for the first 21 months. After that, he'll have to re-negotiate for at least scale-plus-ten if he wants to make any more money on that commercial.

EXCLUSIVITY REVISITED

First, don't confuse "use fees" with "holding fees." Use fees are separate sums paid to you *when the commercial airs*; holding fees are paid to *keep you exclusive whether or not a commercial is aired*. It is indeed possible that you'll get 21 months' worth of holding fees and never see a use fee because the commercial-maker never airs the commercial.

Second, the advertiser will deduct what holding fees he's paid you from what he owes you in use fees if the commercial does air.

Third, the initial session fee he paid you (that also serves as your first holding fee) also "pays for" the first time he airs the commercial — *only* the first time. Your use fees start when he airs the commercial the *second time*.

Fourth, as long as the producer sends you your holding fee *every 13 weeks*, you are held exclusive to him for all of the above kinds of commercials, with the exception *only* of a seasonal. You are *not* exclusive when you do a seasonal. You may do a commercial for a competing product, but you'll need to notify the second advertiser that you've got a seasonal either running or on hold for next year.

Fifth, and most important, you should look at commercials not only as income producers, but as possible blocks to future income. Do a test, for example, and you're cut off from auditioning for all other competing products for as long as you remain exclusive. Maybe no national commercials with competing products will come along during that time for which you would be "right," but maybe one (or many) will — especially if you're a good commercial type. Decisions, decisions.

KEEPING TRACK

How does anyone know if your commercial runs at 4:30 p.m. in Padooka? Do the unions hire little gnomes to sit in front of TV sets all over the country to be sure you get all your units? Who keeps track of all this?

Believe it or not, the very people who pay you. Specifically, the advertising agency, on a more or less "honor system." And it works. Almost all the time. (Since the agency gets a commission from the advertiser every time his commercial is run, it's to the agency's benefit to keep accurate records.)

Still, foul-ups do occur. It wouldn't hurt to contact your friends around the country and ask them to keep a watchful eye out. (It's not all that much of an imposition; people love to spot friends when they appear on the tube. It's exciting to know somebody who's actually "making it" in Hollywood.)

You might even keep a "commercial notification file" of your friends around the USA and, whenever you do a commercial, send them self-addressed postcards asking them to fill in:

"I saw you on a ___PRODUCT___ commercial on ___DAY___ , ___DATE___ , at the approximate time of ___TIME___ ."

If you find you haven't been paid for those units you or your agent can contact the advertiser or the union. Once you've got a starting point — that is, a date and city — it can be checked. Every station, by federal law, must keep a log book of everything they show on that station from sign-on to sign-off.

The cost of the stamps and postcards could ultimately net you some very decent "found" units, and therefore, use payments you didn't even know were owed you. It's happened before.

If it does, you owe your buddy a dozen roses or a six-pack of liquid "units."

VII
OTHER KINDS OF WORK

25 SALAD BAR

*The people who work consistently at Hanna-
Barbera work consistently because they
work consistently.*

Andrea Romano, Voice-Over Casting Director

There's a lot of other acting and related work out there that you might
want to take a bite at. Some of these jobs can be filling to the wallet,
others are only for those in need of some acting exercise.

So, belly up to the bar and think about...

UNION LOW BUDGET/INDEPENDENT FILMS

No appetizer here. And no small piece of the production pie either. In
recent years, independent film production has exploded. (One person in
the know called it "a real startler.") Reasons include the video market,
the way films are financed, etc., but what's important to you is one word:
work.

Since the producer of *Rampaging Math Majors* can rarely afford top
stars, he's going to be far more open to taking a chance on a newcomer
— even in a major part. And just about everyone believes acting jobs
in "indies" are going to increase.

Obviously, the trades are a source for what's casting, and you can find
many producers and directors of independents by using the guides we've
talked about (*Working Actors Guide, Film Directors*, etc. — see Chapter
8). But, if you really want to get out there, mingle and network with people
involved in independent filmmaking, give thought to joining...

- *Independent Feature Project/West (IFP):* Included in what you get
  for your membership fee are screenings and seminars (some free to
  members) and "schmoozes" where members come together and talk
  movie-making. There's also a "skills bank" into which members can
  put their résumés for perusal by producers and directors looking for
  talent. IFP also sends out a monthly newsletter to members. "One
  of the best investments I've made to date is my membership," says
  actress Cynthia Ann Crawford. "You get to mix with people in all

---

*NOTE: For prices, fees, addresses, phone numbers of items mentioned throughout the
book, see Appendix.*

facets and levels in the business. People everyone has heard of and people everyone will be hearing of — producers, directors, writers, fellow actors . . . and they all love show business."

The only excuse for failing to see what a gold mine this organization can be to you is cataracts.

UNION INDUSTRIAL FILMS

Here's another way to get that first break, possibly a SAG card, paid on-the-job-training ("You're polishing your craft at somebody else's expense," says former industrial film producer Don Ciminelli), and film on yourself.

Industrial films break down into three types:

- *Documentaries:* The "star" may be Jacques Cousteau or DNA. The only "actor" is the narrator.

- *Educational material:* Remember snoring through class when they showed How the Dewey Decimal System Can Change Your Life? Remember that fascinating dramatization of the life of Emile Zola on PBS? They're educational films.

- *Corporate image/training:* A car manufacturer wants to excite its salesmen about the new Whizzo. A film is made, showing how the gear shift is also an electric toothbrush. Hordes of rabid dentists are shown, taking numbers just to sit at the wheel. The film is not intended for, and will never be seen by, John Q. Public.

  Except for the narrator (usually a "name"), there are no actors in documentaries. But opportunities for newcomers abound in educational and corporate image/training films because they want "low profile" people. Burt Reynolds playing a rabid dentist would be distracting. And that's where you come in.

  Happily, here's an area where you truly can make the rounds. Besides checking *Drama-Logue* for casting opportunities, drop off your picture and résumé to every industrial film house you can find. (Use the *Working Actors Guide, Studio Blu-Book, Studio Directory,* etc.) Some have in-house casting directors, others don't. But try to wangle appointments with someone at each, and keep in touch.

  However, if you really want to make contacts, your best bet is . . .

- *The Association of Visual Communicators:* Its membership is comprised of people working in all areas of industrials, including acting. When you join, you'll be sent a directory of all members. And who are they? Right, production houses (such as General Telephone, hospitals, etc.) and others who hire actors to do industrials, even slide shows — opportunities many actors don't even know exist.

Also, the association holds monthly meetings which are open to the public — a great way to do a little networking. Call their "hotline" to find out when and where.

One other thing. Besides being a way to get experience, film on yourself and a SAG card, the people you work with on an industrial may well move into major films or TV. "The advancement is extremely rapid," says industrial producer Marsha Jeffer.

NON-UNION FILMS

Union members aren't supposed to do these — you're not protected. The producer can promise the moon and deliver a black hole. He can sign a contract in blood, but, as former industrial producer Don Ciminelli says, "All the paper in the world isn't going to get you paid if the guy doesn't intend to pay you."

If you're going to do one anyway, try to check up on the producer. Certainly ask him politely what he's done in the past and how you'll get paid.

If you're going out of town, get the plane tickets in advance — in *both* directions. And don't forget per diems and hotel rooms. You don't want to arrive in Oshkosh, and hear, "Got your room yet?"

Some actors come out of these deals happy as milk-fed cats. We've also heard horror stories. Be very, very careful — even when you go to the audition. Theatrical agent Miriam Baum says, "If I don't know the people, I tell my clients to bring an extra person with them."

STUDENT FILMS

Unpaid? Only in money. You'll get experience in front of a camera, film on yourself, and make contacts for the future. George Lucas, Steven Spielberg and Francis Ford Coppola — just to name three — were once student filmmakers. "Student films," says theatrical casting director Paul Bengston, "Are summer stock for Hollywood."

To find what's casting, check *Drama-Logue*. Students (usually from the University of Southern California (USC), the University of California, Los Angeles (UCLA), Los Angeles City College, Loyola Marymount, Art Center College of Design and Columbia College) often advertise. Also, nose around bulletin boards of college film and drama departments, acting schools and the unions.

Both union and non-union people may do student films, making competition for parts keen, so don't think all you have to do is show up.

If cast, expect a daytime shoot (especially weekends) and don't be surprised if you're asked to tote a light or move a prop. (Also, ask to watch the editing, looping, and presentation of the film to the class. You'll learn plenty.)

And brother, you'll need patience. Everybody's learning. Your "director" may not know camera right from camera wrong. Things will go slooooooooooooooooooooooooooooooooooooooooooow.

Since you're working for free, the "deal" should include your own copy of the film (or at least the student should let you make a copy). But don't sit back and wait for him to get it to you. Keep at him. Some students would flunk Responsibility 101.

- *SAG/AFI films:* An AFI film is to student films what a Mercedes is to automobiles. To have a shot at being cast, you must be a paid-up member both of SAG and its "Conservatory" program. Then you'll be eligible not only for SAG/AFI casting but a host of other free programs developed for SAG members only (see Chapter 31).

  After joining SAG Conservatory, you can have your photos placed in a book of photographs kept at the prestigious American Film Institute, where filmmakers (called "fellows") from all over the world study. When an AFI fellow is casting (usually a 30-minute tape) he pretty much restricts his casting to Conservatory members. He thumbs through these books, and chooses the actors he wants to have in for an audition.

  But a student director is like anyone else — he likes to work with people he knows. So, to increase your chances of being auditioned, it wouldn't hurt to volunteer to work in the SAG/AFI office once or twice a week. "Fellows" are constantly in and out of the SAG/AFI office, and once they get to know you . . .

EXTRA WORK

"Anyone who says 'Don't do extra work' is crazy," says one casting director. We agree — up to the point mentioned by television stage manager James Hamilton: "When you're first learning it's a great way to get on a set. *But I wouldn't do it too often.*" (Italics ours.)

In other words, pursue extra work on a continual basis? Not if you want to act. Too time-consuming, for one thing. The hours spent registering with the casting agencies, calling them for work, etc., are time taken away from your acting career. Even days spent on a set are wasted except for the paycheck and general knowledge. Networking is difficult and probably not too smart, because, in contrast to New York, where actors go back and forth from acting to extra work with little career damage, in L.A. you're in danger of getting labeled as an extra. That'll do for your career what a heavyweight boxer can do for your stomach.

"When you do extra work, stay in the background," suggests one actor. "Don't be in too much of a hurry to get your face on the screen or to meet the director. If so, they'll think, 'Why should I hire and pay him as an actor if I can get him for what I pay an extra? And, if he's a serious actor, why isn't he pursuing his acting career?'"

Still want to do it? Okay, if you're a paid-up member of AFTRA, send or drop off your photo and résumé to their extra file. Producers and casting directors of AFTRA shows constantly call AFTRA looking for extras. Next, register with any or all of the union casting agencies (union work pays more) that handle extra work. You don't have to be a member of the Screen Extras Guild (SEG) or any union, and these casting agencies won't charge you to register.

Provided you're not a member of any union and are really hot to do extra work, proceed on to the non-union agencies. Some will charge you a registration fee, others won't. Only you can decide if paying their fee is worth it. You're not going to be buying lobster thermador on what you make on a union job, and you're pushing it buying hamburgers on non-union wages.

Whether any casting agency will want you to bring or mail a photo and résumé depends on the agency. Some say to call first, but you'll have as much luck getting through as you do calling a cable company. Just go and tell them you've gotten nothing but busy signals.

The methods of registering and interviewing you also vary, as do the chances of your application being accepted. "According to need" (theirs) was what we heard most often. Two hints: the more special skills you list on your résumé (provided you can do them) and the larger your wardrobe, the better. So, when you go to one of these agencies, dress to the nines.

Of course, it's one thing to register with these places, another to get work. You'll need to call them every day, at least every half-hour or so.

If you can, get to know someone associated with a production, especially the assistant director if it's a movie, the stage manager if it's a taped TV show. He's the one in charge of extras on the set, and he informs the casting agencies what extras are needed. A request from him is like grease to a wheel.

"You'll see wives, girlfriends, fathers of everyone from the cameraman to the make-up artist being extras," says one extra. "There's a lot of politics involved. An electrician says, 'Hey, how about my brother?' to the assistant director, and bingo."

If you're asked to do something like rollerskate, ride a bike, play football, etc., that's a "special ability," and you'll get paid slightly more. If you're a bartender in the show and the star asks you to pour him a drink, that's a "silent bit," and you'll be paid even more. And if you're asked to shout, "Hang him!" you'll be upgraded to a "day player" on the spot (see Chapter 7).

Finally, we've already touched on the pecking order on any set (see Chapter 20), but we'd like to remind you again that extras are at the bottom. As television stage manager James Hamilton observes, though, "It's too negative to say extras are *always* treated like dirt. It depends on the stage manager/assistant director. If he's smart he'll treat extras with respect if for no other reason than they'll be more likely to give him what he wants."

But if you're thinking extra work is an easy way to make a living, listen to what Roy Wallack, past president of the Screen Extras Guild, has to say: "Working as an extra is very tough. Actors have agents, but extras don't. It's work getting work. I would say, of 100 people who start out doing extra work, at the end of a year you'll probably have ten or fifteen left. It's really a rough, rough type of business."

VOICE-OVERS

Of all the performing fields, this is the toughest to break into. "The voice business," says "The Voicecaster" Bob Lloyd (see below), "Is the most lucrative part of show business, and, because of that, it is also the most competitive. You can count on two or three hands the number of new people each year who make a living at it."

However, if you keep hearing that your voice could make Scrooge buy mistletoe, and you want to take a crack at the Voice Biz, first understand, just as every other field, that this is no place for part-time fun and games. Bob Lloyd adds, "My biggest concern with people who are trying to get into it, is that they treat it as an adjunct to everything else. And there's nothing wrong with that, but it's probably pretty much in direct proportion to the rewards you will get from it. Being in the voice business requires a dedication and a work ethic that is perhaps even more difficult than being in the face business. If I had any counsel to give to anyone who wants to get into the voice business, they better damn well figure out how they can put in at least 12 to 20 hours a week working at it."

In any case, your first step is to get yourself into a good voice-over workshop. Regardless of how trained you are as an actor, you need specific training in voice-over technique. Then, when you're ready, the next stop is a recording studio to put together a good demo tape. Note, we said *when you're ready*. "Don't take a voice-over class that promises you a demo tape in six weeks," says voice-over coach Louise Chamis. "That's like promising you a spot in *A Chorus Line* after six weeks of tap dance lessons." On your tape (reel-to reel, 7½ speed), you'll want about three or four "commercials." Use anything from magazine copy to TV or radio ads and gear your choices to the impression your voice gives the listener (called how you "come in"). Can you come in "motherly?" Do a baby powder commercial. Can you sound sexy? Try a perfume spot. Is your voice light and bright? Soda might be a good choice. (Many V/O teachers will go to your session with you to help "direct.")

We didn't mention character voices (old man, wicked witch, etc.) because agents mainly want to hear how well you *vary in your own voice*. They only want to hear character voices at the end of your tape, and you'd better have what the industry calls "good separation": clear distinctions between characters (your Pluto shouldn't sound like your Yogi Bear). If you can do 20 well-separated characters, choose your best six, write a few lines of dialogue for each, and place them at the end of the tape. Just be certain the entire tape is no longer than three minutes, with the first two-and-a-half minutes or so demonstrating variations in your voice. "The people who make the most money in this business are those with one voice, but are able to have 13 variations of that voice (intimate, bright, etc.)," says voice-over agent Don Pitts.

And be sure your tape is not only professionally done, but that you are a pro. If you need more training in voice-overs, get it before you start sending out anything. Arlin Miller, voice-over teacher, sums it up: "You're only going to get one shot in this town. Make it your best shot. Don't rush it. Wait until you can give them something dynamite to hear, because that's what it's going to take. It's going to really have to blow them away. *Good's not good enough*."

Send a copy of your tape to the voice-over agents at those agencies that handle the area. Here's a list of some:

Abrams-Rubaloff & Lawrence
Commercials Unlimited
Cunningham, Escott & Dipene
ICM
Joseph, Heldfond & Rix

William Morris
Sandie Schnarr Talent
Special Artists Agency
Charles H. Stern Agency
Sutton, Barth & Vennari
Talent Group Inc. (TGI)
Herb Tannen & Associates
Arlene Thorton & Associates
Tisherman Agency

To find the name of the specific agent who handles voice-overs, call AFTRA or SAG at the numbers designated for that and ask for "Representation."

If the agent likes what he hears, he'll call you in and have you do some copy live so he'll know it didn't take you six months to put together a decent tape.

Once you're signed, your agent will call you in periodically, along with his other voice-over clients who have the required sound for a particular commercial, to tape your auditions. He sends these for consideration to whomever is doing the commercial. He'll probably also give you a list of production companies, etc. — not only in Los Angeles but all over the country — and ask you to drop off or mail your tape to them. (These can number in the hundreds.)

If hired, you'll do a session and be paid residuals according to the SAG or AFTRA rules covering off-camera and/or radio announcers and actors.

- *"Wallah wallah," "sync," "looping," "foley," etc.*: These are all forms of putting additional sound to a movie or television show. "Sync" is the same as "looping" (see Chapter 20). "Wallah" is "atmosphere noise" — non-scripted background dialogue, grunts, laughs, etc. "Foley" means sound effects — people walking, matches being struck, etc. All of these can provide additional income (usually union scale for a day).

- *Wallah:* Get known in the voice-over community, and you might be allowed to join any one of a number of different "wallah" groups around town. (You'll need to be a good improvisor too.) You find them by working in voice-overs. They're not big on publicizing themselves or in a hurry to get more members, but once they know and trust you, there's a shot.

- *Sync, looping:* You're hired to deliver a specific line. Once again, to find these jobs, get known in the voice-over community.

- *Foley:* An extremely closed area. Your best shot is to try to attach yourself to experienced people, called "walkers," and become an "assistant walker." To find them, check the sound people at the various studios.

- *"The Voicecaster":* Specifically, as referred to above, Bob Lloyd. He's apparently the only full-time voice-over casting director in the country. (There is a voice-over casting outfit in Toronto, Canada, called "Voicecasters." Others, such as on-camera casting directors, occasionally do voice-over casting, but that's all Mr. Lloyd does and he does it all the time.)

  Getting him to give you a listen involves no more than bringing him a professionally-recorded tape. In this case, however, it's irrelevant how long your tape is. You'll want to put every different kind of voice you can do — as long as those voices are, as Mr. Lloyd put it, "competitive" — that is, if they can compete with the already established pros. "My needs are different," he says. "I want to know as much about you (i.e., your voice/s) as possible. So your tape can be three times as long as the typical voice-over tape as long as it keeps telling me different things."

  If he likes what he hears, Mr. Lloyd will retain your tape and put your name in his computer with a description of all the good voices you do. When people (from all over the country) call him asking for, say, a guy who does a great Jimmy Cagney or a gal who can really sound like a Valley Girl, he pulls those names from his computer and, if you're among them, he may call you in.

- *Cartoon voice-overs:* "Voice-overs is the most exclusive area in the entertainment industry, and, with the possible exception of jingle-singing, cartoons are the most exclusive in the voice-over field," says Andrea Romano, casting director for Hanna-Barbera.

  If you want to take a crack at it, you can start by sending her a tape (cassette or reel-to-reel) which, in this case, should only be cartoon voices — "No spokesman stuff," as Ms. Romano puts it, continuing, "Your tape should be about three minutes, certainly no longer than five minutes. I look for versatility — the more versatility the better. But if you do only two good voices that's okay too. And the funnier the better. I listen to a lot of tapes, and if you can get my attention by being funny . . . And watch Saturday morning cartoons. You'll get a good idea of what's selling. And do a little exercise: turn the sound down and make up voices."

Ms. Romano will listen to it, and if you call her she'll give you a critique of your tape.

MODELING

Kinds of modeling work:

- *High-fashion/runway:* Better be a knockout who's very photogenic. With the "greying of America," age for women has become slightly more flexible, with some models still working at the ripe old age of 45. Still, the bulk of the work goes to young women (16 to 21). For men there is now virtually no age restriction, but, again, more jobs go to the young (18 to 22). Women also need to be at least 5'9" and wear a size 6 or 8 dress. Men must be about 6' and wear a size 40 regular suit. "A good barometer," says actress Donna Allen, who models and teaches modeling, "is the cover of *Cosmopolitan.* You'll notice there's a healthy, athletic look — anorexic is out. Today females are permitted to have breasts and hips — as long as they're in proportion."

- *Print:* Includes anything printed for advertising purposes — billboards, magazine ads, etc. The bulk of the work goes to high-fashion models, but you can possibly make a few dollars regardless of your "look," size, weight or age.

- *Commercial:* Non-speaking modeling "roles" on commercials. You can be anything from cute to pretty. Even older and more "real" types occasionally get work.

- *Parts of the body:* Got luscious legs? Handsome hands? Fantastic feet? Totally titillating teeth? Lush, languorous lips?

- *Industrial:* Includes demonstrating products at trade shows, fairs, department stores, supermarkets, and so forth. If you can be cheery, perky, and get along well with people you'll have a shot. If you're a young, beautiful, sexy lady to boot, your chances are better. There's little work for men. None for grumps.

If you really want to pursue any of these fields seriously, go to New York. That's where the modeling action really is.

Wherever you are, the way to start is to send your headshot or composite — even a snapshot will do in this case — to agencies that do modeling and/or print work. Here are only a few to get you started:

Nina Blanchard
East-West Model Management
Elite Model Management
L.A. Model Agency
Alese Marshall Modeling & Commercial Agency
M.A.X.
Joan Mangum Agency
Pacific Artists
Privilege Talent Agency
Wilhelmina Artists' Representatives

While all models have "books" (portfolios of photos), there's no need to throw money at photographers to get one. "I can tell if you're modeling material from a polaroid snapshot," says one modeling agent. Or, as agent Karen DiCenzo says, "I don't think it's right for a person who wants to be a model to go out and spend $500 on a book, because they might not be the right material to be a model. Maybe $100 worth of pictures, but even that's not necessary." If the agent thinks you're promising, he'll send you to various "test photographers" he knows, and they'll shoot you for free. Then you can complete your book gradually, from your assignments.

Enrolling in a modeling school isn't a requirement either. If you're model material you'll get a lot of "on-the-job" training.

Obviously, the kind of money you'll make will depend on the kind of work you do and how well you become known. For a "star model," the sky's the limit.

In the end though, modeling is still a young person's game. And, as Karen DiCenzo puts it, "In most cases, models turn into actors. Actors rarely turn into models."

NIGHTCLUB WORK (AND RELATED)

You'll do far better getting your feet wet in an out-of- the-way bar in Podunk than beginning this part of your career in Hollywood.

There are places, however, where performers can hone their skills in front of an audience, two of the best known being The Comedy Store and The Improvisation. For leads to a new or newly-hot place, check *Drama-Logue* and ask fellow hopefuls standing around waiting to go on. Each place has its own particular rules as to how you go about getting onto its stage, but basically, first you perform on an "off night" and, if you're good, you move up to a more desirable night and time. Then, depending on the policy of the house, you'll be paid or continue to perform for free.

Certainly these places give performers — especially comics — a showcase. Certainly people have been discovered. And certainly they're democratic, in that the best people move up. However, you'll be performing either for nothing or for a very small salary.

Yer don't get yer money and yer makes yer choice.

For paying work, places like Disneyland and Knott's Berry Farm often advertise open calls in the trades.

For versatile performers, including magicians, singers, etc., a good variety agent or personal manger wouldn't hurt. Here are a few agencies:

Devroe Agency
George B. Hunt Agency
International Talent Agency
Variety Artists International

Also, consider joining AGVA (See Chapter 7). Besides health insurance and other benefits, being a member means there's at least one place someone looking for your kind of talent can call. The phones at AGVA ring off the wall and some of those calls come from the studios.

STUNTWORK

"I don't try to act — don't you try to do stunts," says one stuntman. Absolutely. Offered an additional thousand dollars to do a stunt? Terrific. It'll make a great down payment on a wheelchair.

If you're thinking of a career in stunts, it's at least as difficult to become a "star" stuntman (in the sense of earning big money) as it is to become a "star" actor, and there are additional "dues" to be paid in the form of broken bones, bruises and cuts — and that's if you're *lucky*. While the pros take all sorts of precautions, accidents do happen. Stuntmen have died.

In any case, you'll need to get your SAG card (all stuntmen must be SAG), and put together a composite with a résumé that lists all the physically-oriented things you can do. Then make the rounds of the studios, production houses, and especially any producers, directors and stunt coordinators, and hope they'll take a shot on a newcomer.

You can take a stunt workshop, but it isn't vital.

If hired, you'll be paid standard SAG wages for actors, plus a sum for the particular stunt. This usually is negotiated by you and the producer or director right there on the set, and you're paid each time you do it, whether the camera jams or the director "just wants another one." "Stunts such as high falls are often negotiated by the foot," says agent Karen DiCenzo.

And two last words of caution. First, carry insurance — lots of it. (That is, if you can get it.) Second, as an ad once run by a group of stuntmen in the trades said, "No shot is worth a life."

PORNOGRAPHY

Questions of morality aside, if the film is "hard core," it's a career killer. As soon as you become known for grunting your way through the hard stuff, you'll become virtually unhirable for legit films, TV and commercials. Even if you should do one only in a moment of desperation, that film will later cause you ten times more career grief than any amount you were paid. Even "soft core" is iffy.

Pass.

26 THEATRE

I am not going to hire anyone for a sitcom
who has not performed in public.

Andrew McCullough, Director

Hollywood is still Hollywood — not Broadway West. Though second only to New York in the amount of theatre produced, Los Angeles' eye is still focused mainly into the lens of the camera. It's hard to make a career out of paying theatre, but the right theatre role can launch a career — so it's not to be underestimated.

EQUITY WORK

First stop is the Equity offices in Hollywood, where you can pick up lists of Equity-franchised agents, LORT and other Equity-contract theatres, dinner theatres, stock, and theatre for young audiences.

The major touring companies head for the big theatres like the Ahmanson and the Dorothy Chandler Pavillion downtown, the Schubert in Century City, the Pantages, the James A. Doolittle Theatre or the Henry Fonda Theatre in Hollywood. Casting is mainly done in New York, with opportunities for local actors usually limited to "Second Viking, Stage Left." Occasionally secondary parts, even leads, open up. Actors with legit agents have an edge.

There are two League of Resident Theatres (LORT) in Los Angeles: the Mark Taper Forum and L.A. Theatre Center. Each has several stages. In nearby Pasadena, there's the California Musical Theatre and Pasadena Playhouse. Take an hour's drive down the coast, and there's the South Coast Repertory in Costa Mesa. Get a cup of coffee, drive another hour south to San Diego, and you'll find the La Jolla Playhouse, Old Globe Theatre, and San Diego Rep. Turn your headlights north and you'll find San Francisco's American Conservatory Theatre (ACT), only one of a number of Equity theatres in the Bay area.

There are no Equity dinner theatres in Los Angeles, but there are three south of the city: The Grand Dinner Theatre, Anaheim; the Harlequin Dinner Playhouse, Santa Ana; and the Lawrence Welk Village Theatre,

---

NOTE: For a sampling of theatres in L.A. see Theatre Map. For Equity theatre addresses, phone numbers see Appenix.

Escondido. Equity stock theatres include the La Mirada Civic Theatre (Southern California) and the Sacramento Music Circus (Northern California).

These are just a few of the theatres out there. *Drama-Logue*'s "year-end" issue regularly includes a comprehensive list of Southern California theatres. If you don't want to wait, there are a number of directories sold in drama bookstores.

Check with individual theatres for casting policies. Most have general auditions once or twice a year. Almost all maintain casting files, so send photos and résumés and request interviews.

99-SEAT (EQUITY WAIVER) THEATRE

It started because union actors, who aren't permitted to do community theatre (see Chapter 7), needed to showcase themselves to the film industry, sharpen their skills in front of audiences, and feed their souls. It became a Los Angeles "institution" in 1972 when Equity agreed to waive all rules and permit union people to work unpaid as long as the theatre was capable of seating less than 100.

Things stayed that way until 1988, when Equity voted to impose regulations on the Waiver houses regarding actors' payments, casting procedures, rehearsal conditions, etc. Some in the theatre community hail the new rules as an antidote to abuses; others think that some of these regulations are not only too tough, but a threat to the very existence of Waiver theatre.

Ultimately, the question isn't *whether* there will be regulations; it's what the regulations will be. So, for updates and round-to-round coverage of this and all theatre issues, read *Drama-Logue* and other newspapers and contact Equity.

Until recently, 99-seat theatre drew industry people like flies. It's harder now, because many casting directors and agents give these hours to the cold reading showcases where they'll be paid for their time. And too many bad Waiver productions have made audiences more wary and selective. It's still a valuable investment of time, however, so you'll want to think about . . .

THE WHY AND HOW OF DOING THEATRE

Like classes, be clear on your purpose. Are you doing theatre to get experience, to flex your acting muscles, for the sheer joy of it, or to be seen?

Los Angeles Area Theatre Map Key

A sampling of Los Angeles Area theatres and auditoriums. 99-seat (Equity Waiver) theatres are indicated by *.

1. Actors Alley*, 4334 Van Nuys Bl., Sherman Oaks 91403, (818) 986-7440
2. Back Alley Theatre*, 15231 Burbank Bl., Van Nuys 91411, (818) 780-2240.
3. Beverly Hills Playhouse*, 254 S. Robertson Bl., Beverly Hills 90211, (213) 652-6483.
4. California Arts Theatre (California Institute of the Arts), 24700 McBean Pkwy., Valencia 91355, (805) 255-1050.
5. California Theatre of Performing Arts (San Bernadino Civic Light Opera), 562 W. 4th St., San Bernadino 92402, (714) 882-2545.
6. Callboard Theatre*, 8451 Melrose Pl., L.A. 90048, (213) 392-9268.
7. Cast Theatre/Cast-at-the-Circle*, 804/800 N. El Centro Ave., L.A. 90038, (213) 462-0265/462-9872.
8. The Colony/Studio Theatre Playhouse*, 1944 Riverside Dr., L.A., (213) 665-3011.
9. Doolittle Theatre, 1615 N. Vine St., L.A. 90028, (213) 462-6666.
10. East-West Players*, 4424 Santa Monica Bl., L.A. 90029, (213) 660-0336.
11. Ebony Showcase Theatre & Cultural Arts Center, 4718-26 W. Washington Bl., L.A. 90016, (213) 936-1107.
12. Embassy Auditorium, 847 S. Grand Ave., L.A. 90017, (213) 622-4530.
13. Henry Fonda Theatre, 6126 Hollywood Bl., L.A. 90028, (213) 410-1062.
14. The Forum, 3900 W. Manchester, Inglewood 90306, (213) 673-1300.
15. Gaslamp Quarter Theatre, 547 4th Ave., San Diego 92101, (619) 234-9583/232-9608.
16. Will Geer Theatricum Botanicum, 1419 N. Topanga Cyn. Bl., Topanga 90290, (213) 455-3723.
17. Globe Playhouse/Shakespeare Society of America*, 1107 N. Kings Rd., W. Hwd. 90069, (213) 654-5623.
18. Greek Theatre, Griffith Park, 2700 N. Vermont Ave., L.A. 90027, (213) 410-1062.
19. Groundlings Theatre*, 7307 Melrose Ave., W. Hwd. 90046, (213) 934-9700/934-4747.
20. Hollywood Bowl, 2301 N. Highland Ave., L.A. (213) 876-8742/972-7300.
21. Hollywood Palladium, 6215 W. Sunset Bl., L. A. 90028, (213) 466-4311.
22. Los Angeles City College, 855 N. Vermont Ave., L.A. 90029, (213) 669-4000.
23. L.A. Connection Comedy Repertory Theatre*, 13442 Ventura Bl., Sherman Oaks 91423, (818) 784-1868/780-1528.
24. L.A. Inner City Cultural Center*, 1308 S. New Hampshire Ave., L.A. 90006, (213) 387-1161.
25. La Jolla Playhouse, P.O. Box 12039, La Jolla 92037, (619) 534-6760.
26. La Mirada Civic Theatre, 14900 La Mirada Bl., La Mirada 90638, (714) 994-6150.
27. Long Beach Civic Light Opera/Terrace Theatre, P.O. Box 20280, Long Beach 90801, (213) 435-7605.

28. L.A. Theatre Center, 514 S. Spring St., L.A. 90013, (213) 627-6500.
29. Matrix Theatre*, 7657 Melrose Ave., W. Hwd. 90046, (213) 852-1445.
30. McCadden Place Theatre*, 1157 N. McCadden Pl., L.A. 90038, (213) 462-9070.
31. Melrose Theatre*, 733 N. Seward St., L.A. 90038, (213) 465-1885.
32. Music Center of L.A. County (Ahmanson Theatre, Dorothy Chandler Pavillion, Mark Taper Forum), 135 N. Grand Ave. 90012, (213) 972-7211.
33. New Mayfair Theatre, 214 Santa Monica Bl., Santa Monica 90401, (213) 395-8416.
34. Nosotros*, 1314 N. Wilton Pl., L.A. 90028, (213) 465-4167.
35. Odyssey Theatre Ensemble*, 12111 Ohio Ave., L.A. 90025, (213) 826-1626.
36. Old Globe Theatre, Balboa Park, P.O. Box 2171, San Diego 92112, (619) 231-1941.
37. Pacific Conservatory of the Performing Arts/Solvang, P.O. Box 1700, Santa Maria 93456, (805) 925-4009.
38. Pantages Theatre, 6233 Hollywood Bl., L.A. 90028, (213) 468-1700.
39. Pasadena Playhouse, 39 S. El Molino Ave., Pasadena 91101, (818) 792-8672.
40. San Diego Repertory Theatre at the Lyceum, 79 Horton Plaza, San Diego 92101, (619) 235-8025/231-3586.
41. Santa Barbara Theatre Festival, 33 E. Canon Perdido St., Santa Barbara, CA 93101, (805) 963-0761
42. Shrine Auditorium, 3228 Royal St., L.A. 90007, (213) 749-5123/748-5116.
43. Shubert Theatre, 2020 Ave. of the Stars, L.A. 90067, (213) 201-1500.
44. South Coast Repertory Theatre, 655 Town Center Dr., Costa Mesa 92626, (714) 957-4033/957-2602.
45. Lee Strasberg Theatre Institute* (Marilyn Monroe, John Garfield, & Stage/Lee Strasberg theatres), 7936 Santa Monica Bl., L.A. 90046, (213) 461-5333.
46. Theatre Forty*, 241 Moreno Dr., Beverly Hills 90210 (Mailing address P.O. Box 5401, Beverly Hills 90210), (213) 466-6066.
47. Theatre West*, 3333 Cahuenga Bl. W., L.A. 90068, (213) 851-4839.
48. Theatre/Theater Hollywood*, 1713 N. Cahuenga Bl., L.A. 90028, (213) 871-0210/850-6941.
49. Universal Amphitheatre, 100 Universal City Plaza, Universal City, 91608, (818) 980-9421.
50. UCLA, 405 Hilgard, L.A. 90024, (213) 825-2953.
51. USC, University Park, L.A. 90007, (213) 743-7111.
52. Westwood Playhouse, 10886 Le Conte Ave., L.A. 90025, (213) 208-6500.
53. Wilshire Ebell Theatre, 4401 W. 8th St., L.A. 90005, (213) 939-1128.
54. Wilshire Theatre, 8440 Wilshire Bl., Beverly Hills 90211, (213) 653-4490.
55. Wiltern Theatre, 3790 Wilshire Bl., L.A. 90010, (213) 380-5005/388-1400.

- *For the experience:* You're wide open. If you're non-union you can do community theatre and not be disappointed when the only industry person in the audience is an out-of-work lighting technician. (In fact, if you're really inexperienced, that'll be a blessing.) If you're a pro who just wants to shake off some dust, you can do Shakespeare, Pinter, Albee, whatever, at any 99-seat theatre anywhere, without experiencing the futility of trying to get agents to drive all the way to Glendale. So relax and enjoy it. One suggestion from theatrical agent David Westberg: "Make a list of 20 shows that you're right for and you'd like to take a bite at and watch for them."

- *To be seen:* Now you've got to be careful — starting with your choice of play and location. If you want industry people in the audience, whether you're union or not, you'll have to limit yourself to Equity or (more likely) 99-seat theatre. And, regarding the latter, you'll do best following the "play shopping" criteria theatrical casting director Susan Glicksman outlines for herself: "I look for something new. I don't want to see any more *Barefoot in the Parks* or *Lovers and Other Strangers.* I look for something local, preferably a large cast, 12 to 15 people — I don't want to see a two-person show. No Shakespeare."

Next, make hay with the opportunity — both before and after the show. Work to get industry people there (using post-cards, ads, etc. — see Chapter 28), and follow-up after they've come. And, if you're smart, you'll pay careful attention to what entertainment attorney Michael C. Donaldson says: "After an Equity Waiver show you can just see who is going to have a career, and who is always going to be doing Equity-Waiver theatre. Some actors gravitate to their unemployed actor friends. Others go over and meet the agents, producers or directors who were in the audience."

Finally, you'll also have to be a bit of a critic. As rehearsals progress, ask yourself "Do I really want to ask somebody to sit through three hours of this?"

If the play, actors, director — or you — is bad, get out of it or at least don't invite people to see it. Yes, you have a responsibility to the production, but you have an even greater one to yourself. Invite people to see you in a play and you're putting your career on the line. Agents, casting directors, producers and directors have long memories and, as producer Buddy Bregman says, "If it's a bad production it'll permeate the person's psyche and the fallout will drop on your head — even if you were brilliant."

CHOOSING/GETTING IN A THEATRE

- *Choosing:* Reputations wax and wane as people exit and enter, so attend productions and decide if you like what you see. And read the critics; you can learn a lot about how often, how prominently and how favorably theatres are reviewed.

- *Getting in:* It can be as hard to get a part at a quality small theatre as to capture the lead in Andrew Lloyd Webber's next Broadway epic. Besides competing with scores of other actors at auditions, roles are often cast "in-house" long before a casting notice is put out.

  So, if you really want "in," volunteer for tech work. "Actors I can get, but good tech people are hard to find," says one director. Become "one of the boys" first. Then when you show up at an audition they'll be more receptive to you than the stranger who walks in cold. One warning about doing tech: be good, but not *too* good. You don't want miss out on roles because somebody doesn't want to lose a good technician!

A WORD ABOUT BURN-OUT

Can you do too much 99-seat theatre? Not if you need training and/or experience. But if you're a well-trained actor who's doing it mainly to be seen, be careful lest you get burned out and bitter.

"Equity Waiver is the best way to get an agent or be seen by a casting director. Believe me, we go all the time," says theatrical agent David Westberg. "But I think to go out and do Equity Waiver play after play after play is meaningless; something's not working. It's like *Lysistrata*. Why give away the only thing you have to sell — your talent? You can give it away for a certain time or a specific reason, but, after that, don't give it away anymore, because the more you give it away, the less people will be inclined to pay for it."

If you're dragging yourself to yet another read-thru, getting angry because the rehearsal took 15 minutes longer than expected, or if you have a vague feeling you're being ripped-off by, well, *somebody*, you're "waivered." For the sake of your fellow actors, your director, the playwright, your audiences, and, most important, your sanity, take a break. When you remember why you love it, you'll be back.

27 ACTING CLASSES

It doesn't get any better not *doing it.*

Michael Rhodes, Producer

Producer/director Buddy Bregman says, "The only way you can 'stretch' is in a class. You can't 'stretch' on a commercial." Or on a beach.

Maybe it's the air. Or the lack of pulsating, shoulder-to-shoulder humanity. Whatever, as one producer put it, "It never ceases to amaze me how lazy the actors are in L.A."

In New York, you'll find actors hurrying to a different class every night — and apologizing for taking Sundays off. Don't let "laid-back L.A." affect your drive. "Keep active," advises theatrical agent Colee Viedelle. "Our finest surgeons continue to study."

That sentiment was echoed by every single person we interviewed. It's a rare actor who doesn't go stale if he doesn't work at his craft. And that audition call will always come when you're at your stalest. "Acting is like any sport," says theatrical casting director Deborah Barylski. "If you don't keep working, you lose it."

Best training? Theatre. One show will teach you more than six months of training at any acting school. The audience instructs best. "Theatre shows me that the actor has discipline," says director/cinematographer Bruce Logan.

However, theatre alone isn't the answer. You can't learn cold reading, film technique, commercial technique, etc., on a stage. The specialized arts — dance, singing, dialects, mime — also require teachers. "Acting is like being a doctor or a lawyer or anything else; it takes an investment of time and money," says theatrical agent Mary Spencer. "As far as I'm concerned," says voice-over casting director Andrea Romano, "You can't take enough good workshops."

And, perhaps most important, in Hollywood, where memories are long, *a class is the only place where you can go to be bad.*

USING CLASSES PROPERLY

Lesson #1 (The hardest): You learn when you're bad. Always being the Alec Guiness of Acting 101 only teaches you you're not being challenged enough. "Bombing out" in class can be terrific.

NOTE: For a list of some acting schools, teachers, coaches, and their phone numbers, see Appendix.

However, it's not a good idea to "explode" in front of Steven Spielberg. Showcases and classes offering "industry nights" where agents, casting directors, producers, and the like are invited to see what you can do, can be valuable, but as an adjunct to — not a substitute for — the class you take to learn. In other words, first ask yourself why you are taking the class.

To be seen? Fine. Be sure you're ready, play your acting cards very close to the vest, and consider learning anything a bonus.

To grow? Equally fine. But then be certain industry people *don't* attend so you can go out on a limb and stretch your acting to the bombing point.

Don't try to mix the two types of classes together. That's very serious oil and water.

WHICH ONE FIRST?

What a toughie! And so relative to your circumstances.

New to L.A.? Find a class on the business of the business.

New to acting? Get into a good beginning acting class. All other classes pale in significance. "New talent should always be in acting classes. If they're not, I don't even want to talk to them," says personal manager Melissa Tormé-March.

No matter where you are as an actor, a good cold reading workshop is a must. If you're a good commercial type, a commercial workshop is a priority.

Beyond that, play to your weaknesses. (A typical mistake: You're great at comedy. What do you take? That's right, a comedy workshop!) Done a lot of stage? Make a beeline to a film technique class. Done nothing but commercials? Find an acting class that emphasizes truthfulness and forces you to abandon your bag of tricks. Can't even make Neil Simon funny? Look for a comedy workshop. You're a character actor or ethnic type? Go for dialects and accents. Used to relying on exacting stage directors? Improvisation will loosen you up for directors who only say "Play it over there."

And never stop. As theatrical casting director Mike Fenton put it: "Do not vegetate . . . if all you're going to do is sit on your butt, then continue to be a waiter because that is all you will ever do. You must eat, you must be employed . . . drive a cab — but leave yourself time to study."

FINDING A CLASS

That's easy. Besides the teachers we list there are plenty of fine teachers, many of whom advertise in the trades. There are also guides to acting coaches (*The Working Actors Guide*, for example) on sale at your local drama bookstore. And, of course, there are your fellow actors.

Like photographers, it's not a question of finding a class; it's a question of . . .

CHOOSING A CLASS

First, don't get caught up in the "reputation game." A famous Hollywood acting school isn't necessarily any better than a teacher quietly plying his trade in Van Nuys — or vice versa. You learn from teachers — not reputations, institutions, buildings, fancy brochures or neon signs. By the time a school becomes famous, the people who brought it fame are often long gone.

And don't buy price. Someone charging three times more isn't necessarily three times better.

Some suggestions . . .

Does the teacher make promises?

Teachers occasionally help talented students get agents and jobs — but someone who promises this to a stranger is proffering bait; bite, and you're the fish. A good teacher promises one thing only: to train you.

What's the teacher's background?

"The only teachers you should study with are people who have been or are in the industry," says agent Doris Ross. Be sure the teacher knows his stuff. Find out what he's done; where he's gotten his knowledge.

Will he let you audit?

There are perfectly reputable teachers who won't. "You either want to study with me or not," says one. Why? "Lookey-loos." Here's what one well-known acting teacher had to say: "I used to permit audits. Not anymore. I got real tired of dealing with actors who either couldn't make up their minds or who are avoiding the issue by constantly shopping. They're too scared to actually get up and do it, so they constantly shop around, kidding themselves into believing they are working on their craft."

However, our thinking is you shouldn't buy *anything* without looking it over, much less an acting class. By their very nature, these can get pretty darn personal. So, our advice: audit about three classes in the area you're looking for (i.e. cold reading, comedy, etc.) and then, unless you really didn't like any of them, choose one. No class is going to be perfect. You're not joining the Army — if you're unhappy you can always leave.

To that point, the teacher who won't let you audit should at least be willing to give you an easy out if you're not happy with him. His refund policy should be very clear and flexible.

How large?

Fifteen to 18 max. If all you're doing is paying to watch others act, why not stay home and watch TV? it's a helluva lot cheaper. You should be acting in at least three out of four classes.

What's the general level?

Work with people who are at your level, perhaps a little better. "I've got a B.A. in drama," says one actress, "And I got into this class filled with beginners. Talk about frustrating! It drove me crazy to act next to them."

Is videotape employed?

Many excellent classes don't use videotape, but it is enormously helpful to see what you are doing. Also, Hollywood is film-oriented; you should know how you come across on camera.

What goes on?

Ask yourself:

- Is this training practical or artsy-craftsy? Here's what one actor said about his class: "They teach you to be very self-indulgent . . . and a lot of psychotic behavior comes out."

- Is the class too disciplined? Too sloppy? A good laugh can be refreshing, but the class shouldn't be a barrelful of monkeys, either.

- Can the students question the teacher? Do they question him too much? If the teacher turns bright red with anger because a student disagrees, you're dealing with a bush-league Hitler. If there are constant challenges, either the teacher can't control the class or there is an underlying lack of respect for him.

- Does the teacher flatter or criticize too much? His critiques should be honest. Some pretty rotten actors have told us their instructor thought they were just marvy, dahling. We've also seen competent actors seriously damaged by whithering attacks and other "head games" played by their teachers. Listen to your gut. If a little voice tells you something's wrong, leave.

- Does the teacher care? Does he give you the feeling he's more interested in the tuition than the students? Do you get the feeling he's improvising what to do next, because he hasn't prepared for class? Does he constantly talk about himself, and how good he is? (Who cares? You're there to act.) Is he fully aware of the delicacy of his position, dealing with people's emotions, needs and hopes? How does he phrase things? "I don't think that worked because . . ." or "That stinks"? Is he out to show you how rough the business can be? (You know that already. You don't need his "help.") Is he straightforward? Non-manipulative? Bored or involved? Perceptive? Kind?

Remember, keep your classes in perspective. No class is the end-all and be-all of your career. Nobody ever made a dime in an acting class. Your acting teacher is not your: agent, personal manager, buddy, guru, channeler, psychiatrist, group grope specialist, primal-scream therapist, lover or daddy.

MOVING ON

You may find a teacher with whom you'll want to study for the rest of your life, so arbitrary time limits aren't very helpful. Instead of asking "How long?", ask "Why am I still here?"

If the answer involves friendships with your fellow students, the fact that everyone thinks you're soooo good, or your fear of moving on — move on. You're nesting.

At the end of each "semester," ask yourself two questions: Have you grown? Can you learn more from him?

In general, though, move around. You'll learn different approaches, act with a more varied group of people, and, probably, keep your classes more in perspective. (If you find someone you don't want to leave, add other classes.)

And remember, study forever. Well trained? How about a seminar on film production or the emergence of the cable industry? A class on fencing? Dance? Horseback riding? Business? Directing?

Sound like a lot of time and money? You got it. Sounds like an actor never stops learning? You got it again.

VIII
MERRILY YOU ROLL ALONG

28 PUBLICIZING YOURSELF

There's nothing wrong with writing a critic...
especially to thank him for a good review.

John C. Mahoney, Drama Critic

You won't need or be able to afford a publicist until you really get rolling, so you're going to have to be your own. Your main concern will be to become known within the industry — in a positive way. Before you publicize anything, ask yourself, "What am I calling attention to? How will it affect others' perception of me and/or my career?"

GETTING INTO THE TRADES

There are several columns in *Daily Variety* and *The Hollywood Reporter* that provide fertile ground for a little "planting" of your name. It'll take a minimum of effort and a postage stamp.

"Make it as easy to put in the paper as you can," says Ruth Robinson, formerly of *The Hollywood Reporter*. In other words, make proper submissions. And that starts with your agent. Ideally, he should submit news of you (getting cast, re-signing with him, etc. — see below), because the letterhead on his stationary will be more trusted. But if he doesn't, do it yourself. That's standard in this industry. The only no-no is duplicate submissions.

Start by reading the columns. Each has its own style and, if you're smart, you'll follow it down to the punctuation.

Type a short covering letter saying something like: "Dear Sir: Enclosed, information for your _____ column. Thank you." Then, on a separate sheet, type your item as one sentence, double spaced.

It might help if your covering letter has a letterhead on it. "Become a company," suggests a person who deals with the trades all the time. "Is your name Steve Mayfield? Become 'The Steve Company' or 'The Mayfield Company.' Wouldn't hurt." The less devious can settle for decent personal stationary.

Finally, include the name of the column on the envelope. Cumulative time: about ten minutes. Cumulative effect: your name (possibly) in the trades.

NOTE: For prices, fees, addresses, phone numbers of items mentioned throughout the book, see Appendix.

Where to submit what:

- *Cast in a film or TV show?* "Film castings" or "Telecastings," *Daily Variety*; and "Feature Casting" (for both TV and film), *The Hollywood Reporter*.

    (But be sure you aren't jumping the gun. If your part is one or two scenes, no problem. If the role is sizeable, check with the producer and/or publicity department before doing anything.)

- *Cast in a stage production?* Be sure the theatre sends a cast list to "Legit Bits," *Daily Variety*, and "Stage Notes," *Hollywood Reporter*.

- *Traveling?* "Who's Where," *Daily Variety*, and "Travel Log," *Hollywood Reporter*. Warning: burglars can read this and plan their next party.

- *Signed with a new agent or personal manager?* "Agents Alley," *Daily Variety*; and "Artists/Agents," *Hollywood Reporter*.

- *Just tied the knot or added to the world's cast?:* "Hitched" or "Births," *Daily Variety*; "Personal Data," *Hollywood Reporter*.

Until you're well known or doing something really special, you probably won't have a lot of success planting your name in the trade/social columns like Robert Osborne's "Rambling Reporter," Hank Grant's "Off The Cuff," George Christy's "The Great Life" (all in *The Hollywood Reporter*) or Army Archerd's "Just for Variety" (*Daily Variety*). Still, charm and a genuinely novel or amusing anecdote can produce the occasional exception. Unlike the news items, submissions to these columns should be *exclusive* (go to one columnist only).

Finally, if you think this all sounds silly and self-involved, you're missing the point. As publicist Barbara Best says, "It really doesn't matter all that much *why* your name appears in the trades. Most people forget that. They just remember *that* they saw your name."

ADS IN THE TRADES

Are trade ads worth it? Depends. Getting your name before the industry is valuable, but trade ads are expensive. A one-fourth-page ad (about as small as you should go) run once in either *Daily Variety* or *The Hollywood Reporter* will seriously crimp your vacation plans.

Anyway, if you're thinking about buying any ad, ask yourself:

What are you selling?

"Joe Idle, seeking representation" only tells the world you can't get an agent. "Super-Peachy Agency signs Ginger Keeny" (almost always paid for by the actor, by the way), has some value. You're reminding the industry you're alive, flattering your new agent, and telling any casting directors who are paying attention where you are. But you can do this for free in the "agents" columns.

"See Prudence Prindle in 'Jeers'" might be of value if you've got a decent part. But, as theatrical casting director Ron Stephenson says, "Don't take out an ad for a one-line part, *please*."

How are you selling it?

Tacky, amateurish-looking ads are worse than silence in an industry that thrives on style and status. Your ad should at least be one-fourth page (graphics savvy might permit you to go smaller); be uncluttered; contain your photo, name and agent; and sport copy that is not negative, silly, needful or excessively braggadocios.

"Actors usually want to put review after review until nobody will read it," says an account executive for *Daily Variety* (who handles talent ads). "I always tell them 'short and to the point.'"

If you can't afford to have your ad done by a graphics house, the pros in the ad departments of both papers will lay out your ad at no extra charge, as long as it doesn't involve major artwork.

When/where should it go?

Readership is high on days when the production charts are published. That's Tuesdays for *The Hollywood Reporter*, Thursdays (TV) and Fridays (films) for *Daily Variety*.

Unless you're paying for a specific location it's a rare publication that will *guarantee* where your ad will appear. But, what the heck, ask. Good spots: opposite production charts or any major column, on the right-hand side of any page, even, in the case of *Variety*, near the crossword puzzle.

GROUP ADS

Did the critics positively warble over your revival of "*I Never Sang For My Father?*" Get the cast to split the cost of taking out an ad for the production. Include pictures and a rave or two from the critics.

USING THE BREAKDOWN SERVICES

The same Breakdown Service that publishes casting breakdowns and the casting directors guide offers other services as well:

- *The "Go-Between":* For a fee they'll hand-deliver your invitations and announcements to all casting directors; for another fee, to producers. It's a bit expensive, so you might opt for their cheaper alternative of label sets as mentioned in Chapter 8.

- *Delivery service for shows/theatres:* If you're in a show, and your group prints up an 8½" by 11" flyer that includes the names of all cast members, the Breakdown Service will hand-deliver the flyer to agents and personal managers for yet another fee.

WRITING THE CRITICS

It's vital for the producer of an 99-seat theatre play to get someone who knows what he's doing to work on publicity, especially in regard to the critics. Notices should go out two weeks before you open, followed by phone calls a day or so in advance.

"I try to tell people *we don't know they're opening*," says one critic. "Usually an actor is assigned to do publicity who doesn't know a thing about it . . . very often I'll get a call on Thursday night saying, 'Are your coming to our show tonight?' and I answer, '*What show?*' '

If a critic thought you were the cat's meow, there's nothing wrong with sending him a purring thank-you note. "That's no more than reasonable public relations," says Sylvie Drake, a drama critic for *The Los Angeles Times.* "My usual answer to thank-you notes is to tell the actors they have only to thank themselves . . . and the next time, if they get a bad review, they have only to thank themselves, too."

MAILING SERVICES

These services send photos and résumés as direct submissions for roles. They claim they're "selective," but casting directors tell tales of photographs arriving by the *pile.* Certainly these services vary in quality, but even without an agent you can do a lot of this work for yourself for only the cost of stamps and envelopes, and your photo will arrive by itself.

IN GENERAL

Throughout this book we've talked about the importance of letting people know what you're doing through use of letters, postcards, news releases, ads, and even phone calls. Strangely, publicity is often neglected by actors. Take advantage of their foolishness by filling the void with positive, upbeat and continuous mention of your name. Show business is synonymous with publicity.

29 YOUR MANAGEMENT TEAM

Everyone should plan for success.

A. Morgan Maree, Business Manager

Ask an actor how he got a job and the word "friend" continually pops up. ("A friend told me about...," "A friend of my sister knew...") When we talk about the folks below, don't forget they're contacts too. Never underestimate the possibility of anyone helping your career. Entertainment attorney Michael C. Donaldson suggests, "When you hire a CPA invite him to every show you do, so he gets to know and care about you."

Your management team is divided into:

* People to obtain immediately;
* People to obtain later.

IMMEDIATELY

Certified Public Accountant (CPA):

For reasons best left to Merrill-Lynch to analyze, it's often tough to motivate actors to hire a good CPA. If you're at all skeptical as to their value, here's what actor Van Epperson has to say: "For years, we did our own taxes. Finally we decided to try an entertainment CPA. We still went ahead and figured our taxes, just for comparison. Well, he wound up saving us *literally ten times what we would have paid — and that was over and above what it cost us for his services.*" That story is typical. Yes, his services will cost more than a guy seated at one of 33 desks in a storefront operation, but ultimately he'll save you money. Just be sure he's entertainment-oriented.

To find a CPA, ask bright Show Biz people you meet, including your agent, for recommendations.

Attorney

Eventually, someone's going to ask you to sign some gobbledy-gook with a lot of wherefores and whereases. And the worst time to go hunting for an attorney is when you need one. There's no need to pay a retainer, just establish a basic relationship with him for the future. Again, you'll want him to be entertainment-oriented.

NOTE: For prices, fees, addresses, phone numbers of items mentioned throughout the book, see Appendix.

LATER

Personal managers

"The reason an actor needs a personal manager — and this is not meant detrimentally — is that agents are predominantly booking services. They get phone calls from casting directors saying, 'I want so-and-so; send me so-and- so.' In my opinion you need a personal manger and an agent in order to get full attention. A personal manager guides you on every facet of your career. We guide and direct and advise, from business management to publicity to selecting agents to opening bank accounts, you name it," says personal manager Melissa Tormé-March. "I'm sort of an architect, whereas the agent is sort of a realtor," says personal manager Roz Tillman.

Done a lot of theatre? A good personal manager makes sure you have an agent in New York. Sing? He gets you on the nightclub circuit. Offered a part at a theatre in Missouri? He makes sure you're happy with your dressing room. Offered a role on an episodic television show? He advises you whether or not to take it, based on how it may affect your career. Not sure your agent is submitting you? Your PM checks over his own copy of the Breakdown Service and calls you agent to nudge him a little. Need an agent with more clout? He helps you get one. "I do all the things the agent was supposed to have done in the first place," says personal manager Jerry Cohn.

And, on top of all that, he introduces you to important people. He opens doors that might be locked to you and even your agent. There have been cases where a personal manager has introduced a total newcomer to the right producer, and zoooom!

And, once you're earning more than $100,000 a year, a personal manager can very well catapult you into super-stardom. That's why we put them under the category of people to obtain "later," which, frankly, some would question. They'd say get a good personal manager first, have him get you an agent, and stand back and watch your career blossom. Otherwise, you might never get beyond being another drone. "I know an actor who has done 60 films and you still don't know his name," says personal manager Cathryn Jaymes.

However, others have mixed opinions or downright hate personal managers. "I don't think they're very valuable, unless they have access to packaging," says one producer. "They're only helpful if you're a star and they also can provide business advice," says another. "They're nothing more than ambulance chasers," says still another.

Ask an agent what he thinks, and watch smoke come out of his ears. Many agents think of personal managers with a fondness usually reserved for root canal work.

Why the mixed reviews?

Well, anyone can pick up a piece of wood, paint "Personal Manager" on it, and he's in business. He doesn't have to know a thing. He doesn't need a union franchise or a state license. He can charge any fool any percentage he wants. Then he can get on the phone and start making ridiculous demands of agents, casting directors, even producers and directors. The fact that he's destroying a career may never enter his mind.

Next, the going rate for personal managers is 15 percent (and upwards) of your gross income. Since he's not franchised or licensed, he can't negotiate a legal contract unless he (or someone in his office) is an attorney. "There are only three people in the state of California who may negotiate a contract," points out theatrical agent David Westberg, "The artist himself, a certified agent, or a lawyer." In other words, with or without him, you're still going to need an agent.

Add the agent's commission to his and you're paying out (minimum) 25 percent — one quarter — of your income. And, if you think about it, you can do many of the things he does.

Next, even a top-notch personal manager isn't always going to be right. And his mistakes can be dillies. Maybe his demand for that fancy dressing room in Missouri is just enough to make the producer say, "Look, let's skip it." Maybe he nudges your agent once too often, and destroys a relationship you've been working on for years. Maybe he counsels you not to take a part, and you don't work for another year. Maybe he "manages" you right out of the business.

Yes, the general quality of personal managers has improved mostly because the good ones are policing themselves. But there are still a lot of sharks out there and, when it comes to helping you, toothless ones at that.

In any case, if you decide to look for a PM, it'll be easier if you're a teen heartthrob, glamor girl or handsome hunk, or are multi-talented (say, you sing with a band). Lesser beings will probably have to wait until they get hot — if they need one at all. Use the same methods we discussed in "Seeking an Agent." You might start with the Conference of Personal Managers, but bear in mind that not all (good or bad) personal managers are members. Other sources include *The Studio Blu-Book, The Academy Players Directory* (actors often list their managers) or the trades.

If a personal manager expresses interest in you, check him over with a microscope. He should have: been in business for at least a few years; solid connections; at least one relatively well-known client; charge no more than 15 percent; and demand no money up front. Most agents and casting directors should know and respect him. He should have a maximum of 10 to 15 clients. And, most important, his judgment should be solid and well-informed — that's really what you hire him for.

There's just no clear-cut answer to the value of a personal manager. In fact, only one thing is certain. As business manager A. Morgan Maree puts it, "Unfortunately today you get for 25 percent what you used to get for 10."

Business Manager

His title tells you what he does — he manages your business, helps you pre-plan tax deductions, suggests possible investments, arranges loans, puts together your portfolio and annual financial statement, etc. He should make his entrance when you're making upwards of $100,000 a year, and, if he's good, help you keep it and maybe make more.

Develop a good relationship with a CPA; he can offer business advice now and act as your business manager or refer you to one later. Some personal management firms also offer business management services.

With or without a business manager, learn some business. Stars have lost their shirts either through their own bad investments or those of a bad/shyster business manager. In college and thinking of becoming an actor? A major or minor in business will give you something to fall back on if it doesn't work out, and the background to make the most of your earnings if it does. Out of college? There are plenty of community college business courses and seminars available.

Publicist

Get rolling and a publicist can be invaluable. Through strategic planning, he can keep your name before the public, and, more important, the industry, for weeks, months and even years ahead. "Some publicists get you out to all the right parties," notes theatrical agent David Westberg. He can keep everybody convinced you just never stop working and are in constant demand. As publicist Barbara Best puts it, "You'll know your publicist is doing a good job when people come up to you and tell you how well you're doing."

However, even if you can afford his monthly fee, no publicist can help if you're not doing anything worth publicizing. And a community theatre production of *Carousel* doesn't qualify. If you're thinking of hiring a "publicist" who claims he can get you on Johnny Carson just because you're so cute, put your money on the longest shot at Hollywood Park instead. Besides, as editor Ruth Robinson put it, "Until you're famous, you can probably do the same things for yourself as any publicist."

30 GENERAL FINANCIAL

*I know it's not very exciting or glamorous,
but if you want my best advice, keep records.*

David Perren, Certified Public Accountant with
the firm of Barkin, Perren & Associates

TAXES

- *Withholding:* When figuring your withholding, your employer follows a tax table that assumes you make what you're being paid for that acting job every week of the year. Chomp! There goes a substantial portion of your paycheck.

  You may get that money back in your tax refund, but don't you need the money now? And why "rent" money to the federal government for free?

  To avoid this bite, in past years some actors claimed 99 exemptions or wrote "exempt" on their tax forms. The employer then withheld nothing. No more. Oh, you can do it, but if you claim more than ten exemptions, or that you're exempt, your employer must immediately send that form to the IRS. The IRS can match it against your tax return, and if you don't qualify for what you've claimed, they'll send you a letter asking you to substantiate your claim. If you can't or don't respond to that letter, they'll tell your employer to withhold tax based on your being single, claiming zero exemptions. That will do for your paycheck what Bruce the Shark does for legs.

  There is, however, one thing you can do:

- *"Part-Year Employment Method of Withholding":* That's the name of the form to request. On it, you're telling your employer that in that year you anticipate: working no more than 245 days; earning no more than $30,000; and you use a calendar-year method of accounting (January 1 to December 31). With that in hand, your employer will take less withholding.

- *What's your line?:* It's a bit of a gray area as to when you can call yourself an actor on your tax return. Certainly you can if acting is your chief source of income. But if the amount of money made in any given year were to be the sole criteria to putting "actor" on your

---

NOTE: For a list of "typical" tax deductions and other financiall information see Appendix.

return, we don't have to tell you most actors wouldn't qualify. Therefore, the question seems to be: How much time did you spend trying to make money as an actor?

- *Keeping track:* Way back, we mentioned the importance of a daily diary in regard to filing your income tax. At least once a week, enter into your diary all the expenses you incurred as an actor. Did you "do" lunch with your agent on Thursday? Enter it. Did you buy *Your Film Acting Career* on Friday? Write it in. Not only will that diary serve you well if you're audited, but often it will remind you of forgotten expenses.

  And keep receipts — even for items purchased by check or credit card. Without receipts, your deductions, no matter how legitimate, can be disallowed. Try attaching receipts directly onto the daily diary next to the expense. "It gives the diary more substance," says CPA Mel Blank.

- *Per diems:* When on location, you get a per diem for expenses, which your employer reports to the IRS. You must report that expense money as income. If your expenses on location equal the per diem, they cancel each other out. If your expenses were greater, that's an additional deduction. If they were less, that's taxable income. So keep records.

- *In case of an audit:* Don't jump off a bridge. Nobody's going to reserve a room for you at San Quentin unless you're defrauding the government, which has nothing to do with this book. Your return will be checked and you'll be asked to substantiate deductions. When notified about an audit, call your CPA. He'll advise you what to do, perhaps even take a power of attorney and go to the audit with your records, all by himself. The IRS will then: declare a "no change" (return accepted as filed); disallow certain deductions (for which you have the right to be billed at a later time); or maybe even give you a refund.

INVESTING

Ever hear of the concept of "paying yourself first?" Each month you pay your bills saying, "Well, I'll just use whatever's left over on myself." Reverse that. *Pay yourself first.* Before you pay any bill, put a ten spot in a savings account. Drop a fiver in a piggy bank.

And, if you get a small or large windfall, extend the concept. Before you buy shares in a diamond mine in New Guinea, invest in yourself. New pictures, an ad in *Variety*, that class you've been putting off, a good presentation tape, etc., will pay more dividends than stock on the Big Board.

A. Morgan Maree, business manager, suggests this order of investment:

1. You;
2. Insurance (especially if you have dependents);
3. A place in which you'd be comfortable living;
4. Other investments (and seek competent advice).

If the windfall is small, and you feel you might need the money sooner rather than later, you might look into a money market fund. These funds pay higher interest rates and you can withdraw your money when needed. Some require a minimal initial deposit, others don't; the same is true for any succeeding deposits or withdrawals.

A WORD ABOUT INSURANCE

Achieve even a modicum of success and you may need more insurance on your car, house, etc. because actors are "target risks." See, it's a given that all actors are rich, so slam into someone with your car, have him recognize your face, and don't be surprised if he starts shouting, "Whiplash! Whiplash!" Ain't fame grand?

UNEMPLOYMENT COMPENSATION

We don't have the space to go into all the rules and regulations. Just don't view it as charity — you earned the money. As one actor put it, "I think of unemployment compensation as the national endowment for the arts."

To start, go down to any branch office of the State of California Employment Development Department. You'll be interviewed and notified of your "award" — how much money you'll be getting each week. It's computed like this: First, go back six months — you can't get unemployment on monies earned more recently. For the year prior to that time, your award will be based on the most money you earned in any quarter (January-March; April-June; July-September; October-December) of that 12-month period. Every two weeks you'll fill out another form and receive a check. You'll also occasionally be asked to go in person for a "work search review."

Bear in mind that, when you're receiving unemployment compensation, you must report any work and any income you get. That includes residuals, holding fees, etc. Don't fail to report a single dime. It can mean big trouble.

31 MISCELLANEOUS

*Each actor is responsible for his own career
and I invite you to assume that responsibility.
It's your career. It's your business.*

Roz Tillman, Personal Manager

SAG CONSERVATORY

A lulu of a bargain. Join (for how-to see Chapter 25) and you may participate in a host of free Conservatory programs held at the American Film Institute, put together by fellow union members. A sampler:

- *Monday/Wednesday workshops:* Free feedback on your audition technique. Monday evening you and about ten other members (separately) will videotape a spokesman commercial. Your performance will be critiqued by an experienced SAG volunteer. Wednesday evening, you'll repeat the process doing a typical theatrical interview and cold reading. Not a substitute for a good commercial or cold reading workshop (you only get to do this once), but a great way to stay fresh if you know what you're doing, and a revelation if you don't.

- *Tuesday seminars:* Guest speakers range from casting directors to agents, even financial planners. Conservatory members make a reservation, show up and learn.

- *Summer seminars:* Happens once a year over a weekend. Two day-long series of interviews, lectures and "Q&A" sessions with industry people. Besides the information, there's a wonderful feeling of camaraderie, warmth and excitement as you bustle from one session to the next. Bring your lunch and enjoy.

UNION SHOWCASES

If you read Chapter 18, you know the importance of showcasing for casting directors, agents, etc. Well, both AFTRA and SAG offer showcases too, but with one slight difference: they're free to paid-up members. The rules for doing these vary slightly between each union, but both hold prepared scene showcases, most often for casting directors. And don't

---

NOTE: For prices, fees, addresses, phone numbers of items mentioned throughout the book, see Appendix.

think there are necessarily hundreds of actors in line ahead of you. We were told by a union volunteer that it was surprising how few actors take advantage of this. It's the "dateless beautiful blonde syndrome": All the guys figure she's already got a date. Contact the respective union and ask her out.

AFTRA/SAG FEDERAL CREDIT UNION

"The actor's savings and loan." You must be a member of SAG or AFTRA to open an account. Benefits include a slightly higher rate of interest on savings; lower interest on loans; interest checking, etc., all federally insured by NCUA. Best thing is that it's run by and for SAG/AFTRA members. That means they'll be a little more understanding if you get into trouble, and they'll even consider a part of your unemployment compensation as income when you apply for a loan. Try and get *that* from Louie the Loan-Shark.

SAG FILM SOCIETY

It's open only to paid-up SAG members and sells out fast. (Don't wait when you see the ad for it in the SAG newsletter.) For your membership, you and a guest get to see a first-run movie every other Friday or Saturday. Figure about 52 admissions to 26 new movies. That comes to about a buck a ticket. Last time you saw a bargain like this was when Eisenhower fretted over his golf score. Two drawbacks, one minor, the other major. Minor: you don't get to select the movies. Major: no popcorn.

GAME SHOWS

Brainless. Oh, not the shows — the financially-strapped actor who refuses to do them. In one month we met three actors whose winnings, added together, were over $100,000. Each was then able to pursue his career on a full-time basis for at least a year, without having to live on peanut butter. Actress Jan Hoag, who won $38,000 (her winnings are separate from the above-mentioned figure), says, "You still have to peel me off the ceiling. It certainly takes a weight off my shoulders for a while."

Aha, now you're interested. Okay, how do you get on a game show? Just pick up a phone. They really do need contestants and union members may play. AFTRA's news magazine *Diallog* includes a listing of game shows and their phone numbers. There are also a couple of books out on the subject (see Appendix). And, of course, a phone number is usually announced during the shows themselves.

But before you pick up that receiver, study the shows. Decide which show is best for you. Do they pay ten big ones to people who know the difference between a femur and a lemur? Do you? Do their contestants get apoplectic at the drop of a toaster? Can you? If you're slow hitting buzzers, pass on "Buzzing For Bucks!" You're limited to three game-show appearances so don't waste one.

Also, skip the shows that give more prizes than money. A new coffee table might be nice, but you're looking to support yourself — go for the gold.

What *they'll* be looking for, naturally, depends on the program. But they *all* want happy, warm, full-of-beans types with, above all, perk. It may be quiet perk, medium perk, or THE SCREAMING PERK FROM HELL — but perk.

Finally, once you know you're going to "COME ON DOWN!", practice. Rehearse like you're opening on Broadway. After all, if you're a "hit" it'll probably pay a helluva lot more.

AFTRA-SAG YOUNG PERFORMERS HANDBOOK

If Baby June is making goo-goos about getting into the Biz, she and her parents can benefit from this absolutely super booklet put together jointly by members of SAG and AFTRA. Includes parental do's and don'ts, child labor laws, info on unemployment insurance (yep, kids can qualify), etc.

Pick one up at either union, or simply write them for a copy. It's free.

THE NATIONAL BLACK TALENT DIRECTORY

Being listed in *Academy Players Directory* and the *New York Players Guide* is usually sufficient. Here's a *possible* exception.

This brand-new talent guide is for black artists — both on and behind the camera. A one-year listing costs the same as the APD, and to be included all you need is the fee and a photo.

"FREE" PHOTOS

If you're broke but need new pictures (modeling or standard headshots), try swapping posing services for cash at places such as the Art Center College of Design in Pasadena. You'll "donate" some hours of posing (no nudity) for student photographers, in return for which they'll give you a headshot session and some free prints.

SEMINARS

College extension courses, open to the general public, can be a great way to fill gaps in your knowledge. So can classes offered by Contemporary Concepts, The Learning Tree The Learning Annex, etc. You can learn anything from low-budget film production to belly dancing. Ask to be placed on their mailing lists. Periodically, *The Beverly Hills Bar Association* presents an all-day seminar for the actor. Watch for their ads.

ACADEMY (OF MOTION PICTURES ARTS AND SCIENCES) FOUNDATION

Besides handing out the little gold statuettes you may have heard of, and publishing *The Academy Players Directory*, the Academy has a research library on the film industry and the Academy Foundation which holds seminars, interviews, retrospectives, etc., many open to the public. For a small fee you can be put on their mailing list.

WOMEN IN FILM

An "old girl network" for career women in film and TV. Membership includes newsletters, guest speakers, workshops and the like. To get in, you'll need three years' pro experience in the industry and two WIF sponsors.

HOTLINES

For hot tips on what's doing, perhaps a lead on free theatre tickets, or even an audition, all three unions offer hotlines for union members.

STARTING YOUR OWN NETWORK

Throughout this book we've tried to point out the importance of taking your career in your own hands. Certainly one way is to get a group of actors together to form your own showcase, theatre, information-getting organization or what have you. It's been done in the past and can be done again. Also, you'd be amazed at the serendipity that occurs when you take on a project. You're working on project A and, bing!, someone comes along with project B. Work begets work, projects beget projects, ideas beget ideas. You're only limited by your imagination.

Some time ago, a group of guys got together to take their future into their own hands. The result was a little production called the U.S.A.

32 ASSESSING YOUR CAREER

In this industry you're either on the rise or
falling — there's no standing still.

David Westberg, Theatrical Agent

We don't believe in arbitrary time limits, but at some point you'll need to examine where you are. Let's assume it's New Year's Day. Between toasts or kick-offs, you wander away for a mull. You have:

- *Gotten a good amount of work;*
- *Gotten some work;*
- *Gotten work in the past, but somehow your career has stopped;*
- *Gotten nothing.*

A GOOD AMOUNT OF WORK

Congratulations. If you earned $15,000 or more last year, you're in the upper ten percent of the Screen Actors Guild. Think over what you've been doing right and plan to keep doing it. Then go back and toast yourself.

SOME WORK

Before you climb all over your own back, bear in mind that if you earned more than $5,000 last year, you're in the top 20 percent of your class. Make that a pat on the back instead.

Now: how to get more work? Look at the jobs you got. How'd you get them? What did you do right? Next, make a list of any career weak points and plan to solve them. Break that plan into weekly and daily goals. Need a new agent? Pictures? Are you showcasing yourself enough — especially in those cold reading showcases and 99-seat theatre? Are you keeping in touch with past employers? How about new contacts — did you nurture them? If you blow auditions, how about taking a cold reading workshop? A commercial workshop? A class in improvisation? Lost a role because you can't ride a horse? Or dance? Or do a French accent?

YOU WERE GETTING WORK, BUT YOUR CAREER HAS JUST "STOPPED"

We can't think of a more frustrating turn of events. If it helps, this is a phase all actors go through periodically. Everything is going swimmingly, then glub! Somebody pulls the plug out of the pool.

First, try figuring out what happened — unemotionally. Agent gone cold on you? Why? Been sitting back, waiting for him to do it all? Was your type "out" this season? Were there union strikes? Have you priced yourself out of the market? Maybe you need new pictures. Maybe you need to do a 99-seat theatre play. And maybe, just maybe, you've become, through no fault of your own . . .

Yesterday's mashed potatoes:

Hollywood is addicted to the new. Producers go anywhere from East Bochaboora to South Wales looking for "new faces"; all the while there are thousands of better-trained "faces" sitting idle in their own back yard.

It's as though you're given an indeterminate amount of time to become a "hot item." Exceed it, or "merely" become a pro who consistently does good work, and you may wake up to find you're passé. Old news. "Out." And typed to boot.

If that's you, you'll need to do one of two things:

- *Double your efforts:* Especially to meet new people. You're not passé to them. Find a play that shows you being different. Done nothing on TV but scroungy villains? Play a doctor reeking with distinction. Typed as a bookish accountant? Buckle a swash or two. Tired of playing Miss Goody Two-Shoes? Don't just say it, try doing: *Nuts.* Get "discovered" by those who don't know you, and "re-discovered" by those who do.

  You mean to say an established actor has to go back to work getting work? All the time. Otherwise you can really become past tense.

- *Turn bicoastal:* "The place to go is New York," says personal manager Larry Fonseca. "There, they'll take shots on people. The talent is what counts. Out here, they'll go for a name, or the (casting) precedent has been set." Selling like cold pancakes and sensing that casting directors yawn, "Oh, *him*?" Head east. You'll be new to an entire city. Even better, if you've got film/TV credits, you'll find it easier to interest agents. (A *lot* easier. Just as Hollywood goes ga-ga over New York credits, New York — whether it admits it or not — at least goes "ga" over Hollywood credits.)

Eventually, you'll get in a play, some Hollywood producer will see you, bring you out to L.A. for his next picture, and everyone will ask, "Where have you been hiding all this time?"

YOU'VE GOTTEN NOTHING

We don't have to tell you something's wrong. You're probably aching inside. Should you quit? Give it six more months? Keep going indefinitely? First, as voice-over casting director Andrea Romano puts it, "If you really want to do it, don't give up. There's always room for somebody new, if they're talented."

But, if you're beginning to feel, well, just not happy any more, note what theatrical agent Joel Rudnick has to say: "My biggest frustration is with actors who are unhappy. If it's always tense, and you always want to kill yourself if you don't get a job, and, when you do get a job you're unhappy with the dressing room . . . well, I mean, I just don't think it's worth it if it doesn't make you happy."

It boils down to one word: *love*. Still love it? You bet it's still worth it. As producer/director Buddy Bregman says, "After you've been at it a year or so, if you find it's totally negative and your ambition is *metza-metza*, it's time to think about whether you should carry on or not. Because sometimes persevering against a brick wall is a waste of time. But if you really think you've got the talent, and this is all you want, then don't stop; it would be wrong to stop."

If you decide to quit, happily quit. You're not a failure. If all you're doing is scratching, there's nothing wrong with racking your cue. This just wasn't your game. So what?

Besides, you took your shot. The rest of your life will be free from tortuous "What ifs?" That alone is an enormous gift to yourself — ask those who didn't try.

And remember, you're being relieved of all the problems, nonsense, and all those receivers being hung up in your ear. And, if you return home to another state, you'll be free from smog, traffic and gold chains. And you'll never again have to hear, "Let's *take* a meeting."

And one other thing. Leaving acting doesn't have to mean exiting the film industry. You tried playing second base; how about catcher or shortstop? How about becoming an agent, casting director, gaffer, makeup artist, producer, director, stage-manager, writer, personal manager, continuity person, editor, lighting technician . . . there are hundreds of other industry jobs. Ultimately, you may find far greater satisfaction wearing a different hat. That's exactly what former actor, now theatrical agent, David Westberg did. Here's what he has to say: "I had been struggling with that decision for a long time. I mean, I loved acting, but it was between the jobs that drove me up the wall. I found myself becoming very negative and cynical about things. There seemed to be so many decisions that were out of my control. Finally, I reached an age when I didn't want to sit around for two, three months between jobs. And I decided that I could do more with my brain than wait for calls to come in. So I stopped acting. And, as soon as that happened, it opened up a whole range, a whole spectrum of colors came into play that I had never seen because I had always been so tunnel-visioned about acting. I could make decisions. And, all of a sudden I found myself receptive to people on entirely different levels. It was very exciting for me as a human being. And I love what I'm doing."

Just remember, the industry can always use more happy set decorators, fewer miserable actors.

33 CONCLUSION

*Concentrate on your career, but have a
personally enriched life along with it,
which means dating... marriage...
and having some fun.*

Viola Kates Stimpson, Actress

He lives in the South, working a typical nine-to-five job. He's a true fan of a famous actress. He even sent her a dozen roses once, when she won an Academy Award.

While he's talented and enjoys acting in community theatre, he has no plans to pursue a career as a professional actor. He's a rather shy person, reticent around strangers, so his interview technique needs some work. His cold reading technique, moreover, is nonexistent. He'll admit if he doesn't get the script long enough to memorize it, he doesn't have a chance.

He's non-union. He doesn't have any résumé shots or résumés — after all, what does he need them for? He never goes to L.A. or New York seeking work...

...And, on top of all that, he's partially handicapped.

One day, a local director asks him if he'd like to appear in a show being produced in that southern city...

Cut to: Manhattan. He's appeared on stage in a hit show for two years. His face has appeared on the front page of *The New York Times'* theatre section, and he's gotten excellent reviews.

He's been on a European tour, including performing for and meeting the Prince of Wales.

And, one night, his favorite actress happens to be in the audience. After the show, she goes backstage, tells him how much she enjoyed his performance...

...And then she gives him a kiss.

Sound like the script for a B movie?

It's all true. We know; it happened to a friend. Call it Fate, the Karmic Kosmos, or more things than are dreamt of by us Horatios. The point is, this business is just plain magically nutsy.

You can stand at a corner with a comic book in your hand, turn left, and bump into a guy with his shirt open to his navel who says, "You! You're perfect!" And zoooom.

Or you can be at the same corner with this book under your arm, turn right, and wind up struggling for 20 years.

Well, that's the job-getting business. At least you know the game a little better, which will cut the odds a bit.

In any case, whether you have that unlikely instant luck or the usual period of struggle, we hope you'll never forget the sheer joy of: a mustard-slavered hot dog at the ballpark; kissing your loved one for no good reason whatsoever; or just plain having a good laugh.

We also hope your acting coach never asks you why you secretly hate your little brother. We hope your agent calls you once a month desperate for more pictures. We hope the receptionists you run up against don't give you terminal frostbite. We hope casting directors sensitively understand why your hands are so clammy. We hope producers pay you all your meal penalties and directors only shoot you in close-up.

And, finally, we hope that blowhard who told you you'll "never make it" is backstage when your favorite actress walks up to you, tells you how wonderful you were . . .

. . . And gives you a kiss.

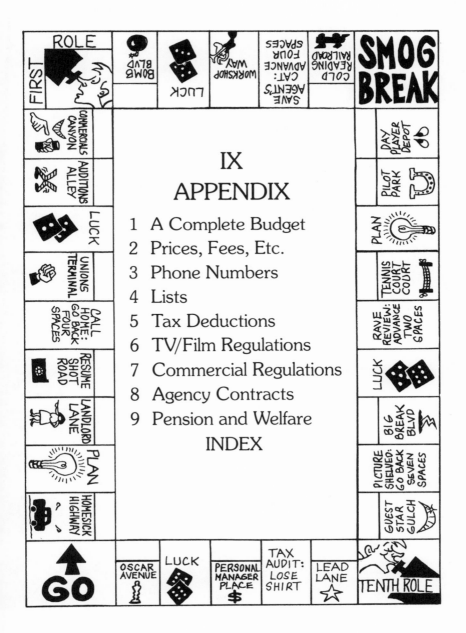

IX
APPENDIX

FIRST ROLE
BOMB BLVD
LUCK
WORKSHOP WAY
SAVE AGENT'S CAT: ADVANCE FOUR SPACES
COLD READING RAILROAD
SMOG BREAK

COMMERCIALS CANYON
AUDITIONS ALLEY
LUCK
UNIONS TERMINAL
CALL HOME: GO BACK FOUR SPACES
RESUME SHOT ROAD
LANDLORD LANE
PLAN
HOMESICK HIGHWAY

DAY PLAYER DEPOT
PILOT PARK
PLAN
TENNIS COURT COURT
RAVE REVIEW: ADVANCE TWO SPACES
LUCK
BIG BREAK BLVD
PICTURE SHELVED: GO BACK SEVEN SPACES
GUEST STAR GULCH

GO
OSCAR AVENUE
LUCK
PERSONAL MANAGER PLACE
TAX AUDIT: LOSE SHIRT
LEAD LANE
TENTH ROLE

APPENDIX

1 A COMPLETE BUDGET

In many cases these are average figures, all rounded off. You can raise or lower them to some extent.

- **THE MUSTS**

Telephone ($40 month, installation) $500
Headshot session $150
Headshot printing (500 theatrical, 500 commercial) $250
Résumés (typing, printing 500) $100
AFTRA initiation $600
Equity initiation $500
SAG initiation $796
Union dues (assumes two unions) $130
Postage (500 @ $25 per 100) $125
Envelopes (good-looking manila, some regular) $50
Academy Players Directory listing (one year) $45
Answering device $100
Good stationery $75
Thank-you notes $25
SAG agency list (free to members) $1
Datebook $20
Theatre, showcases, classes $1,500

TOTAL $4,967

- **OTHER ITEMS**

Composite session $300
Composite printing $150
Card file & notebook $20
Directories $100
Working Actors Guide $28
Trade subscriptions $125

Postcards $250
Typewriter $200
Labels (blank or pre-addressed) $30
Videocassette (including air-check, stock, editing) $150
Passport $40

TOTAL $1,393

Total (The Musts) $4,967
Total (Other Items) $1,393

GRAND TOTAL $6,360

• CHICKEN SOUP

Desk $100
Computer $1,500
VCR $250
Video camera $1,200

TOTAL $3,050

Total (The Musts) $4,967
Total (Other Items) $1,393
Total (Chicken Soup) $3,050

DELUXE GRAND TOTAL $9,410

2 ALPHABETICAL LISTING OF PRICES, FEES, ETC.

Academy Foundation (mailing list for public programs): $4
Academy Players Directory (per edition): $15
Academy Players Directory (per year): $45
Accent tapes (David Alan Stern's, per tape): $15
Actors Equity Association (AEA) initiation: $500
Actors Equity Association semi-annual minimum dues: $26
Actors Equity Membership Candidate Program: $100
AFTRA initiation: $600
AFTRA semi-annual minimum dues: $32.50
AFTRA scale (principal, daily): $379
AFTRA scale (principal, weekly): $1,319
AFTRA scale ("special ability," per day): $145
AFTRA scale (extra per day): $102
AFTRA scale (session fee radio, solo performer): $142
AFTRA/SAG Federal Credit Union (minimum first deposit): $50
AGMA initiation: $500
AGMA semi-annual dues: $26
AGVA initiation: $300
AGVA (three-times-yearly dues): $24
Airlink: $6.50
Answering service (average, monthly): $15
Apartments (single, one-bedroom): .... $450-$1,000
Apartment finders/real estate services (minimum): $40
Association of Visual Communicators: $75
Auto gas (average, unleaded, gallon): $1
Auto registration (add 2% of market value to): $35
Back Stage, newsstands: $1.50
Back Stage, one-year subscription: $50
The National Black Talent Guide (one-year listing): $45
Breakdown Services *Agency Guide*: $10.65
Breakdown Services "Go-Between" (agts., cast. dirs.): $60
Breakdown Services "Go-Between" (producers): $80
Breakdown Services (deliver flyers, agts., pers. mgrs.): $60
Breakdown Services *C/D Guide* (per issue): $5.30
Breakdown Services *C/D Guide* (per year): $35
Breakdown Services labels (L.A. agents): $21.30

Breakdown Services labels (L.A. casting directors): $16
Breakdown Services labels (L.A. comm. cast. dirs.): $12.80
Breakdown Services labels (N.Y. casting directors): $12.80
Buses (RTD): $1.10
Buses (transfers): .... $.25
Buses (monthly passes): $42
Car rental (average "cheapie," per day): $20
Cold reading showcases (average, per session): $25
Commercial audition (every 30 mins. over 1 hour): $20.85
Commercial callback (3rd): $83.30
Commercial callback (4th): $183.30
Commercial creative fee, improv. audition: $132
Commercial scale for session, holding fees: $366.60
Computer/printer (possibly less): $1,000
Daily Variety, newsstand: .... $.75
Daily Variety, one-year subscription: $85
Daily Variety, quarter-page talent ad: $330
Disneyland (adults): $21.50
Disneyland (kids): $16.50
Drama-Logue, newsstand: $1.50
Drama-Logue, one-year subscription (52 wks.): $45
Driver's license: $10
Equity-franchised agents (list): .... $.25
Equity-contract theatres (each list of LORT, etc.): .... $.25
Equity initiation: $500
Equity semi-annual minimum dues: $26
Equity Membership Candidate Program: $100
Electricity bill (apartment, average month): $40
Film Directors — A Complete Guide: $44.95
Flyaway (Van Nuys): $4.50
Gas (apartment, average month): $8
The Hollywood Reporter, newsstand: .... $.75
The Hollywood Reporter, one-year subscription: $89
The Hollywood Reporter quarter-page talent ad: $325
Independent Feature Project/West (IFP) (per year): $60
Knotts Berry Farm (adults): $17.95
Knotts Berry Farm (kids): $13.95
La Brea Tar Pits (admission): $3
Los Angeles Herald Examiner, newsstands: .... $.25
Los Angeles Times, newsstands: .... $.25

Magic Mountain (adults): $20
Magic Mountain (kids): $10
Mailbox rental (average, monthly): $14
The National Black Talent Guide (see above)
Pacific Coast Studio Directory: $7
Publicists monthly fee (average, minimum): $1,000
Resume typing (average): $25
Ross Reports Television (one edition): $3.75
Ross Reports Television (one-year subscription): $17.10
Scene partner ad (1"), *Drama-Logue*: $22
SAG Agency List (free to members): $1
SAG Calendar Datebook: $12
SAG Calendar Datebook (refills): $6
SAG Conservatory: $10
SAG Film Society: $60
SAG initiation (is double day scale, see below): $796
SAG semi-annual minimum dues: $42.50
SAG scale (daily): $398
SAG scale (3-day TV only): $1,009
SAG scale (weekly): $1,385
"Scale plus ten": .... Add ten percent to scale
Screen Extras Guild (SEG) initiation: $600
Screen Extras Guild (SEG) semi-annual minimum dues: $55
The Hollywood Reporter's Studio Blu-Book: $40
Theatre tickets (average, Equity Waiver): $10
Theatre tickets (average, major theatre): $40
Thomas Bros. Maps: $13
Union dues reductions (approx.): .... $10-$20
Universal Studios Tour (adults): $17.95
Universal Studios Tour (kids): $12.95
Van Nuys Flyaway: $4.50
VCR: $300
Women in Film (first-year membership): $150
Women in Film (yearly membership): $100
Working Actors Guide: $27.50
YMCA (Hollywood branch): .... $27 per night

3 ALPHABETICAL LISTING
OF PHONE NUMBERS

Academy Foundation	(213) 278-8990
Academy Players Directory	(213) 278-8990
AFTRA	(213) 461-8111
AFTRA Health & Retirement Fund	(213) 462-3244
AFTRA Hotline	(213) 462-8505
AFTRA, specific voice-over agents	(213) 461-7145
AFTRA/SAG Federal Credit Union	(213) 461-3041
AGMA	(818) 907-8986
AGVA	(818) 508-9984
Airlink	(714) 778-3141
Airport Transportation Information	(213) 646-5252
Airport (24-hour recording)	(818) AIRPORT
AMTRAK	(800) USA-RAIL
Art Center College of Design (ACCD)	(818) 584-5000
ACCD for "free" modeling photos	(818) 584-5111
ACCD For "free" résumé shots	(818) 584-5111
ACCD for student films	(818) 584-5125
Association of Visual Communicators	(818) 441-2274
Assoc. of Visual Communicators Hotline	(818) 905-4540
Back Stage	(213) 936-5200
The National Black Talent Guide	(213) 463-8033
Breakdown Services, Inc.	(213) 658-5684
Buses (RTD) (L.A.)	(213) 626-4455
Columbia College	(213) 851-0550
The Comedy Store	(213) 656-6225
Conference of Personal Managers	(213) 667-2888
Daily Variety	(213) 464-7411
Dept. Motor Vehicles (DMV)	(213) 271-4585
Dept. Water & Power (DWP) (electricity)	(213) 481-5411
Director's Guild of America (DGA)	(213) 656-1220
Disneyland	(714) 999-4565
Drama-Logue	(213) 464-5079
Larry Edmunds Bookshop (Hollywood)	(213) 463-3273
Larry Edmunds Bookshop (Studio City)	(818) 508-7511
Equity (AEA)	(213) 462-2334
Equity Hotline	(213) 462-8505

Samuel French's Bookshop (Hollywood)	(213) 876-0570
Samuel French's Bookshop (Studio City)	(818) 762-0535
Flyaway (Van Nuys)	(818) 994-5554
Info Line–Los Angeles	(213) 686-0950
Greyhound/Trailways	(800) 237-8211
Hanna-Barbera Studios (Andrea Romano)	(213) 851-5000
The Hollywood Reporter	(213) 464-7411
The Improvisation	(213) 651-2583
Independent Feature Project/West (IFP)	(213) 451-8075
Knotts Berry Farm	(714) 220-5200
La Brea Tar Pits	(213) 936-2230
Los Angeles Herald Examiner	(213) 744-8000
Los Angeles Times	(213) 237-5000
Magic Mountain	(805) 255-4111
The Oakwood	(800) 421-6654
Andrea Romano (at Hanna-Barbera)	(213) 851-5000
SAG	(213) 465-4600
SAG Affirmative Action	(213) 856-6821
SAG Agency Information	(213) 856-6737
SAG Conservatory (at AFI)	(213) 856-7600
SAG Dental (Traveler's Ins. Co.)	(800) 245-4557
SAG Film Society	(213) 856-6655
SAG Hotline	(213) 461-1023
SAG New Membership	(213) 856-6750
SAG Pension & Welfare	(818) 954-9400
SAG Residuals	(213) 856-6700
SAG, specific voice-over agents	(213) 856-6739
SEG	(213) 851-4301
Southern Calif. Gas Company	(213) 390-7983
Hollywood Stuntmen Association	(818) 446-2268
UCLA	(213) 825-4321
Universal Studios Tour	(818) 508-9600
USC	(213) 743-2311
The Voicecaster (Bob Lloyd)	(818) 841-5300
Women in Film	(213) 463-6040
YMCA (Hollywood Branch)	(213) 874-6643

4 LISTS

1. Acting classes
2. Agents
3. Answering services
4. Bargains
5. Bookstores/newsstands
6. Equity theatres
7. Extra casting offices (union/no fee)
8. Photographers
9. Photographic print shops
10. Print shops (résumés, etc.)
11. Recommended reading
12. Showcases and cold reading workshops
13. Trade publications
14. Union branch offices
15. Videotaping services
16. Miscellaneous

1. ACTING CLASSES

There are scores more good ones than we have room to list.

COACHES/WORKSHOPS

A number of coaches and workshops have classes in more categories than are listed here.

- *Acting (general)*

Jeff Corey
(213) 456-3319

Paul Gleason
(213) 874-9967

Robert Hanley
(818) 907-6276

Milton Katselas
(213) 855-1556

M.K. Lewis
(213) 826-8118/394-2511

Tracy Roberts
(213) 271-2730

• *Cold reading*

Charles Conrad
(818) 846-9010

M.K. Lewis
(213) 826-8118/394-2511

Michael Shurtleff
(213) 469-8745

• *Commercials*

Pamela Campus
(213) 659-5013

Randy Kirby
(213) 469-5727

Beverly Long & Assocs.
(213) 466-0770

Bobbi Morris
(213) 278-1030

Tepper-Gallegos
(213) 469-3577

• *Dance*

Dupree Dance Academy
(213) 655-0336

Stanley Holden Dance Center
(213) 475-1725

Steven Peck Studios
(213) 837-3775

• *Dialects*

Robert Easton
(213) 463-4811

George Gilbert
(213) 463-3586

David Alan Stern (Ph.D)
(213) 467-7301

• *Extension courses*

Contemporary Concepts
(213) 276-2000

The Learning Annex
(213) 478-6677

Learning Tree University
(818) 882-5599

UCLA
(213) 825-8895

USC
(213) 743-4343

- *Film technique*

    Jackie Benton
    (213) 392-4229

    M.K. Lewis
    (213) 826-8118/394-2511

    David Macklin
    (213) 654-7044

    Mike Muscat
    The Reel Acting Workshop
    (818) 765-3747

- *Improvisation/comedy*

    The Groundlings
    (213) 934-4747

    L.A. Connection
    (818) 784-1868

    Harvey Lembeck
    Comedy Workshop
    (213) 271-2831

- *Musical theatre/opera*

    David Craig
    (213) 462-8448

American Center for Music
Theatre Training
(818) 792-0776
This used to be the
music theatre workshop
of the Los Angeles
Civic Light Opera.

- *Savvy/seminars*

    Actors Center of Los Angeles
    (818) 505-9400

    M.K. Lewis' Hollywood
    Actors Survival Seminar
    (213) 826-8118/394-2511

    Beverly Hills Bar Assn.
    Actors Symposium
    (Every 4 years; watch for ads)

    Professional Artists Group, Inc.
    (213) 871-2222

- *Vocal*

    Natalie Limonick
    (213) 934-7472

    Harper MacKay
    (213) 851-3193

Carlos Noble
(213) 876-9618

Giorgio Tozzi
(602) 998-4962
The above number is
in Scottsdale, Arizona;
however, Mr. Tozzi
teaches in Los Angeles.

- *Voice-overs*

Louise Chamis
(818) 985-0130

Andrea Romano
(213) 462-4318

Dave Sebastian Williams
(213) 960-7833

OTHER ACTING WORKSHOPS

There are many other well-known acting coaches and workshops in L.A., including Actors Center of Los Angeles, Stella Adler (commutes from New York once or twice yearly), American Theatre Arts, Joan Darling, Film Industry Workshops, Estelle Harman Studio, Gordon Hunt, Loft Studio (William Traylor), Jose Quintero, Professional Artists Group, George Shdanoff, Lee Strasberg Theatre Institute, Weist-Barron-Hill, etc.

COLLEGES/CONSERVATORIES

American Conservatory
Theatre (ACT)
450 Geary St.
San Francisco 94102
Degrees: MFA, Certificates

California Institute of the Arts
24700 McBean Pkwy.
Valencia 91355
BFA, MFA, Certificates

Los Angeles City College
855 N. Vermont Ave.
Los Angeles 90029
AA, Certificates

Loyola Marymount
Loyola Blvd. at W. 80th
Los Angeles, 90045
BA (MA in film only)

Pacific Conservatory for the
Performing Arts/Solvang
P.O. Box 1700
Santa Maria 93456
Certificates

South Coast Repertory Theatre
P.O. Box 2197
Costa Mesa 92626
Certificates

University of California,
Los Angeles (UCLA)
308 Westwood Blvd.
Los Angeles, CA 90024
BA, MA, MFA, Ph.D

University of Southern California
(USC)
University Park
Los Angeles 90007
BA, BFA, MFA

2. AGENTS

Below is a list of SAG-franchised actors' agents in the Los Angeles metropolitan area. We make no recommendations. Don't assume an agency not listed below is unfranchised until you've checked with SAG, as revisions are frequent.

CODE KEY:

Theatrical (Film/TV) = T
Commercial = C
Youngsters = Y (Usually, in addition to adults)
Equity-franchised = E

2 A Total Acting Experience, 6736 Laurel Cyn. Bl. #300, N. Hwd. 91606, (818) 765-7244 (TCYE)

Aaron, Sally, 5301 Laurel Cyn. Bl. #116, N. Hwd. 91607, (818) 980-6719 (TCE)

Abrams Artists & Assoc., 9200 Sunset Bl. #625, L.A. 90069, (213) 859-0625 (TE)

- Abrams-Rubaloff & Lawrence, 8075 W. 3rd, L.A. 90048, (213) 935-1700 (TCY)

Actors Group Agency, 8285 Sunset Bl. #2, L.A. 90069, (213) 650-2224 (T)

Agency, The, 10351 Santa Monica Bl. #211, L.A. 90025, (213) 551-3000 (T)

Agency for Creative Talent, 8500 Melrose Ave., L.A. 90048, (213) 657-5304 (TE)

Agency for Performing Arts, 9000 Sunset Bl. #315, L.A. 90069, (213) 273-0744 (TCE)

Aimee Entertainment, 13743 Victory Bl., Van Nuys 91401, (818) 994-9354 (T)

Alexander, Willard, 9229 Sunset Bl. #801, L.A. 90069, (213), 278-8220 (TCY)

All Talent Agency, 2437 E. Washington, Pasadena 91104, (818) 797-2422 (TCYE)

Alvardo, Carlos, 8820 Sunset Bl., L.A. 90069, (213) 652-0272 (TCY)

Amaral Agency, Pat, 10000 Riverside Dr. #11, Toluca Lake 91602, (818) 980-1013 (TC)

Ambiance Agency, 901 Dove St. #235, Newport Bch., 92660, (714) 720-7416 (TC)

Ambrosio/Mortimer, 9000 Sunset Bl. #900, L.A. 90069, (213) 274-4274 (TYE)

Amsel, Fred, 6310 San Vicente Bl. #407, L.A. 90048, (213) 939-1188 (TE)

Arnold, Maxine, 8350 Santa Monica Bl. #103, L.A. 90069, (213) 650-4999 (TC)

Arthur Assoc., Irvin, 9363 Wilshire Bl. #212, Beverly Hills 90210, (213) 278-5934 (TC)

Artistic Enterprises, Inc., 6290 Sunset Bl. #403, L.A. 90028, (213) 469-4555 (TC)

Artists Agency, 10000 Santa Monica Bl. #305, L.A. 90067, (213) 277-7779 (TE)

2 Artists First, Inc., 8230 Beverly Bl., L.A. 90048, (213) 653- 5640 (TCE)

Artists Group, Ltd., 1930 Century Park West #303, L.A. 90067, (213) 552-1100 (TYE)

Associated Talent Intl., 9744 Wilshire Bl. #312, B.H. 90212, (213) 271-4662 (TY)

Atkins & Assoc., 208 S. Beverly Bl. #8, B.H. 90212, (213) 271-5188 (TYE)

Atkins Talent Agency, Sonya, 1636 Cahuenga Bl. #203, L.A. 90028, (213) 469-7115 (TCY)

Badgley, McQueeney & Connor, 9229 Sunset Bl., L.A. 90069, (213) 278-9313 (TE)

2 Ball, Bobby, 6290 Sunset Bl. #304, L.A. 90028, (213) 465-7522 (TCE)

Barr, Rickey, 8350 Santa Monica Bl. #206A, L.A. 90069, (213) 650-8525 (TE)

Barskin Agency, 120 S. Victory Bl., Burbank 91502, (818) 848-5536 (T)

Bauer-Benedek Agency, 9255 Sunset Bl. #716, L.A. 90069, (213) 275-2421 (T)

Bauman, Hiller & Assoc., 9220 Sunset Bl. #202, L.A. 90069, (213) 271-5601 (TE)

Beakel & Debord, 10637 Burbank Bl., Burbank 91601, (818) 506-7615 (TE)

Belson & Klass, 211 S. Beverly Dr., B.H. 90210, (213) 274-9169 (T)

Benson, Lois J., 2221 W. Olive, Burbank 91502, (818) 849-5647 (T)

Berzon, Marian, 336 E. 17th, Costa Mesa 92627, (714) 631-5936 or (213) 207-5256 (TCY)

Bikoff, Yvette, 9255 Sunset Bl. #510, L.A. 90069, (213) 278-7490 (TE)

Blanchard, Nina, 7060 Hollywood Bl. #1010, L.A. 90028, (213) 462-7274 (C)

Bloom, J. Michael, 9200 Sunset Bl. #710, L.A. 90069, (213) 275-6800 (TCYE)

Borinstein-Bogart, 9100 Sunset Bl. #210, L.A. 90069, (213) 278-2555 (TE)

Bresler, Kelly & Assocs., 15760 Ventura Bl. #1730, Encino 91436, (818) 905-1155 (TE)

Brewis, Alex, 4721 Laurel Cyn. Bl. #211, N.Hwd. 91607, (818) 509-0831 (T)

Bridges Talent Agency, Jim, 1607 N. El Centro #22, L.A. 90028, (213) 874-3274 (TCY)

Brooke, Dunn & Oliver, 9165 Sunset Bl. #202, L.A. 90069, (213) 859-1405 (TE)

Burkett & Kear, 3100 Airway Ave. #113, Costa Mesa 92626, (714) 546-4166 (TCY)

Burton, Iris, 1450 Belfast Dr., L.A. 90069, (213) 652-0954 (TCY)

Bush & Ross Talents, 4942 Vineland Ave., N.Hwd. 91601, (818) 762-0096 (TCYE)

𝒵 C.L. Inc. (Cassell/Levy), 843 N. Sycamore Ave., L.A. 90038, (213) 461-3971 (C)

Calder Agency, 4150 Riverside Dr., Burbank 91505 (818) 845-7434 (T)

Camden Artists, 2121 Ave. of the Stars 90067, (213) 556-2022 (TE)

Career Artists Intl., 11030 Ventura Bl. #3, Studio City 91604, (818) 980-1315/ 980-1316 (T)

Carroll, William, 120 S. Victory Bl., Burbank 91502, (818) 848-9948 (TC)

Carter, Mary J., 6525 Sunset Bl., #502, L.A. 90028, (213) 467-2662 (TCYE)

𝓏 Castle-Hill, 11526 Burbank #3, N.Hwd. 91601, (818) 653-3535 (TCY)

Cavaleri & Assoc., 6605 Hollywood Bl. #220, L.A. 90028, (213) 461-2940 (TCYE)

Ceder, Paula, 8303 Melrose Ave. #3, L.A. 90069, (213) 273-8603 (T)

Century Artists, Ltd., 9744 Wilshire Bl. #308, B.H. 90212, (213) 273-4366 (TE)

Cereghetti Agency, 9538 Brighton Way, #327, B.H. 90212, (213) 278-0556 (TC)

Charter Management, 9000 Sunset Bl., L.A. 90069, (213) 278-1690 (TE)

Chasin Agency, 190 N. Canon #201, B.H. 90210, (213) 278-7505 (T)

Chiz, Terry, 5761 Whitnall Hwy. #E, N.Hwd. 91601, (818) 506-0994 (T)

Clark W. Randolph, 6464 Sunset Bl. #1050, L.A. 90028, (213) 465-7140 (TCY)

Clarke, Kathy, 2030 E. 4th #102, Santa Ana 92705, (714) 667-0222 (C)

CNA, 8721 Sunset Bl. #102, L.A. 90069, (213) 657-2063 (TCE)

Coast to Coast, 12711 Ventura Bl. #460, Studio City 91604, (818) 508-3434 (TCY)

Colton, Kingsley, 16661 Ventura Bl. #400, Encino 91436, (818) 788-6043 (T)

– Commercials Unltd. Inc., Sonjia W. Brandon's, 7461 Beverly Bl., L.A. 90036, (213) 937-2220 (TCY)

Contemporary Artists, 132 Lasky Dr., B.H. 90212, (213) 278-8250 (TCYE)

Coralie Jr., 4789 Vineland Ave. #100, N.Hwd. 91602, (818) 766-9501 (TCYE)

Cosden, Robert, 1680 N. Vine St., L.A. 90028, (213) 856-9000 (TCE)

Craig Agency, 8485 Melrose Pl. #E, L.A. 90069, (213) 655-0236 (TE)

𝓏 Creative Artists Agency, 1888 Century Park East #1400, L.A. 90067, (213) 277-4545 (TCY)

Cumber, Lil, 6515 Sunset Bl. #300A, L.A. 90028, (213) 469-1919 (TCYE)

– Cunningham, Escott & Dipene, 261 S. Robertson Bl., B.H. 90211, (213) 855-1700 (TCY)

Dade/Rosen/Schultz, 15010 Ventura Bl. #219, Sherman Oaks 91403, (818) 907-9877 (TE)

Diamond Artists, Ltd., 9200 Sunset Bl. #909, L.A. 90069, (213) 278-8146 (TE)

Dietrich Agency, 10850 Riverside Dr. #501, N.Hwd. 91602, (818) 985-4824 (T)

Douglass, Adie J., 4605 Lankershim #800, N.Hwd. 91602, (818) 763-3188 (TCY)

Eastwest Model Mgmt., 6922 Hollywood Bl. #302, L.A. 90028, (213) 463-7575 (TC)

Elias & Assoc., Thomas G., 23501 Park Sorrento #218, Calabasas 91302, (818) 888-4608 (TC)

Emerald Artists, 6565 Sunset Bl. #525, L.A. 90028, (213) 465-2974 (TC)

Exclusive Artists, 2501 W. Burbank #304, Burbank 91505, (818) 846-0262 (TE)

Farrell Talent Agency, Eileen, 10500 Magnolia Bl., N.Hwd. 91601, (818) 762-6994 (TCY)

Feature Players Agency, 4051 Radford Ave. #A, Studio City 91604, (818) 508-6691 (T)

Felber, William, 2126 Cahuenga Bl., L.A. 90068, (213) 466-7629 (TCY)

Film Artists Assoc., 470 N. San Vicente, L.A. 90048, (213) 651-1700 (TCYE)

First Artists, 427 N. Canon #203, B.H. 90210, (213) 276-7090

Flick East-West Talents, Inc., 6671 Sunset Bl. #1580, L.A. 90028, (213) 273-7666 (T)

Fontaine Agency, Judith, 7060 Hollywood Bl., L.A. 90028, (213) 467-6288 (C)

Fox, Beverly, 4655 Kingswell #203, L.A. 90027, (213) 661-6347 (TCY)

ㄴ Freed, Barry, 9255 Sunset Bl. #603, L.A. 90069, (213) 274-6898 (TCYE)

Frings Agency, Kurt, 139 S. Beverly Dr., B.H. 90212, (213) 277-1103 (TE)

Gage Group, The, 9229 Sunset Bl. #103, L.A. 90069, (213) 859-8777 (TE)

Garrett, Helen, 6525 Sunset Bl. #205, L.A. 90028, (213) 871-8707 (TCYE)

Garrick, Dale, 8831 Sunset Bl., L.A. 90069, (213) 657-2661

Geddes Agency, 8457 Melrose Pl. #200, L.A. 90069, (213) 651-2401 (T)

Gelff, Laya, 16000 Ventura Bl. #500, Encino 91436, (818) 906-0925 (T)

Gerard Talent Agency, Paul, 2918 Alta Vista Dr., Newport Bch. 92660, (714) 644-7950 (T)

Gerler, Don, 3575 Cahuenga Bl. West #252. L.A. 90068, (213) 850-3309 (TY)

Gerritsen Intl., 8721 Sunset Bl. #203, L.A. 90069, (213) 659-8414 (T)

Gersh Agency, Phil, 222 N. Canon Dr., B.H. 90210, (213) 274-6611 (TCYE)

Gibson, J. Carter, 9000 Sunset Bl. #811, L.A. 90069, (213) 274-8813 (T)

Gilly, Talent Agency, Georgia, 8721 Sunset Bl. #103, L.A. 90069, (213) 657-5660 (TE)

G.M.A., 1741 N. Ivar #119, L.A. 90028, (213) 466-7161

Gold, Harry Talent Agency, 12725 Ventura Bl. #E, Studio City 91604, (818) 769-5003 (TCYE)

Goldin Talent Agency, Sue, 6380 Wilshire Bl. #1600, L.A. 90048, (213) 852-1441 (TCYE)

Goldstein & Assoc., Allen, 15010 Ventura Bl. #234, Sherman Oaks 91403, (818) 905-7771 (TE)

Gores/Fields, 10100 Santa Monica Bl. #700, L.A. 90067, (213) 277-4400 (TE)

Gray, Joshua & Assoc., 6736 Laurel Cyn. #306, N.Hwd. 91606, (818) 982-2510 (TCE)

Gray, Stephen, 205 S. Beverly Dr. #210, B.H. 90210, (213) 276-7070 (TCY)

Greenvine Agency, 9021 Melrose Ave. #304, L.A. 90069, (213) 278-5800 (TE)

Gurian Agency, The, 920 S. Robertson Bl. #4, L.A. 90035, 550-0400

Hanzer Holdings, 415 N. Barrington Ave., L.A. 90049, (213) 476-3089 (TC)

Harris & Goldberg, 2121 Ave. of the Stars #950, L.A. 90067, (213) 553-5200 (TE)

Hart, Vaughn D., 200 N. Robertson Bl. #219, B.H. 90211, (213) 273-7887 (T)

ㄴ Hecht Agency, Beverly, 8949 Sunset Bl., L.A. 90069, (213) 278-3544 (TCY)

Henderson/Hogan Agency, 247 S. Beverly Dr., B.H. 90212, (213) 274-7815 (TE)

Hunter & Assoc., Ray, 1901 Ave. of the Stars #1774, L.A. 90067, (213) 277-8161 (C)

Int'l. Contemporary Artists, 19301 Ventura Bl. #203, Tarzana 91356, (818) 342-3618 (TCY)

ㄴ International Creative Mgmt., 8899 Beverly Bl., L.A. 90048, (213) 550-4000 (TCYE)

International Talent, 241 E. Angelino Ave., Burbank 91502, (818) 842-1204 (TCY)

Jackman & Taussig, 1815 Butler #120, L.A. 90025, (213) 478-6641 (TCY)

Jay, George, 6269 Selma Ave. #15, L.A. 90028, (213) 465-0232

J E Talent, 429 Santa Monica Bl. #640, Santa Monica 90401, (213) 394-4676 (TCY)

Jennings & Assoc., Tom, 427 N. Canon Dr. #205, B.H. 90210, (213) 274-5418 (T)

→ Joseph, Heldfond & Rix, 1717 N. Highland Ave. #414, L.A. 90028, (213) 466-9111 (CYE)

Joseph/Knight, 6331 Hollywood Bl. #1016, L.A. 90028, (213) 465-5474 (T)

Kaplan, Len, 439 S. La Cienega #210, L.A. 90048, (213) 274-8889 (TE)

Kelly-Blue, 1234 6th St. #204, S.M. 90401, (213) 395-3548 (T)

Kelman/Arletta, 7813 Sunset Bl. 90046, (213) 851-8822 (TCYE)

Kemp, Sharon, 9701 Wilshire Bl. #850, B.H. 90212, (213) 553-9486 (T)

Kerwin Agency, William, 1605 N. Cahuenga Bl. #202, L.A. 90028, (213) 469-5155 (TE)

Kjar, Tyler, 8961 Sunset Bl. #B, L.A. 90069, (213) 278-0912 (TCYE)

Kohner Inc., Paul, 9169 Sunset Bl., L.A. 90069, (213) 550-1060 (TE)

L.A. Artists, 10920 Wilshire Bl. #220, L.A. 90024, (213) 824-2444 (TYE)

L.A. Models, 8335 Sunset Bl., L.A. 90069, (213) 656-9572 (C)

L.A. Talent, 8335 Sunset Bl., L.A. 90069, (213) 656-3722 (TC)

Labelle Agency, El Paso Studio 110, Santa Barbara 93102, (805) 965-4575 (TCY)

Lane, Stacy, 13455 Ventura Bl. #223, Sherman Oaks 91423, (818) 501-2668 (TCY)

Lani Talent Agency, Moya, 1589 East Date St., San Bernadino 92412, (714) 882-5215 (TCY)

Lantz Office Inc. The, 9255 Sunset Bl. #505, L.A. 90069, (213) 858-1144 (TE)

LaRocca Talent Group, 3907 W. Alameda, Burbank 91505, (818) 941-8000 (TY)

Lawrence Agency, 3575 Cahuenga Bl. West #125, L.A. 90028, (213) 851-7711 (TY)

Lawrence, Fred & Assoc., 9044 Melrose Ave., L.A. 90069, (213) 273-5255 (T)

Leading Artists, 445 N. Bedford, B.H. 90210, (213) 858-1999 (T)

Levin Assoc., Mark, 1341 Ocean, Santa Monica 90401, (213) 458-9965 (TCE)

Levin, Sid, 1680 N. Vine St. #821, L.A. 90028, (213) 461-4789 (TC)

Liberty, Glennis Agency, 10845 Lindbrook Ave. #203A, L.A. 90024, (213) 824-7937 (TC)

Lichtman, Terry, 12456 Ventura Bl. #1, Studio City 91604, (818) 761-4808 (T)

Light, Gordon, Rosson Co., 901 Bringham Ave., L.A. 90049 826-2230 (TCYE)

Lloyd Talent Agency, Johnny, 6404 Hollywood Bl. #219, L.A. 90028, (213) 464-2738

Lockwood Agency, The, 9777 Wilshire Bl. #707, B.H. 90212, (213) 824-3396 (TY)

Loo Agency, Bessie, 8235 Santa Monica Bl. #202, L.A. 90046, (213) 650-1300 (TCYE)

Lovell & Assoc., 1350 N. Highland Ave., L.A. 90028, (213) 462-1672 (TE)

Lynne & Reilly, 6290 Sunset Bl. #326, L.A. 90028, (213) 461-2828 (TCY)

Marie's Modeling & Talent Agency, Linda, 6472 Santa Monica Bl. #206, L.A. 90028, (213) 465-3218 (TCY)

Maris Agency, 17620 Sherman Way #8, Van Nuys 91406, (818) 708-2493 (T)

Marshak, Wyckoff & Assoc., 280 S. Beverly Dr. #400 B.H. 90212, (213) 278-7222 (T)

Marshall Agency, 2330 Westwood Bl. #203, L.A. 90064, (213) 272-1290 (T)

Marshall, Alese Model & Coml., 24050 Vista Montana, Torrance 90505, (213) 378-1223 (TCY)

Martel Agency, 7813 Sunset Bl., L.A. 90046, (213) 874-8131 (TCE)

M.A.X., 9230 Olympic Bl. #203, B.H. 90212, (213) 550-8858 (TCY)

Maxine's Talent Agency, 4830 Encino Ave., Encino 91316, (818) 986-2946 (TC)

McCartt-Oreck-Barrett, 10390 Santa Monica Bl. #300, L.A. 90025, (213) 553-2600 (TCE)

McHugh Agency, James, 8150 Beverly Bl. #303, L.A. 90048, (213) 651-2770 (TCE)

McMillan, Hazel, 126 N. Doheny, B.H. 90211, (213) 276-9823 (TCY)

Media Artists Group, 6255 Sunset Bl. 90028, (213) 463-5610 (TCY)

M.E.W. Inc., 151 San Vicente, B.H. 90211, (213) 653-4731 (TCY)

MGA/Mary Grady, 150 E. Olive Ave. #111, Burbank 91502, (818) 843-1511 (TCYE)

Miller, Lee, 5000 Lankershim #5, N.Hwd. 91601, (818) 505-0077 (T)

Minkoff Agency, The, 12001 Ventura Place, Suite 335, Studio City 91604, (818) 760-4501 (T)

Mishkin Agency, 2355 Benedict Cyn, B.H. 90210, (213) 274-5261 (TE)

Mitchell, F. Sterling, 1718 N. La Brea 90046, (213) 203-0738 (TCY)

Morris, William, 151 El Camino Dr., B.H. 90212, (213) 274-7451 (TCYE)

Moss Agency, Burton, 113 San Vicente Bl. #202, B.H. 90211, (213) 655-1156 (TE)

Moss & Assoc., H. David, 8019 1/2 Melrose #3, L.A. 90046, (213) 653-2900 (TE)

Murphy Talent Agency, Mary, 12001 Ventura Pl. #304, Studio City 91604, (818) 506-3874

My Talent Agency, 1806 Wright St., Pomona 91777, (714) 622-8228 (TCY)

Nathe, Susan & Assoc., C.P.C., 121 N. Robertson Bl. #B, B.H. 90211, (213) 659-6671 (TC)

New World Artists, 200 N. Robertson Bl. #308, B.H. 90210 (213) 276-2494 (TCY)

Pacific Artists, 515 N. La Cienega Bl., L.A. 90048, (213) 657-5990 (TC)

Perillo Talent Agency, Victor, 9229 Sunset Bl. #611, L.A. 90069, (213) 278-0251 (TE)

Prescott, Guy, 8920 Wonderland Ave., L.A. 90046, (213) 656-1963 (T)

Prima Model Mgmt, Inc., 832 N. La Brea Ave., L.A. 90038, (213) 465-8511 (TCY)

Privilege Talent, 8344 Beverly Bl., L.A. 90048, (213) 658-8781 (TC)

Progressive Artists, 400 So. Beverly Dr., B.H. 90212, (213) 553-8561 (TE)

Rainford Agency, 7471 Melrose #14, L.A. 90046, (213) 655-1404 (T)

Raison Agency, Ltd., Robert, 10000 Washington Bl. #400, Culver City 90232, (213) 475-3253 (T)

Rappa Agency, Ray, 7471 Melrose Ave. #11, L.A. 90046, (213) 653-7000 (T)

Rispoi, Gina, 16042 Ventura Bl. #203, Encino 91316, (818) 784-1120 (TCY)

Rose Agency, Jack, 6430 Sunset Bl. 90028, (213) 463-7300 (TCYE)

Rosson Agency, Natalie, 11712 Moorpark St. #205B, Studio City 91604, (818) 508-1445 (TCY)

Rothberg, Howard & Assoc., 3060 Greentree Ct., L.A. 90077 (213) 858-3000 (TC)

Sanders Agency, The, 721 N. La Brea Ave., #200, L.A. 90038, (213) 938-9113 (TCE)

Savage Agency, The, 6212 Banner Ave. 90038 L.A. (213) 461-8316 (TCE)

Scagnetti Talent Agency, Jack, 5330 Lankershim Bl. #210 N.Hwd. 91601, (818) 762-3871 (TC)

Schaefer, Peggy, 10850 Riverside Dr. N.Hwd. 91602, (818) 985-5547 (C)

Schallert Enterprises, 9350 Wilshire Bl. #214, B.H. 90212, (213) 276-2044 (T)

Schechter Co., Irv., 9300 Wilshire Bl. #410, B.H. 90212, (213) 278-8070 (TE)

Schiowitz & Assoc., 7080 Hollywood Bl. #720, L.A. 90028, (213) 461-0152 (TE)

Schnarr, Sandie, 121 N. Robertson Bl. #B, B.H. 90211, (213) 855-1722 (C)

Schut Agency, Booh, 11350 Ventura Bl. #206, Studio City 91604, (818) 760-6669 (TCY)

Schwartz & Assoc., Don, 8749 Sunset Bl., L.A. 90069, (213) 657-8910 (TCYE)

Screen Children's Agency, 12444 Ventura Bl., Studio City 91604, (818) 985-6131 (TCY)

Sekura, John/A Talent Agency, 7469 Melrose Ave. #30, L.A. 90046, (213) 653-5005 (TE)

Selected Artists Agency, 13111 Ventura Bl. #204, Studio City 91604, (818) 877-0055 (TCE)

Shapira & Assoc., David 15301 Ventura Bl. #345, Sherman Oaks, 91403, (818) 906-0322 (TCE)

Sherrell Agency, Ltd., Lew, 7060 Hollywood Bl. 90028, (213) 461-9955 (TC)

Shiffrin Artists, Inc., 7466 Beverly Bl. #205, L.A. 90036, (213) 937-3937 (TE)

Shreve Artists Manager, Dorothy, 729 W. 16th, Costa Mesa 92627, (714) 642-3050 (TCY)

Shumaker Agency, The, 6533 Hollywood Bl. #301, L.A. 90028, (213) 464-0745 (TCYE)

Sidell Canavan Agency, 11530 Sunset Bl., L.A. 90049 (213) 472-5205 (TCY)

Smith-Freedman & Assoc., 121 N. San Vicente Bl., B.H. 90211, (213) 852-4777 (TYE)

Special Artists Agency, 8730 Sunset Bl. #400, L.A. 90069, (213) 855-1803 (C)

St. Louis, Dolores, 12021 Magnolia Bl. #102, N.Hwd. 91607, (818) 762-8422 (TC)

Star Talent, 17502 Parthenia, Northridge 91325, (818) 701-7471 (CY)

Starwil Talent, 6565 Sunset Bl., L.A. 90028, (213) 874-1239 (TCY)

STE Representation, Ltd., 9301 Wilshire Bl. #312, B.H. 90210 550-3982 (TCE)

Stern Agency, Charles H., 9220 Sunset Bl., L.A. 90069, (213) 273-6890 (TC)

Stone-Manners, 9113 Sunset Bl., L.A. 90069, (213) 275-9599 (T)

Strand, Winifred, 439 S. La Cienega #117, L.A. 90048, (213) 278-1561 (TCE)

Striemer & Co., 2040 Ave. of the Stars, 4th Fl., L.A. 90067, (213) 556-3137 (TE)

Sturdivant & Assoc., 3050 W. 7th, L.A. 90005, (213) 382-8483 (TCY)

Sutton, Barth & Vennari, Inc., 8322 Beverly Bl., L.A. 90048, (213) 653-8322 (CYE)

Talent Bank, 1617 N. El Centro Ave. #9, L.A. 90028, (213) 466-5983 (TCY)

Talent Enterprises, 1607 N. El Centro #2, L.A. 90028, (213) 462-0913 (TC)

Talent Group, Inc., 9250 Wilshire Bl., B.H. 90212, (213) 273-9559 (CY)

Talent Network Intl., 9000 Sunset Bl. #807, L.A. 90069, (213) 271-8048

Tannen & Assoc., Herb, 6640 Sunset Bl., L.A. 90028, (213) 466-6191 (TCY)

Thompson, Willie, 6381 Hollywood Bl. #450, L.A. 90028, (213) 461-6594 (TCY)

Thornton & Assoc., Arlene, 5757 Wilshire Bl. #493, L.A. 90036, (213) 939-5757 (C)

Tisherman Agency, 6767 Forest Lawn Dr., L.A. 90028, (213) 850-6767 (TCY)

Tobias & Assoc., 1901 Ave. of the Stars #840, L.A. 90067, (213) 277-6211 (TE)

Tolbert Booking, 6363 Sunset Bl. #530, L.A. 90028, (213) 469-8859 (TCY)

Triad Artists, 10100 Santa Monica Bl. 16th Flr., L.A. 90067, (213) 556-2727 (TCE)

Turtle Agency, The, 15010 Ventura Bl. #219A, Sherman Oaks 91403, (818) 907-9892 (TY)

Twentieth Century Artists, 3800 Barham Bl. #303, L.A. 90028, (213) 850-5516 (TYE)

V.A.M.P., 713 E. La Loma Ave. Office 1, Camarillo 93010, (805) 485-2001 (TCY)

Vaughn Agency, 9155 Sunset #7, L.A. 90069, (213) 273-9544 (CY)

Vivid Intl., 3575 Cahuenga Bl. W. #240, L.A. 90028, (213) 850-3340

Wain Agency, Erika, 1418 N. Highland Ave. #102, L.A. 90028, (213) 460-4224 (T)

Wallack & Assoc., 1717 N. Highland Ave. #701, L.A. 90028, (213) 465-8004 (TCY)

Waugh, Ann, 4731 Laurel Cyn Rd. #5, N.Hwd. 91607, (818) 980-0141 (TE)

Webb Ent. Inc., Ruth, 7500 Devista Dr., L.A. 90046, (213) 874-1700 (TCYE)

Wilder Agency, The, 3151 Cahuenga Bl. West #310, L.A. 90028, (213) 969-9641 (TC)

⟵ Wilhelmina Artists' Reps. Inc., 6430 Sunset Bl. #701, L.A. 90028, (213) 464-8577 (TCE)

Wilmar Talent, 14329 Victory Bl., Van Nuys 91401, (818) 781-8539 (T)

Wilson Agency, Shirley, 291 S. La Cienega Bl. #306, B.H. 90211, (213) 659-7030 (TCY)

Witzer, Ted, 1900 Ave. of the Stars #2850, L.A. 90067, (213) 552-9521 (TCE)

Wright Talent Agency, Carter, 6533 Hollywood Bl., L.A. 90028, (213) 469-0944 (TCE)

Writers & Artists Agency, 11726 San Vicente Bl. #300, L.A. 90049, (213) 820-2240 (TCE)

Wunsch/Ostroff, 9200 Sunset Bl. #212, L.A. 90069, (213) 278-1955 (TC)

Yanez Talent Agency, Bob, 1607 N. El Centro Ave. #23, L.A. 90028, (213) 461-0298 (TCY)

Zadeh & Assoc., Stella, 11759 Iowa Ave., L.A. 90025, (213) 207-4114 (T)

Zolton Talent, 1636 Cahuenga Bl. #206, L.A. 90028, (213) 871-0190 (TCY)

3. ANSWERING SERVICES

A Better Connection
(213) 462-2200

Actorfone West
(213) 462-6565

Nationwide Paging
(800) USA-BEEP

4. BARGAINS

- *Guides to bargains*

  Glad Rags II
  (women's clothing)
  Leigh Charlton &
  Annette Swanberg

  *Guide to the Los Angeles
  Garment District*
  Barbara Moe

  L.A. Weekly (newspaper)
  Los Angeles and Valley editions;
  lots of ads for bargains.

  The Recycler
  Weekly classified newspaper,
  published every Thursday.

- *Clothing*

Garment District, downtown, roughly bordered by 7th St. on the north, the Santa Monica Fwy. (I-10) on the south, Broadway on the west, Maple Ave. on the east. S. Los Angeles is its "main street." Parking, however, is no bargain.

The Cooper Building
860 S. Los Angeles St.,
Garment Dist.
Seven floors of discount shops.

Loehmann's
6220 W. Third St., L.A./
other locations
(213) 933-5675
Women's wear

The Re-Take Room
3953 Laurel Grove Ave.,
Studio City
(818) 508-7762
Men's & women's wear
from studio wardrobe
departments.

- *General merchandise*

Adray's
5575 Wilshire Bl., L.A./
other locations
(213) 935-8191

Circuit City
1839 S. La Cienega Bl., L.A./
other locations
(213) 280-0700
Appliances & electronics.

Fedco Inc.
3535 S. La Cienega Bl., L.A.
(213) 837-4481
14920 Raymer, Van Nuys
(818) 786-6863

Federated
7050 W. Sunset Bl., Hwd./
other locations
(213) 871-0895
Electronics.

Pic 'N' Save
1341 Vine St., Hwd.
(213) 464-3505

The Slauson Home Club
4925 W. Slauson Ave.
(213) 298-1155

5. BOOKSTORES/NEWSSTANDS

- *Bookstores*

Samuel French's Theatre
& Film Bookshops
7623 Sunset Bl., Hollywood
(213) 876-0570
11963 Ventura Bl., Studio City
(818) 762-0535
Toll-free, California:
(800) 7-ACT NOW
Toll-free, U.S.:
(800) 8-ACT NOW

Larry Edmunds Bookshops
6658 Hollywood Bl., Hollywood
(213) 463-3273
11969 Ventura Bl., Studio City
(818) 508-7511

The Collectors Bookstore
1708 N. Vine St., Hollywood
(213) 467-3296

Movie World
212 N. Golden Mall, Burbank
(818) 846-0459

- *Newsstands*

Al's Newsstand
370 N. Fairfax Ave., L.A.
(213) 935-8525

Universal News Agency
1655 N. Las Palmas Ave., Hwd.
(213) 467-3850

Centerfold Newsstand
716 N. Fairfax Ave., L.A.
(213) 651-4822

Victory Bl. Newsstand
Victory & Van Nuys Bls.,
Van Nuys
(818) 782-2446

Sherman Oaks Newsstand
Van Nuys & Ventura Bls.,
Sherman Oaks
(818) 995-0632

World Book & News Co.
1652 Cahuenga Bl., Hwd.
(213) 465-4352

6. EQUITY THEATRES

EQUITY DINNER THEATRES

Category 1: $250
Category 2: $270.50
Category 3: $309

Category 4: $380
Category 5: $394.50

Harlequin Dinner Playhouse
3503 S. Harbor Bl.
Santa Ana, CA 92704
(714) 979-7550
Category 4

Lawrence Welk Village Theatre*
8845 Lawrence Welk Dr.
Escondido, CA 92026
(619) 749-3000
Category 3

The Grand Dinner Theatre*
Grand Hotel — One Hotel Way
Anaheim, CA 92802
(714) 772-7710
Category 4

*Member, American Dinner Theatre Institute

LEAGUE OF RESIDENT THEATRES (LORT CONTRACT)

"A" size house: $442   *"C" size house: $399*
"B+" size house: $431   *"D" size house: $364*
"B" size house: $420   *"Experimental": $261*

American Conservatory Theatre
450 Geary St.
San Francisco, CA 94102
(415) 771-3880
"A" house

Berkeley Repertory Theatre
2025 Addison St.
Berkeley, CA 94704
(415) 841-6108
"C" house

Berkeley Shakespeare Festival
Box 969
Berkeley, CA 94701
(415) 548-4322
"D" house

California Musical Theatre
30 N. Raymond Ave., Ste. 608
Pasadena, CA 91103
(818) 792-8672
"B" house

La Jolla Playhouse
P.O. Box 12039
La Jolla, CA 92037
(619) 452-6760
Two houses, "B/C" & "D"
Submit photos/résumés to:
Pagano/Bialy, 1680 N. Vine St.,
Ste.904, Hwd. 90028 (L.A.) or
Stanley Soble, 1776 Broadway,
Ste. 503, N.Y. 10019 (N.Y.)

L.A. Theatre Center
514 S. Spring St.
Los Angeles, CA 90013
(213) 627-6500
Three "D" houses

Old Globe Theatre
Balboa Park
P.O. Box 2171
San Diego, CA 92112
(619) 231-1941
Three houses, "B+", "B" & "C"

Pasadena Playhouse
39 S. El Molino
Pasadena, CA 91101
(818) 792-8672
"B" house

San Diego Repertory Theatre
at the Lyceum
79 Horton Plaza
San Diego, CA 92101
(619) 231-3586
"D" house

San Jose Repertory Theatre
Box 2399
San Jose, CA 95109-2399
(408) 294-7572
"C" house

Santa Barbara Theatre Festival
E. Canon Perdido St.
Santa Barbara, CA 93101
(805) 963-0761
"B" house

South Coast Repertory Theatre
655 Town Center Dr.
P.O.Box 2197
Costa Mesa, CA 92626
(714) 957-2602
Two houses, "B" & "D"

Mark Taper Forum
L.A. Music Center
135 N. Grand Ave.
Los Angeles, CA 90012
(213) 972-7384
Two houses, "A" & "Exp."

EQUITY STOCK

La Mirada Civic Theatre
14900 La Mirada Bl.
La Mirada, CA 90637
(714) 994-6310
Non-resident dramatic stock
(COST) & indoor musical
stock (small): $408.81

Sacramento Music Circus
P.O. Box 2347
Sacramento, CA 95811
(916) 446-5880
Resident musical: $459.63

7. EXTRA CASTING OFFICES (UNION/NO FEE)

Cast & Crew
4201 W. Burbank Bl., Burbank
(818) 848-0906

Central Casting
2600 W. Olive St., Burbank
(818) 569-5200

Disc Casting
3601 W. Olive St., Burbank
(818) 841-0687

Intercontinental Casting Inc.
8489 W. Third St., #1008, L.A.
(213) 651-4365

L.A. Casting
2000 W. Magnolia Bl., #209, Burbank
(818) 766-2296

Producers Casting Agency
P.O. Box 1527,
Pacific Palisades 90272
(213) 459-0229

8. PHOTOGRAPHERS

Ray Bengston	Kevyn Major Howard	John Sanchez
(818) 506-6868	(213) 662-5611	(213) 399-5544
Charles Fretzin	Tama Rothschild	Herb Weil
(818) 966-1600	(213) 658-7862	(213) 874-8492
John Gibson	Buddy Rosenberg	Dick Wieand
(213) 666-6238	(213) 464-9475	(818) 785-5995

9. PHOTOGRAPHIC PRINT SHOPS

Anderson Graphics
6037-45 Woodman Ave., Van Nuys
(818) 909-9100

Custom Print Shop
1759 N. Las Palmas, Hwd.
(213) 461-3001

Duplicate Photo Labs
1522 N. Highland Ave., Hwd.
(213) 466-7544
11969 Ventura Bl., Studio City
(818) 505-8595

Libbea Watkins Litho
152 N. La Brea Ave., Hwd.
(213) 936-4156

Prints Charm'n
8600 Melrose Ave., W. Hwd.
(213) 657-8600

Quality Custom Photo Lab
142 N. La Brea Ave., Hwd.
(213) 938-0174

10. PRINT SHOPS (RÉSUMÉS, ETC.)

Copy Mat
6301 Sunset Bl., Hwd.
(213) 461-1222
11988 Wilshire Bl., W. L.A.
(213) 207-5952
Hwd. location open 24 hrs.

Copy Spot, Inc.
712 Wilshire Bl., Santa Monica
(213) 393-0693

Kinko's Copies
13322 Burbank Bl., Van Nuys
(818) 787-7271
Open 24 hours.

Kwik-Kopy
3915 Riverside Dr., Burbank
(818) 843-2679
(213) 849-3278

11. RECOMMENDED READING

- *About L.A.*

  LA/Access
  Richard Saul Wurman

  The Best of L.A.
  L.A. Weekly Staff &
  Mary Beth Crain, Ed.

- *Acting*

  Acting Is Believing
  Charles McGaw

  *An Actor Prepares &
  Building a Character*
  Constantin Stanislavski

  Respect for Acting
  Uta Hagen

  Sanford Meisner on Acting
  Sanford Meisner &
  Dennis Longwell

- *Auditioning*

  Audition
  Michael Shurtleff

  Be a TV Game Show Winner!
  Marla Schram Schwartz

  How to Audition
  Gordon Hunt

  *How to Become a Game Show
  Contestant - An Insider's Guide*
  Greg Muntean &
  Gregg Silverman

- *Commercials/voice-overs*

  *Acting in Television
  Commercials*
  Squire Fridell

  *Acting in the
  Million Dollar Minute*
  Tom Logan

  Word of Mouth
  Susan Blu & Molly Ann Mullin

- *General insight*

  Actors on Acting
  Toby Cole, Helen Krich Chinoy,
  Eds.

  The Cool Fire
  Bob Shanks

  Final Cut
  Steven Bach

  Reel Power
  Mark Litwak

• *Others*

Body Language by Julius Fast; *How to Read a Person Like a Book*, Gerard I. Nierenberg; *Power of Positive Thinking*, Norman Vincent Peale; *Think and Grow Rich*, Napoleon Hill; *The 1988 What Color Is Your Parachute?*, Richard Nelson Bolles, and any book on salesmanship.

12. SHOWCASES & COLD READING WORKSHOPS

The Actors Center
of Los Angeles
11969 Ventura Bl., Studio City
(818) 505-9400
By audition.

The Cold Reading Workshop
1953 Cahuenga Bl., L.A.
(213) 464-0795
Particularly welcomes comics,
improv and crossover talent.
By recommendation.

One on One Productions
10761 Burbank, #7, N. Hwd.
(818) 761-6099
By audition.

Professional Artists Group, Inc.
845 N. Highland Ave., L.A.
(213) 871-2222
By audition.

**Note: For Studios see Studio Map,
Chapter 3.**

**For Theatres see Theatre
Map, Chapter 26.**

13. TRADE PUBLICATIONS

KEY: (N) = Newsstand sales   *(S)* = Subscription

Back Stage (N/S)
Subscriptions: P.O. Box 2078
Mahopac, NY 10541-9900

Daily Variety/
Weekly Variety (N/S)
1400 N. Cahuenga Blvd.
Los Angeles 90028
(213) 469-1141

Drama-Logue (N/S)
1456 N. Gordon St.
Los Angeles 90028
(213) 464-5079
Mailing: P.O. Box 38771
Los Angeles 90028-0771

Hollywood Reporter (N/S)
6715 Sunset Bl.
Hollywood 90028
(213) 464-7411

OTHER TRADES OF INTEREST

American Film (N/S)
American Premiere (N/S)
Broadcasting (S)
Casting Call (N/S)
Diallog (S) (AFTRA publication)
Screen Actor (S) (SAG publication)

SAG Newsletter (S)
 (SAG publication)
State of the Arts (S):
 California Arts Council
 1901 Broadway, Suite A,
 Sacramento 95818

14. UNION BRANCH OFFICES

ACTORS' EQUITY ASSOCIATION (AEA)
6430 Sunset Blvd.
Los Angeles, CA 90028
(213) 462-2334

165 W. 46th St.
New York, NY 10036
(212) 869-8530

MIDWESTERN:

203 N. Wabash Ave.
Chicago, IL 60601
(312) 641-0393

SAN FRANCISCO:

100 Bush St.
San Francisco, CA 94104
(415) 391-7510

THE AMERICAN FEDERATION OF TELEVISION AND RADIO ARTISTS
6922 Hollywood Bl.
Hollywood, CA 90028
(213) 461-8111

260 Madison Ave.
New York, NY 10016
(212) 265-7700

Excepting New York and L.A., SAG offices listed below also handle AFTRA. Call AFTRA or Information for AFTRA hotines in Cincinnati/Columbus/Dayton, Indianapolis, Kansas City, Louisville, New Orleans, Pittsburgh, Portland and Rochester.

AMERICAN GUILD OF MUSICAL ARTISTS

10859 Fruitland Dr., #10
Studio City, CA 91604
(818) 506-8883

1717 Broadway
New York, NY 10019
(212) 265-3687

Write New York office for list of AGMA branches nationwide.

AMERICAN GUILD OF VARIETY ARTISTS

4741 Laurel Canyon Bl., #028
North Hollywood, CA 91607
(818) 508-9984

184 Fifth Avenue
New York, NY 10010
(212) 675-1003

For regional offices, write AGVA in New York.

THE SCREEN ACTORS GUILD

7065 Hollywood Bl.
Hollywood, CA 90028
(213) 465-4600

1515 Broadway, 44th Fl.
New York, NY 10036
(212) 944-1030

ARIZONA:

5150 N. 16th St. #C-255
Phoenix, AZ 85016
(602) 279-9975

ATLANTA:

1627 Peachtree St. N.E., #210
Atlanta, GA 30309
(404) 897-1335

BOSTON:

11 Beacon St. #512
Boston, MA 02108
(617) 742-2688

CHICAGO:

307 N. Michigan Ave.
Chicago, IL 60601
(312) 372-8081

CLEVELAND:

1367 E. 6th St. #229
Cleveland, OH 44114
(216) 579-9305

DALLAS:

Two Dallas Communications Complex
6309 N. O'Connor Rd. #111-LB 25
Irving, TX 75039-3510
(214) 869-9400

DENVER:

950 S. Cherry St. #502
Denver, CO 80222
(303) 757-6226

DETROIT:

28690 Southfield Rd.
Lathrup Village, MI 48076
(313) 559-9540

FLORIDA:

145 Madeira Ave. #317
Coral Gables, FL 33134
(305) 444-7677

HAWAII:

949 Kapiolani Bl. #105
Honolulu, HI 96814
(808) 538-6122

HOUSTON:

2650 Fountainview #325
Houston, TX 77057
(713) 972-1806

MINNEAPOLIS/ST. PAUL:

15 S. 9th St. #485
Minneapolis, MN 55402
(612) 371-9120

NASHVILLE:

1108 17th Ave. South
Nashville, TN 37212
(615) 327-2958

PHILADELPHIA:

230 S. Broad St., 10th Fl.
Philadelphia, PA 19102
(215) 545-3150

ST. LOUIS:

906 Olive St. #1006
St. Louis, MO 63101
(314) 231-8410

SAN DIEGO:

3045 Rosecrans Ave. #308
San Diego, CA 92110
(619) 222-3996

SAN FRANCISCO:

100 Bush St., 16th Fl.
San Francisco, CA 94104
(415) 391-7510

SEATTLE:

601 Valley St., #200
Seattle, WA 98109
(206) 728-9999

WASH. D.C.:

The Highland House
5480 Wisconsin Ave. #201
Chevy Chase, MD 20815
(301) 657-2560

THE SCREEN EXTRAS GUILD

3629 Cahuenga Bl. West
Los Angeles, CA 90068
(213) 851-4301

HAWAII:

1127 Eleventh Ave., #205
Honolulu, HI 96816
(808) 737-2211

MIAMI:

1190 N.E. 125th St., #130
Miami, FL 33161
(305) 891-9714

SAN DIEGO:

3045 Rosencrans St., #308
San Diego, CA 92110
(619) 222-6059

SAN FRANCISCO:

100 Bush St.
San Francisco, CA 94104
(415) 391-7510

15. VIDEOTAPING SERVICES — "AIR CHECKS"

Angus Lake Productions
10859 Fruitland Dr., #10
Studio City, CA 91604
(818) 506-8883/8744

Jan's Video
1800 N. Argyle, Suite 300, Hwd.
(213) 462-5511

16. MISCELLANEOUS

Academy Players Directory
Academy of Motion Picture
Arts & Sciences
8949 Wilshire Bl., Beverly Hills 90211
(213) 278-8990

The American Film Institute
2021 N. Western Ave., Hwd. 90027
(213) 856-7600

Breakdown Services, Ltd.
8242 W. Third St., Ste. 250, L.A. 90048
(213) 658-5684

Greater L.A. Visitors &
Convention Bureau
505 S. Flower St., L.A. 90071
(213) 624-7300

Hollywood YMCA
1553 Hudson Ave., Hwd. 90028
(213) 467-4161

"The Voicecaster"
(Bob Lloyd)
3413 Cahuenga Bl. West, L.A. 90068
(213) 874-1933

5 "TYPICAL" TAX DEDUCTIONS OF THE PROFESSIONAL ACTOR

We're not accountants or attorneys, and we don't expect you to use this material in place of a good CPA. Nor do we claim that these deductions are written in concrete. With the tax changes Congress is making in recent years, it's possible that, by the time you read this, none of these deductions will still be valid. Remember too that all deductions — in fact, your entire tax return — depend on your circumstances.

While some of these items may be totally deductible (your union dues and initiation, for example), others (such as your phone bill) are partially deductible depending on how much of the expense/use is business-related. Once again, what those portions may be depend on your facts and circumstances.

Also, certain items, such as television sets, typewriters, etc., may be wholly deductible in one year or they may have to be "capitalized" over a period of years — that is, a portion of the expense will be deductible each year, say, for seven years. ("Capitalizing" may ultimately prove more beneficial to you anyway.)

Also, for performers there are special rules involving "above the line" versus "below the line" deductions that are simply too complicated to go into here. Your CPA can explain this to you.

Finally, all deductions are applicable only to the extent that the cost *exceeds* any reimbursements, and certain expenses may only be 80 percent deductible.

- *Admissions to plays and movies:* Save your ticket stubs.

- *Attorneys/legal fees:* Only if the work pertains to your acting career.

- *Auto expenses:* First, you'll need to estimate how much you use your car for business purposes. An example: You're going out to make the rounds of studios. The drive to the first stop is *not* tax-deductible — that's part of your "normal commute." However, each stop after that is business use and therefore deductible, until the last stop. From the last stop to home is *not* deductible — again, it's part of your commute.

    Here, too, keeping a daily dairy can come in mighty handy. At the end of the year, look through it and figure out your deduction, based on one of the following two methods:

    1. *The mileage method:* If you've got an older car, this is generally the best "tax break" way. Estimate the number of business miles you put on the car and multiply that figure times whatever the IRS is allowing

for business miles that year. That's your deduction. (The IRS will not ask for receipts.)

2. *The usage method:* If you have a newer car, this may be more beneficial than using the mileage method. Along with your daily dairy, keep receipts for everything — gas receipts, repair bills, insurance payments, etc. Add those receipts together and, using your daily diary, estimate the percentage of business use you put on the car. Take that percentage of your bills — that's your deduction.

- *Books:* As long as they pertain to the industry. *War and Peace*, no; *Your Film Acting Career*, yes.

- *Business gifts:* All gifts to agents, personal managers, etc., up to $25 per person per year.

- *Business meals:* This can be a picky area with the IRS. You'll need the receipt for the meal, a record of who was there, how that person or persons relate to your position in the industry, and, basically, what you talked about. Your daily diary can be worth its weight in gold here. If the meal was under $25, you don't have to have a receipt, but the IRS still will want to know why you deducted it. Be sure you can explain each and every deduction. (These expenses may only be 80 percent deductible.)

- *Classes:* Once established as an actor, classes that maintain or improve your skills as a professional actor are generally deductible.

- *Commissions:* paid to agents, personal managers, etc.

- *Hairstyling/haircuts:* As long as it's directly related to a role.

- *Industry parties:* Probably the most difficult area to get the IRS to approve as a deduction. Not only do you need to be able to prove that the party had a direct bearing on your position in the industry, but you will have to keep a guest list and be able to explain how those guests have a direct bearing on your career. A *very* touchy area.

- *Magazine and trade publications: Daily Variety, Hollywood Reporter, Drama-Logue,* etc., and any others as long as at least a portion of the publication pertains to the industry. If you buy these on the newsstands, get receipts and attach them to your daily dairy. If you don't, an auditor could disallow these deductions.

- *Mailing expenses:* Stamps, envelopes, labels, etc.

- *Makeup.*

- *Office supplies:* Typewriter, staples, writing paper, etc.

- *Phonograph records.*

- *Plays.*

- *Publicity materials:* Anything·that publicizes you as an actor. Presentation tapes, *Academy Players Directory* listing, postcards, ads in the trades, etc.

- *Résumés:* Typing, printing, and/or photocopying.

- *Résumé shots:* Session and printing costs.

- *Tapes.*

- *Telephone and related:* Your telephone bill, depending on how much it's used for business. Also answering devices and answering services.

- *Television and related:* The set itself, repairs, cable or pay TV, VCRs, videotapes, *TV Guide,* or other television magazines.

- *Union dues/initiations.*

- *Wardrobe:* See hairstyling.

- *Wardrobe maintenance:* See hairstyling.

...And anything else that is directly related to or associated with your profession. You'll need: receipts, a daily diary, and a good CPA (also see Chapter 30).

6 TV & FILM REGULATIONS

(This material is based on the current contract, which expires July 1, 1989.)

WARDROBE FITTINGS

First, for all actors, if the fitting is on the same day you work, there's no additional pay, but the hour(s) you spend being fitted count as part of your workday.

- *Day player, $600 or less:* If you're called in for a fitting you get a one-hour minimum payment. Stay beyond one hour, and you're paid for each additional 15-minute period.

  Be sure to get and sign a voucher (indicating time in and time out) from the costumer.

- *Day player, more than $600 per day:* Sorry, no additional pay for being called in.

- *Three-day contract, television only:* The producer can call you in for two hours' "free" fitting time on one day.

- *Free-lance weekly:* Producer can call you in for four hours' "free" fitting time on two days if it's a film and three hours' time on two days if it's a TV show.

The agent only gets a commission on fees for wardrobe fittings if you're making more than scale.

WARDROBE ALLOWANCE

For supplying your own wardrobe: $10 per outfit, $15 formal wear.
Your agent gets no commission.

MEAL PERIODS/PENALTIES

Meal periods (up to one hour) don't count as time worked. Your first meal break has to come six hours after you're called. (Six hours after returning to work from the first meal break, you must be given a second meal break.) If not, you're paid: $25 first half-hour, $35 second half-hour, $50 each half-hour thereafter.
Your agent gets no commission.

STUDIO/NEARBY LOCATION/OVERNIGHT LOCATION

- *Studio work:* That's working on a lot.

- *Nearby location:* Any place within a 30-mile radius of Beverly and La Cienega Boulevards (called the Hollywood Studio Zone) is a "nearby location." Either you'll report directly there or to the studio and be taken to the location by car or bus. In the former case, you're paid 30 cents per mile, based on the distance from the studio to the nearby location. If they're shooting next door you still must be paid as though you had driven from the studio to the location. Mileage can be paid in cash on the set or be included in your check.

  Your agent gets no commission.

- *Overnight location:* That's Georgia, Paris, Thailand, whatever. The producer must pay your transportation and your expenses (more later).

TRAVEL TIME/PAY

- *Studio:* Just like a regular job. You're paid nothing to get yourself there.

- *Nearby location:* If you're transported, the time spent traveling back and forth counts as a part of your day. If traveling takes you into overtime, it's paid at time-and-a-half.

- *Overnight location:* Depends on your contract:

  1. *Day player:* You get a full day's pay for traveling to the location and a full day's pay for returning.

  2. *Three-day contract $2,100 or less, TV only:* You go on salary the day you leave and remain on salary till the day you return.

  3. *Weekly player, $3,500 or less:* Same as 2.

  4. *Weekly player, over $3,500:* Get to the location within 24 hours and you'll go on salary when put "on call." However, you can't go on salary any later than 24 hours after reaching the location.

COMPUTING OVERTIME

Your work day starts at the time you were first called and ends when you're excused. (Meal breaks don't count.) Whether or not you're due overtime depends on your contract and, in some cases, whether you're at a studio or on an overnight location.

- *Day player, $900 or less:* Overtime starts on the ninth hour, at time-and-a-half for the ninth and tenth hours. After that, its double time. It's paid in "hourly units." That is, work 15 minutes overtime and you're paid for an entire hour.

- *Day player, more than $900:* Overtime starts on the ninth hour, but there's no double time. All overtime is time-and-a-half. Further, it's based on a maximum of $900 per day, regardless of how much more your salary might be. It's paid in hourly units.

- *Three-day player, $2,100 or less:* Overtime only starts after the tenth hour and goes immediately to double time, in hourly units. Also, if you work more than 24 hours (straight time) over the three days, you get overtime, at time-and-a-half, but it's computed in six-minute units.

- *Three-day player, more than $2,100:* Overtime starts after ten hours. It's paid in hourly units at double time, but will be based on $2,100 no matter how much more you may be making. Actually, that's $175 per hour.

- *Weekly/series players earning $3,500 or less, TV only:*

  1. *Studio week:* At a studio or a nearby location, your week is five days, 44 hours. If you work more than ten hours on any day, your overtime is paid in hourly units at double time. For two days, you may work up to ten hours without getting overtime. However, work more than eight hours on a third, fourth, and/or fifth day and you're paid overtime at time-and-a-half, in half-hour units, for the ninth and tenth hours. Past ten hours is double time, in hourly units.

  2. *Overnight location:* Your week is six days, 48 hours. Daily overtime is the same as a studio week. The longer week, however, requires the producer to pay a bonus four hours' overtime, whether you work those four hours or not. (That's the equivalent of a 44-hour week plus four hours' "automatic" overtime.) This "location premium" applies whether you work the full week or not.

- *Weekly player, $3,500 or less, movie work:* Work beyond ten hours a day is paid in hourly units at double time. Work beyond 44 hours in five days is paid in six-minute units at time-and-a-half. An overnight location workweek (six days) requires the producer to pay you four hours overtime, whether you work or not.

- *Weekly players, more than $3,500 films and TV:* Daily overtime is paid after ten hours, in hourly units, at double time figured on the basis of $3,500 (that's $159.10).

- *"Pro rata":* When you're on a three-day or weekly contract, that's what the producer is actually paying you per day. He'll use that figure to pay you if you work a day or more beyond what you've actually been contracted for.

Your agent gets a commission on overtime.

DROP AND PICK UP (DAY-PLAYER CONTRACT ONLY)

This option may be used only once, and can't used at all if you start out on a weekly contract.

Let's say you'll be needed on March 21, but not again until May 24. To avoid keeping you on the payroll, "drop and pick up" is employed. You'll work March 21 and be dropped until May 24. You must be given an exact "pick up" date and must go back on payroll on that date, regardless of whether they use you or not. Also, at least ten days must intervene from drop day to pick up day. They may pick you up on either a daily or a weekly contract.

REST PERIODS

- *Daily:* You must be given 12 hours of rest between workdays, with one exception: If you're working outdoors ("exterior photography"), rest period may be reduced to ten hours once every fourth consecutive day. No reduction is allowed on the first day, however.

- *Weekly:* Besides your daily rest periods, on a five-day week you must be given one weekly rest period of 58 hours. One exception: shooting at night, primarily exterior, that can be reduced to 56 hours as long as your call is not earlier than three P.M. and you're dismissed before midnight Friday.

   On a six-day location week, your weekly rest period is 36 hours.

   Violation of rest periods is called a "forced call." Penalty is one day's pay or $950, whichever is less.

   To find out if you're on a "forced call," check "Time Dismissed Studio" against your next call.

   Your agent gets no commission on rest period penalties.

EXPENSES

On an overnight location, you must be provided:

- First-class transportation (you fly first class).
- $100,000 travel insurance (by plane).
- $250,000 travel insurance (by helicopter).
- A private single room.

- Meal allowances (per diems) of: $8 breakfast, $12 lunch, $22 dinner. Total: $42. The producer may deduct any meals he supplies. If the location is expensive (Tokyo, London etc.), the producer must adjust per diems upward.

Agent gets no commission on any of above.

SIGNING OUT

When wrapped, the second assistant director will hand you either a time card or a production time report, with times written in under the following headings:

- Date Worked
- First Time Call
- Time Arrived Location
- Lunch
- Dinner
- Time Dismissed Location
- Time Dismissed Studio

Be sure all times entered are in ink and correct. If on a nearby location, be sure he's given you enough traveling time from location to studio.

GETTING PAID

- *Day player:* Check must be postmarked within five days after your last day of work.

- *All others:* You get your check no later than the studio payroll date (usually Thursday) of the following week.

Late-payment damages are $10 a day up to 20 days. Then, SAG will contact the producer by mail. If he fails to respond in five days, damages accrue at $2.50 per day.

Your agent gets no commission on late penalties.

GO GET YOUR MONEY — BUT USE COMMON SENSE

If your check is "light," go after what's coming to you. Explain it to your agent and have him call the accounting office or producer. If he's reluctant, do it yourself and think about changing agents. If there's a dispute, don't do battle alone — go to the union.

However, sometimes it's wise to back off: An actor's check was missing a one-hour fitting fee and a 45-minute meal-period violation. He called SAG and was assured he was due the money. Then, the actor called his agent, who, after checking said, "Look, they say the wardrobe fee was an 'oversight,' but they're getting *very* uptight about the meal penalty. If you want, I'll go after the meal penalty, but it just may make them angry enough never to hire you again." The actor swallowed and said, "Skip it."

If a producer is one day late with your check, don't start screaming, "I want my ten dollars in damages!" Use your head.

A NOTE ABOUT AFTRA SHOWS

If the program is run on network prime time the work rules are almost exactly the same. However, daytime soap operas, syndicated shows — anything not shown on network prime time — have different rules and pay scales for each type of show. Call AFTRA for further information.

As mentioned earlier, there's a movement toward merger with SAG, which would make things more uniform.

RESIDUALS

The producer is entitled to one run of the show. After that, you're into "subsequent runs" (re-runs). That's where residuals come in. What you're paid depends.

- *Television pictures, network prime time:* If your TV picture is re-run on network television between eight and eleven P.M. (that's "prime time"), you get 100 percent of your salary subject to "ceilings" (the most you can get):

Length of Show	Ceiling
½ hour	$1,600
1 hour	2,200
1½ hours	2,400
2 hours	2,600
2 hours+	3,000

- *TV, network, non-prime time:* If the TV picture is re-run on a network but not in prime time, you get a percentage of *what union scale was when you worked,* regardless of what you actually were paid. If you worked one week in 1988 and were paid $5,000, you'll get a percentage of $1,385 as that was union scale for a week in 1988.

- *Syndication:* When a show goes into syndication, it's usually shown on independent stations. Again you'll get a percentage of union scale at the time you worked, and the percentages are slightly smaller.

- *Feature films to TV/cable TV:* You want complicated? Boy, do we got complicated! The important thing is pointed out by Mark Locher, public relations director of SAG: "A lot of actors believe every time their film is shown on television, they'll get a payment. Not necessarily."

  Here, you get a percentage of your total salary when the producer's grosses hit certain plateaus. Now you could get SAG's latest figures on the producer's worldwide grosses, but then you'd have to know how to figure out how much of the percentage allotted to the entire cast is allotted to you. Just rely on SAG.

- *Foreign telecasts:* Occasionally you'll get small residual checks from a five-year-old show that's currently running in Zanzibar. The method of computing what you get is again too complicated to explain, but you won't get rich. (There's a bar in town that gives free drinks for silly residual checks. The record? One cent!)

- *Agents' commissions:* A theatrical agent gets a commission *only* on prime time network residuals of television shows. Nothing else.

- *When/how you're paid:* With network re-runs, the producer's got 30 days from air date to mail the check. In syndication, he's got up to four months. Foreign telecasts mean up to six months. Since residuals are first sent to the unions, add at least another two weeks for handling. Hold off on the party.

We've barely scratched the surface of items that affect your pocketbook. We simply chose the most common rules. Obtain the digests of rules and regulations of SAG, AFTRA, and Equity and read them. Your banker will love you for it.

7 COMMERCIAL REGULATIONS

(This material is based on the current contract, which expires February 6, 1991.)

WORKDAY AND OTHER RULES

The rules governing a workday in commercials are almost exactly the same as those of a day player earning $900 or less. One major difference: should the advertiser shoot more than one commercial on your workday, you must be paid an additional session fee for each additional commercial shot.

EXCLUSIVITY/HOLDING FEES (OTHER POINTS)

- Holding fees are due each 13-week anniversary of the day you shot the commercial. (These 13-week periods are called "fixed cycles." There are a maximum of seven during 21 months). The advertiser must send your "holding fee" within 12 working days of the beginning of each fixed cycle. If he fails to do this, his right of exclusivity is cancelled. (You don't need a release letter. However, have your agent call the advertiser just to be sure there haven't been any foul-ups.)

- You may permit the advertiser to later reinstate the commercial provided you haven't done a commercial for a competing company in the meantime. If you allow reinstatement, he must pay you a one-time double holding fee.

USE CYCLES

When a commercial first airs, that date starts what is called "use cycles." Therefore, if the advertiser airs the commercial, you'll have two different cycles running — a fixed cycle (for holding fees) and a use cycle (for "residuals" — use fees) and payments for each will be on different dates. However, the advertiser may credit only one holding fee against use fees in any fixed cycle.

USE FEES ("RESIDUALS")

- *Program usage commercial:* The commercial is shown on "interconnecting stations." You're paid each time it airs. Payments must be sent within 15 working days of the end of each week the commercial runs. What you're paid depends on whether the commercial is a Class A, B, or C:

Class A: It airs in more than 20 cities.

Class B: It airs in six to 20 cities

Class C: It airs in one to five cities.

- *Dealer commercials:* You're paid a flat fee that entitles the dealer to unlimited use of that commercial for *six months.* The fee depends on whether the commercial is a "Type A" (dealership is *not* owned by the manufacturer of the product) or "Type B" (dealership *is* owned by the manufacturer of the product) and where the commercial is shown.

  Your contract must stipulate that the commercial is to be used as a "dealer commercial" (as well as "test commercial" or a "seasonal commercial" — see below). In the upper- right-hand corner you'll see various boxes to be checked off telling you if that's the case. Farther down, there's another box to check if you don't consent.

- *Test commercials:* Your contract must stipulate you're doing a "test," and you must be told that *at your audition.*

  Since use fees are small, your agent probably will negotiate an "over-scale" session fee. Instead of the usual $366.60 payment, he'll try to get you say, $600 — and will try to negotiate the payment of that $600 every 13 weeks as your "holding fee."

  Usually you're released in the first 13 to 26 weeks or the commercial goes national, but in actuality one of three things can happen:

  1. The advertiser tests the commercial, decides he hates it and drops it. You're released.

  2. The advertiser continues to pay your holding fee every 13 weeks, keeping you exclusive for the maximum-use period of 21 months. (He may or may not use or decide to go national with it.) Sometimes your agent will negotiate a deal that gives you a guaranteed cut-off date prior to 21 months.

  3. The advertiser loves the commercial and goes national with it (called a "rollout"). It might then even go to program usage and wild spot.

- *Seasonal commercials:* This kind of commercial may only be used for 13 to 15 weeks. The advertiser may opt to pay you an additional holding fee and, the following year, reuse the commercial for one more cycle of 13 weeks. (That holding fee may not be applied against use.) After that, the advertiser may not use the commercial again without your permission.

AGENT'S COMMISSION

Your commercial agent gets 10 percent commission on all session, holding, and use fees for the first 21 months. Then he must notify the advertiser (sometime between 120 to 60 days before the end of the maximum period of use) that the commercial is coming up for renegotiation. If he fails to do this, the commercial can automatically go into a second 21-month period with no change in terms. Should that occur, your agent no longer has a right to a commission.

If he wishes to continue to get his 10 percent, the agent must renegotiate the terms of that commercial to above scale — at least "scale plus ten" (percent). You, of course, have the right to accept or reject any terms or simply say no to any deal.

8 AGENCY CONTRACTS

THEATRICAL

You'll sign three different contracts (three copies of each):

1. *Television Motion Picture Talent Agency Contract:* Covers his representation of you in films made for TV. (We'll call this SAG-TV.)

2. *Theatrical Motion Picture Artists Manager Contract (Agency Contract):* Covers his representation of you in movies. (We'll call this SAG-Film.)

3. *Standard AFTRA Exclusive Agency Contract Under Rule 12- B:* Covers his representation of you for taped TV shows and radio — not commercials. (We'll call this AFTRA.)

All three contracts are standard, with no "fine print." They protect you and the agent. Provisions in one contract are often similar to provisions in the others, although they may be found in different places.

Nonetheless, carefully read any contract. We're not attorneys, and we haven't the space to go into each contract point. Also, these contracts can change.

TOP OF THE CONTRACTS

At the beginning of all three contracts, you'll find:

This Agreement, made and entered at ___(LOS ANGELES)___ by and between __(NAME OF THE AGENCY)__ , hereinafter called the "AGENT" and ____(YOUR NAME)____ , Social Security No. ___(YOUR SS#)___

TERM OF CONTRACT

Also on page one of all three contracts — Paragraph (2) SAG-TV and SAG-Film; Paragraph (3), AFTRA:

The term of this contract shall be for a period of ___(ONE YEAR)___ , commencing the ___(DAY OF MONTH)___ day of ___(MONTH)___ , 19 ___(YEAR)___ .

Your agent can't ask you to initially sign for longer than a year. Later, he may want you to sign for three years.

10 PERCENT PROVISION

On the first page of all three contracts — Paragraph (3), SAG-TV and SAG-Film; Paragraph (4), AFTRA — the number ten is typed in. That's his commission. No other number should be there.

Following this are paragraphs labeled alphabetically, (a) through (j) on SAG-TV; (a) through (h) on SAG-Film; (a) through (g) on AFTRA. These provisions include: when the agent gets no commission (wardrobe fees, meal penalties, etc.); that the agent only gets money if you do; fire an agent and you still owe him a commission on work obtained through his services; and so on.

91-15 PROVISION — PARAGRAPH 6 (ALL THREE CONTRACTS)

Perhaps the most important provision. It's the "out" we discussed in Chapter 12. Edited, it reads: "...If during any period of 91 days... the actor fails to be employed... for fifteen (15) days... the actor or agent may terminate... employment... of the agent... by written notice to the other party...". In SAG contracts, Saturdays and Sundays are included.

Actually, the two SAG contracts permit you to fire an agent when you reach the 77th day — on the 77th day it would be impossible for you to get 15 days' work in 91 days. However, this 77-day provision isn't in the AFTRA contract.

Following this are exceptions and additions to the provision. These include but aren't limited to:

- Leaves of absence don't count.

- You owe him commissions on work he helped you obtain.

- If you turn down a job while signed with your "old" agent, and later (within a time limit) accept it when signed with your "new" agent, you owe the "old" agent the commission. Time limit on both SAG contracts is 60 days. However, on the AFTRA contract, it's 90 days, and is a separate provision, Paragraph (5).

- If you turn down a job at your "usual salary," and the job offer came "from an employer commensurate with the actor's prestige," as all three contracts put it, the days you *would* have worked are counted as days you *actually* worked (Paragraph (c), SAG-TV; Paragraph (k), SAG-Film; Paragraph (c), AFTRA).

PARAGRAPH (8) — ALL THREE CONTRACTS

There's a blank space to write in the name of the agent or agents representing you.

LAST PAGE — ALL THREE CONTRACTS

That's where you and the agent sign and date the contract. Below this, look for:

1. Your agent is licensed by the Labor Commissioner of California.
2. Your agency is franchised with SAG (or AFTRA).
3. The contract has been approved by the Labor Commissioner.
4. The contract has been approved by SAG (or AFTRA).

DIFFERENCES

There are differences between SAG and AFTRA contracts. We've touched on some, but there are others — including how your "usual salary" is computed (see Paragraph (6)(a), (b), (c) on SAG-Film as an example). One major difference is:

- *One year anniversary:* It's Paragraph (10) on both SAG contracts. If you've signed a multi-year contract (usually three years), you may fire your agent on the anniversary of the day you signed by giving him 30 days' notice in writing — *regardless if you are working or not.* However, this provision isn't in the AFTRA contract.

PRODUCERS RELEASE FORM

Call it "commission insurance." This form authorizes a producer to send your checks directly to your agent, and releases the producer from responsibility if the check is mishandled. The agent deposits your check into a "Client Account" and writes two checks against it — his check for ten percent and a check to you for the balance. He sends you this second check, along with your pay stub.

There's nothing wrong with asking you to sign this form. You can check his figures against your pay stub. Do you have to sign it? Well, no... and yes. As one agent put it, "If you refuse to sign it, as far as I'm concerned, you don't trust me. And if you don't trust me, I don't want you for a client."

COMMERCIAL

You'll sign the AFTRA contract mentioned above and the SAG Commercial Agency contract, large sections of which have been "borrowed" from the SAG Theatrical & TV contracts.

Because of this similarity, we'll only touch on two points:

- *Paragraph (3)(b):* Here's where it says that the agent gets no commission after the first 21-month "maximum use period." Immediately following are the exceptions, including if he notifies the advertiser no more than 120 days in advance that the commercial is coming up for renegotiation; renegotiates the deal above scale, etc.

- *Paragraph (6):* The idea is the same as the theatrical and TV contracts, but the number of days has been replaced with a dollar amount. You must receive $2,000 in fees (use and holding) in 91 days or you may fire the agent.

9 PENSION AND WELFARE

The major unions each have their own plans, eligibility requirements, etc. We've chosen SAG as a fairly typical example. (AFTRA's is almost identical to SAG's.) Obviously, we can't go into minor points or exceptions. Call the respective union for booklets and information. Percentages listed are what the plan pays.

HEALTH/DENTAL BENEFITS — BLUE CROSS

- *Eligibility:* Minimum earnings of $3,200 (salaries, residuals) over four consecutive three-month quarters.
- *Coverage:* You, spouse, and dependent children under 19.
- *Hospitalization:* 100 percent semi-private room (you pay phone, TV).
- *Doctor/medical bills:* 80 percent $160 deductible per person, up to a maximum deductible of $320.
- *Dental:* 75 percent, $25 deductible basic stuff (exams, cleaning, etc.) 50 percent, $50 deductible major work.

PENSION

- *Eligibility:* Minimum earnings of $2,000 in each of a cumulative number of ten years.
- *Benefits start:* Age 65 (Early retirement: age 55).
- *Benefit range:* $187 to $3,000 per month.

DEATH BENEFIT

- *Not on job:* $10,000 ("On the job" has other benefits).

INDEX

M.K. LEWIS OFFERS CLASSES IN:

- On-camera acting
- Film technique
- Cold reading
- Survival seminar

For Information: M.K. Lewis Workshops
1513 Sixth St. #203
Santa Monica, CA 90401
(213) 394-2511/826-8118

Phone Orders for YOUR FILM ACTING CAREER: (213) 393-0590

ORDER FORM: YOUR FILM ACTING CAREER

Please rush me ☐ copies of YOUR FILM ACTING CAREER.

YOUR FILM ACTING CAREER:	$ 12.95
Add $.84 sales tax (California only):	_____
Shipping and handling: $3.00 for the first book, $1 for each additional book:	_____

(Allow 4 to 6 weeks for delivery.)

☐ (First Class Mail · add $1)   TOTAL: _____

Name _____ Phone _____

Address _____

City _____ State _____ ZIP _____

Here is my: ☐ Check
☐ Money Order in the amount of $_____

Charge my: ☐ Visa
☐ MasterCard

Card # _____ Expiration date _____

Signature _____

Checks payable to: Gorham House Publishing
2210 Wilshire Blvd.
Suite 777
Santa Monica, CA 90403
Telephone: (213) 393-0590